CONTI
&
EUROPEAN
COMMERCIAL LAW

CONTRACT & EUROPEAN COMMERCIAL LAW

A. Lewis

M.A. (T.C.D.), Barrister-At-Law

TUDOR

© A. Lewis 1992

First published in Great Britain by Tudor Business Publishing Limited. Sole distributors worldwide, Hodder and Stoughton (Publishers) Ltd, Mill Road, Dunton Green, Sevenoaks, Kent, TN13 2XX.

British Library Cataloguing in Publication Data

Lewis, A. (Arthur)
 Principles of contract and European commercial law. –
 (Management series)
 1. Europe. Commercial law
 I. Title II. Series
 344.067

ISBN 1-872807-25-9

All rights reserved. No part of this publication may be reproduced, stored in a retrieval system, or transmitted in any form or by any means, electronic, mechanical, photocopying, recording, or otherwise without prior permission of Tudor Business Publishing Ltd. at Stanton House, Eastham Village Road, Eastham, Wirral, Merseyside L62 8AD.

Typeset by Deltatype Ltd, Ellesmere Port, Cheshire
Printed and bound by Billing & Sons Ltd, Worcester.

Contents

Table of Cases — vii
Table of Statutes — xv
Introduction — xix

PART ONE. PERSONS
1. Law of Agency — 1
2. Law of Partnership — 15
3. Law of Companies — 25
4. Borrowing by a Company — 45
5. Arbitration – resolving disputes — 62

PART TWO. RELATIONSHIPS
6. Formation of a contract — 73
7. Mistake, Misrepresentation and Illegality — 88
8. Terms of a contract — 105
9. Discharge of a contract — 115
10. Sale of goods — 129
11. Transfer of property in the goods — 140
12. Consumer Protection/Product Liability — 161
13. Insurance — 168
14. Intellectual Property — 173

PART THREE. FINANCIAL
15. Consumer Credit Act 1974 — 193
16. Financial Services Act 1986 — 209
17. Data Protection Act 1984 — 222
18. Negotiable Instruments – generally — 227
19. Cheques – in particular — 240
20. Insolvency — 268

PART FOUR. INTERNATIONAL
21. European Community Law — 299
22. Sources and Application of Community Law — 312
23. European rules relating to competition — 322
24. Foundations of the European Community — 341
25. Conflict of Laws — 358

General Index — 367

Dedication

To Betty – my wife

Table of Cases

Ailsa Craig Fishing Co Ltd v Malvern Fishing Co Ltd (1983)	114
Aluminium Industrie Vaasen BV v Romalpa Aluminium Ltd (1976)	54, 144
American Cyanamid v Ethicon (1975)	178
Anderson v Edie (1795)	169
Arata Potato Co Ltd v Egyptian Navigation Co (The El Amria) (1980)	64
Ashley v Ashley (1829)	169
The Assunzioni (1854)	362
Astro Vencedor Compania Naviera SA of Panama v Mabanaft GmbH (The Damianos) (1971)	68
Atlas Express Ltd v Kafco Ltd (1989)	100
Auchteroni and Co v Midland Bank Ltd (1928)	252
BTC v Gowley (1956)	125
Baines v National Provincial Bank (1927)	251
Baldry v Marshall Ltd (1924)	139
Balfour v Balfour (1919)	75
Bank of England v Vagliano Brothers (1891)	247
Bartlett v Sydney Marcus Ltd (1965)	138
Beale v Taylor (1967)	137
Bell v Lever Brothers Ltd (1932)	89
Bernstein v Pamsons Motors (Golders Green) (1986)	152
Bettini v Gye (1876)	120
Bevan v National Bank Ltd (1906)	242
Bishopsgate Motor Finance Corporation v Transport Brakes Ltd (1949)	146
Bissett v Wilkinson (1927)	94

viii   *Table of Cases*

Boissevain v Weil (1949)	361
Re Bond Worth Ltd (1908)	145
Bondina Ltd v Rollaway Shower Blinds Ltd (1986)	6, 35
Borden (UK) Ltd v Scottish Timber Products Ltd (1981)	54
Brace v Calder (1895)	125
British Eagle International Airlines Ltd v	
H P Bulmer Ltd v Bollinger S A (1974)	319
Burnett v Westminster Bank Ltd (1965)	241
Bute v Barclays Bank Ltd (1954)	260
Butler Machine Tool Co Ltd v Ex-Cell-o Corporation Ltd (1979)	108
Byrne v Van Tienhoven (1882)	78
Car & Universal Finance Co Ltd v Caldwell	92, 99, 146
Carlill v Carbolic Smoke Ball Co (1893)	76
Carmichael v Evans (1904)	22
Carpenters Co v British Mutual Banking Co (1937)	262
Cassis de Dijon (1979) (120/78)	342, 344
Cellulose Acetate Silk Co v Widnes Foundry (1933)	124
Centrafarm v American Home Products (1979)	188
Centrafarm BV v Stirling Drug Inc (1974)	187
Centrafarm v Winthrop BV (1974)	187
Central London Property Trust v High Trees House (1947)	83
Chapman v Smethurst (1909)	6
Chappell v Nestle and Company (1959)	85
Chapelton v Barry UDC (1940)	109
Chaplin v Hicks (1911)	126
Chartr v Sullivan (1957)	126, 156
Clough Mill Ltd v Martin (1985)	54, 145
Coggs v Bernard (1703)	12
Combe v Combe (1951)	83
Commission v Ireland (249/81)	344
Compagnie Nationale Air France (1975)	285
Consten S A and Grundig v EC Commission (56 & 58/64)	328
Cowan v Le Tresor Public (186/87)	345

Table of Cases

Cox v Cox and Co (1921)	246
Crowther v Shannon Motor Co Ltd (1975)	139
Cuckmere Brick Co Ltd v Mutual Finance Ltd (1971)	290
Cundy v Lindsay (1878)	90, 91
Curtice v London City and Midland Bank Ltd (1908)	244
Curtis v Chemical Cleaning & Dyeing Co (1951)	107
Czarnikow Ltd v Koutos (The Heron II) (1969)	123
Delber v Caisse d'allocations familiales (114/88)	345
Deutsche Grammophon GmbH v Metro SB Grossmarkte (78/70)	187
Donoghue v Stevenson (1932)	161
Eley Positive Assurance Co (1876)	32
Elliot v Bax-Ironside (1925)	6
L'Estrange v F Graucob Ltd (1934)	107
Evans v London and Provincial Bank (1917)	246
Re F	10
Falcke v Gray (1859)	155
The Fehmarn (1957)	63
Felixstowe Dock & Railway Company v British Transport Docks Board (1976)	319
Felthouse v Bindley (1862)	82
Fisher v Bell (1961)	77
Fitch v Dewes (1921)	103
Garner v Murray (1904)	23
Garnett v McKewan (1872)	241
Gaunt v Taylor (1843)	243
Grad v Finanzamt Traunstein (9/70)	313, 317
Re Gray's Inn Construction Co Ltd (1980)	285
Great Western Railway Co v London and County Banking Co Ld (1901)	257
R W Green Ltd v Cade Bros Farmers (1978)	114

x *Table of Cases*

Hadley v Baxendale (1854)	122
Halford v Kymer (1830)	169
Harris v Nickerson (1873)	77
Harz v Deutsche Tradex GmbH (79/83)	315
Hebdon v West (1863)	169
Hedley Byrne & Company Ltd v Heller & Partners Ltd (1964)	94, 96
R V Henn (1981)	310
Hibernian Bank v Gysin and Hanson (1939)	243
Hochster v De la Tour (1853)	120
Hoenig v Isaac (1952)	116
Horsfall v Thomas (1862)	95
Household Fire Insurance Co v Grant (1879)	81
Hurley v Dyke (1979)	97
Hyde v Wrench (1840)	80
Internationale Handelsgesellshaft mbH v Einfuhr – und Vorratsstelle fur Getreide und Futtermittes (11/70)	318
Re Introductions Ltd (1969)	41
Irish Aerospace (Belgium) NV v European Organisation for the Safety of Air Navigation (1991)	322
Re K	10
Keighley, Maxsted & Co v Durant (1901)	7
Kelner v Baxter (1866)	7
Kemble v Farren (1829)	124
Kirkham v Attenborough (1897)	142
Re K M Kushler (1943)	288
Ladbroke v Todd (1914)	257, 261
Lagunas Nitrate Company v Lagunas Syndicate (1899)	98, 128
Lewis v Averay (1971)	91, 146
Litster v Forth Dry Docks Engineering Co Ltd (1989)	316, 319
London Assurance v Mansel (1879)	98

Table of Cases xi

London Joint Stock Bank Ltd v Macmillan and Arthur (1918)	240
London Provincial and South Western Bank Ltd v Buszard (1918)	244
Lumsden & Co v London Trustee Savings Bank (1971)	258
Macarthy's Ltd v Smith (1979)	319
MacKenzie v Coulson (1869)	93
Marfani & Co v Midland Bank Ltd (1927)	258
Marshall v Southampton : South West Hampshire Area Health Authority (Teaching) (152/84)	314
Mendelsohn v Nomera Ltd (1979)	107
Merck & Co Inc v Stephar BV (1981)	188
Microbeads AG v Vinhurst Road Markings (1975)	136
Miller v Karlinski (1945)	102
G Mitchell (Chesterhall) Ltd v Finney Lock Seeds Ltd (1983)	114
Re Moore Landauer & Co (1921)	136, 150
Mutual Life Insurance Company of New York v North and South Wales Bank v Macbeth (1908)	248
Norwich Pharmacal v Customs and Excise (1954)	178
Nova (Jersey) Knit Ltd v Kammgarn Spinnerei GmbH (1977)	64
Nu-Stilo Footwear Ltd v Lloyds Bank Ltd (1956)	262
Officier van Justitie v Kolpinghuis Nijmegen (80/86)	316
Olley v Marlborough Court Ltd (1949)	110
Ontario Metal Products Co (1925)	170
Orbit Mining and Trading Co Ltd v Westminster Bank Ltd (1962)	249
Pao On v Lau Yiu Long (1979)	100
Pearce v Brookes (1866)	102
Pharmaceutical Society of Great Britain v Boots (1953)	77

xii *Table of Cases*

Phillips v Brooks (1919)	99
Pignataro v Gilroy (1919)	143
Pioneer Shipping Ltd v BTP Tioxide Ltd (The Nema) (1982)	66
Re Pressdee Ltd (1985)	285
Procureur du Roi v Dassonville (8/74)	343
Publico Ministero v Ratti (148/78)	314
Raffles v Wichelhaus (1864)	88
Re Rampgill Mill Ltd (1967)	294
Ramsgate Victoria Hotel Company v Montefiore (1886)	79
Rasbora Ltd v JCL Marine Ltd (1977)	112
Reading v Att Gen (1951)	11
Regent OHG Aisenstadt und Barig v Francesco of Jermyn Street Ltd (1981)	151
Rewe-Zentral AG v Bundes monopolverwaltung fur Branntwein (120/78)	342, 344
Richards Ltd v Oppenheim (1950)	121
Roe v R A Naylor Ltd (1971)	106
Rose and Frank Company v Crompton and Brothers Ltd (1923)	74
Ross v London County, Westminster and Parr's Bank Ltd (1919)	260
Rowland v Divall (1923)	136
Royal British Bank v Turquand (1855)	34
Salford Corporation v Lever (1891)	11
Salomon v A Salomon & Co Ltd (1897)	25
Saunders v Anglia Building Society (1970)	92
Savory & Co v Lloyds Bank (1932)	259
Schloh v Auto Controle Technique Sprl (50/84)	344
Scott v Coulson (1903)	89
Scriven Brothers & Company v Hindley & Company (1930)	90
Sika Contracts Ltd v B L Gill and Closeglen Properties Ltd (1979)	5
Simmenthas SpA v Commission (92/78)	318

Simpkins v Pays (1955)	76
Smith v Hughes (1871)	89
Smith v Wilson (1832)	105
Springer v Great Western Railway (1921)	8
Stilk v Myrick (1809)	85
Taylor v Caldwell (1863)	119
Technograph Printed Circuits Ltd v Mills & Rockley (Electronics) Ltd (1972)	175
Re Thomas Mortimer Ltd (1967)	294
Thompson Ltd v Robinson Gunmakers Ltd (1955)	126, 156
Thornton v Shoe Lane Parking Ltd (1971)	110
Tower Cabinet Co v Ingram (1949)	21
Re Tramway Building and Construction Co Ltd (1988)	285
Tritonia Shipping Inc v South Nelson Forest Product Corp (1966)	67
Turpin v Bilton (1843)	12
Tzortzis v Monark Line A/B (1968)	361
Re Unit 2 Windows Ltd (1985)	295
Universal Guarantee Property Ltd v National Bank of Australasia (1965)	243
Universal Steam Navigation Co Ltd v Mckelvie and Co (1923)	5
Van Gend en Loos v Nederlandse Administratie der Belastingen (26/62)	317
Van Zuylen Freres v Hag AG (1974)	188
Victoria Laundries v Newman Industries Ltd (1949)	123
Victors Ltd v Lingard (1927)	37
Vinden v Hughes (1905)	247
Von Colson v Land Nordrhein – Westfalen (14/83)	315
White v Bluett (1853)	85
Warner Bros Pictures Inc v Nelson (1937)	127

Warninck v Townend (1980)	183
Watteau v Fenwick (1893)	78
Westminster Bank v Zang (1905)	264
Westminster Bank Ltd v Hilton (1926)	244
Re Williams C Leitch Brothers Ltd (1932)	36
With v O'Flanagan (1936)	97
Re Yeovil Glove Co Ltd (1965)	55
Yonge v Toynbee (1910)	14
Re Yorkshire Woolcombers Association (1903)	53

Table of Statutes

Advertisements (Hire Purchase) Act 1967	193
Arbitration Act 1950	62
Arbitration Act 1975	64
Arbitration Act 1979	65
Bills of Exchange Act 1882	5, 231, 243
Business Names Act 1985	17
Cheques Act 1957	253
Civil Liability (Contribution) Act 1978	19, 164
Community Patent Convention 1975 (CPC)	174
Companies Act 1985	26, 27, 270
Companies Act 1989	28, 30
Company Directors Disqualification Act 1986	36
Company Securities (Insider Dealings) Act 1985	209
Consumer Credit Act 1974	193
Consumer Protection Act 1987	113, 162
Contracts (Applicable Law) Act 1990	363
Companies Act 1981	17
Copyright Act 1956	179, 182
Copyright Design and Patents Act 1988	179
Data Protection Act 1984	222
Enduring Powers of Attorney Act 1985	10
Enduring Powers of Attorney (Prescribed Forms) Regulations 1986	10
European Communities Act 1972	317
European Patent Convention 1973 (EPC)	174

xvi *Table of Statutes*

Financial Services Act 1986	209
Gaming Acts 1835–1968	169
Hire Purchase Act 1964	148
Hire Purchase Act 1965	193
Insolvency Act 1986	36, 55, 270
Insolvent Partnerships Order 1986	23
Law of Property Act 1925	52
Law of Property (Miscellaneous Provisions) Act 1989	9, 87
Law Reform (Frustrated Contracts) Act 1943	119
Law Reform (Miscellaneous Provisions) Act 1970	75
Life Assurance Act 1774	101, 169
Matrimonial Homes Act 1983	284
Mental Health Act 1983	22
Misrepresentation Act 1967	96
Moneylenders Acts 1900–1927	193
Partnerships Act 1890	15, 16, 20
Patent Co-operation Treaty (PCT) 1970	174
Patents Act 1977	174
Pawnbrokers Act 1872–1960	193
Powers of Attorney Act 1971	9
Prevention of Corruption Act 1906	11
Prevention of Fraud (Investments) Acts 1939–1958	209
Registered Designs Act 1949	182
Registration of Business Names Act 1916	12
Restrictive Trade Practices Act 1976	104
Rome Convention 1981	363
Sale of Goods Act 1979	105, 129, 140

Single European Act 1986	300, 304
Stamp Act 1891	254
Supply of Goods and Services Act 1982	132
Trademarks Act 1938	183, 184
Treaty of Rome 1957	299, 312
Unfair Contract Terms Act 1977	111, 133, 165
Vienna Convention 1980	366

Introduction

It is obvious that the law of the European Community will have an increasingly important impact on the business activities of this country. This book therefore is intended to serve as an introduction to some important aspects of European law as well as covering the usual topics to be found in any book on commerical law.

It deals with contract, agency and sale of good and goes into some detail on the European purchasing directives. Certain topics have to some extent been affected either directly or indirectly by European law and so intellectual property, product liability, companies, data protection and the Financial Services Act 1986 are covered.

This book will be suitable for all students of business law on degree and professional courses as well as managers in sales, purchasing and industry generally.

It will also be suitable for the general reader who wishes to see how the law of this country is being, and will continue to be affected by the law of the European Community.

Of course it is not intended to be an exhaustive treatise on European law but merely provides an introduction to that subject which can be studied in greater depth in other books.

It should be remembered that European law in particular is constantly and quickly changing and so although every effort has been made to ensure that what is written is up to date, it may be that events have overtaken the publication. Finally my thanks are due to authors who have written in the same area because inevitably every book written owes a great debt to the books which have been published before it. In particular, mention must be made of *'Law and the Institutions of the European Community'* by *Lasok and Bridge* and *'Textbook on EC Law'* by *Josephine Steiner*.

I also acknowledge the assistance of the Royal Bank of Scotland plc., Barclays Bank plc., and National Westminister Bank plc., in allowing me to use and copy some of their documents, in which of course they retain the copyright.

A. Lewis 1992

Part 1

Persons

Part 1 is concerned with persons because it is persons who are involved in any legal situation.

Persons include, a single human being, an association of human beings as in a partnership or an artificial legal person known as a corporation of which the best known example is a company.

All these persons human or artificial may sometimes act through another person and so we look at the Law of Agency.

Chapter One

The Law of Agency

The examples of agencies that exist are commonplace and everyone probably appreciates their purpose. An estate agent is someone who acts on behalf of another to sell or buy his house or land. Theatrical artistes have agents who negotiate terms with producers of theatrical or TV shows. The agents are people who bring their principals into contractual relationship with third parties. In other words they make contracts with people; but these contracts will be binding not on themselves but on the people they are representing. In a typical agency relationship the agent makes the contract and then disappears, leaving the contract proper between the principal and the third party.

```
Principal
  |\
  | \
  |  \ CONTRACT
  |   \
  |    \
Agent ——————————> 3rd Party
```

Of course there may probably be a contract between the principal and the agent but this is not the main contract – the important one is that between the principal and the third party.

The purpose of the law of Agency is to establish whether or not the agency relationship exists. Depending on the answer to that question the rights and duties of the parties can be determined.

As always the law seeks to determine the rights and liabilities of the parties. Is the agent himself to be liable, may the third party sue the principal or may the principal sue the third party?

Liability of the Agent

From a practical point of view one should consider the matter from the point of view of the third party. Does he know that he is dealing with an agent? That depends on whether or not he is informed on this point. Quite obviously an agent does not go round wearing a cap bearing the word "Agent" on it. So only if the agent notifies the person he is dealing with that he is an agent will the third party know this fact.

The normal agency situation is when the agent informs the third party that he is an agent acting for a certain principal. In that case the third party knows the position and the contract will be between the principal and the third party.

Looking at the agency relationship from the point of view of the principal – as a general rule it all depends on whether or not he has authorised the agent as to whether he will be liable or not. Thus if the agent is authorised to enter into a contract and the third party knows that he is dealing with an agent and maybe knows the identity of the principal then the contract when made will lie between the principal and the third party. The agent will have neither rights nor duties under the contract.

If the third party does not know he is dealing with an agent, because the agent has not informed him of the fact, then the third party will naturally conclude that he is dealing with the person who is the agent in his own right. Consequently the third party may only sue the agent, if the need arises. However if he later does discover the existence of the principal and his identity then he may sue him. He cannot of course sue both agent and principal. In this case the third party will believe he is dealing with the agent in his own right because he has not been informed that he is an agent. This is sometimes referred to as the doctrine of the undisclosed principal.

Another situation may arise when the agent informs the third party that he is an agent but does not identify his principal. This may occur when a large important company is wishing to buy certain property and if it became known that such a wealthy client had an interest in acquiring the property the price might become inflated. In this case the third party knows he is dealing with an agent and so it is up to him whether he continues to deal with a principal whose identity he does not know. At any rate the agent will have no liability in the matter.

Signatures

An agent may be liable if he signs a document, but it depends on the manner in which he signs it.

1. The agent may sign in his own name. In that case it is probably true to say that the agent has accepted liability unless of course he makes it clear that he is signing as agent. However he must be careful to make sure that he is not merely describing his relationship to his principal e.g. A signs in his own name and adds "Chartered Civil Engineer". *Sika Contacts Ltd v B L Gill and Closeglen Properties Ltd (1978)*. It was held that A was liable as he had merely described his occupation.

    However in *Universal Steam Navigation Co Ltd v Mckelvie and Co (1923)* A was not liable when he signed in his own name "as agents".

    Section 26 of the Bills of Exchange Act 1882 provides:

    a. Where a person signs a bill as a drawer, indorser or acceptor, and adds words to his signature, indicating that he signs for or on behalf of a principal or in a representative character, he is not personally liable thereon; but the mere addition to his signature of words describing him as an agent, or as filling a representative character, does not exempt him from personal liability.

b. In determining whether a signature on a bill is that of the principal or that of the agent by whose hand it is written, the construction most favourable to the validity of the instrument shall be adopted.

The effect of this is that where an agent signs, in his own name, a deed or a bill of exchange then he will be liable on these documents. P will not be liable if his name does not appear on these documents. An exception would be if A signed a deed and was authorised by a power of attorney.

2. If a person signs "per procurationem" then it indicates that he has only a limited authority. Often a person will sign in this way on behalf of a company. The principal therefore will only be liable if the agent is acting within his actual authority.
3. The principal may of course authorise the agent to sign using his (the principal's) name. This is in order.
4. No one has a proprietary right to any name, unless it is subject to the trade mark rules. Therefore a person may use any name that he wishes so long as there is no dishonest intent.

In *Chapman v Smethurst (1909)* a promissory note was signed by the managing director who signed it "S Ltd. – S. M.D." The court held that this showed that the company S Ltd was to be bound and not S.

In *Elliott v Bax-Ironside (1925)* two directors signed a cheque as "I and M directors F Ltd" and on the back they indorsed it by signing "F Ltd." "I and M – directors". The two directors were held liable for the second signatures because they had merely indicated their occupations and the company was already liable because of the signatures on the front.

In *Bondina Ltd v Rollaway Shower Blinds Ltd (1986)*

The printed cheque form of a company contained its name, the branch of the bank and the number of the cheque. It was signed by two directors who added their names (W,M). It was held that the directors had adopted all the printing on the cheque including the name of the company and so the directors were not liable.

Liability of Principal

From the principal's point of view he will usually only be liable if he has authorised the agent to enter into his contract. This is known as the express appointment of an agent.

However an agency relationship may arise in other ways e.g.

1. If the principal holds out the agent as having his authority. That means the principal gives the third party the impression that the agent has the authority of the principal to make the contract he is making with the third party.

    A case in point here is *Watteau v Fenwick (1893)* where a firm of brewers forbade the manager of a public house to buy cigars for the business. The manager did in fact buy cigars in disobedience of this order and the court held that the brewers were nevertheless still liable. They had held out the manager as having the normal authority of a manager of a public house which was to buy cigars for the business and had not communicated their restriction on his authority to the seller of the cigars.

2. The agent may have exceeded his authority but nevertheless the principal decides to adopt his contract. This is called "ratification" and is only possible if the agent notified the third party that he was an agent.

    In *Keighley, Maxsted & Co v Durant (1901)* no ratification was possible because the agent had contracted in his own name.

    Also in order for the principal to ratify an unauthorised contract of his agent, he must have had contractual capacity both at the time the contract was made and when it was ratified. Finally if the principal was a company then it must have been in existence when the contract was made. Thus a pre-incorporation contract will not bind a company when it is later incorporated – *Kelner v Baxter (1866)*.

3. The agent is a carrier and is carrying perishable goods belonging to the principal. Something occurs to prevent their delivery and so the carrier must do something immediately otherwise the goods are going to become worthless. He sells the goods in order to minimise the principal's loss. On the face of it he will be liable to the principal, however if he can show that he tried to get in touch with him and failed and it was an emergency then he will be declared to be an "agent of necessity".

In *Springer v G W Railway (1921)* the delivery of a consignment of tomatoes was delayed and so the carrier sold the perishable goods and the question arose – was he liable for interfering with the goods of another and did the purchasers get a good title to the goods which they bought? The court held that an agency of necessity had arisen and so the carrier was not liable to the owner, and the purchasers of the goods acquired good title to them.

Thus it can be seen that sometimes it can be said that an agent has been appointed expressly. In other cases the agency relationship merely arises because of circumstances – a relationship e.g. husband and wife; a situation e.g. perishable goods prevented from being delivered and the carrier sells them; or the holding out of a person as having the authority of another as in *Watteau v Fenwick (1893)*.

Where a man and a woman are living together (not necessarily as man and wife) then the woman has the right to pledge the man's credit for the purchase of necessaries i.e. food and certain articles for the home. This is the common law position and it is interesting to consider how this position may be affected by the modern approach to sexual equality.

There is one case when an agent must be appointed by a deed and that is when his principal expects him to execute a deed. The deed appointing the agent is called a power of attorney and often old people incapable of acting for themselves appoint some other person to deal with their affairs.

Power of Attorney

A power of attorney is required by the agent if it may become necessary for him to make a transaction by deed. In this case the attorney or agent must himself be appointed by deed. The law has always treated a transaction by deed in a special way. A deed was quite simply a document to which had been affixed a seal. At one time a seal was a large piece of wax on which a person's coat of arms would be impressed when the wax was in a molten state. It was necessary for the person executing the deed to state, with his finger on the seal, "I deliver this as my act and deed". Since the *Law of Property (Miscellaneous Provisions) Act 1989* a seal is not necessary but it must be made clear in the document that it is intended to be a deed. Nevertheless certain transactions will have no legal effect unless contained in a deed e.g. conveyance of the legal estate in land, or a legal mortgage of property.

Powers of Attorney Act 1971
Signature and sealing may be by a person other than the donor if in his presence and by his direction – in this case 2 witnesses are necessary. The power of attorney must be stamped within 30 days of its execution.

The advantage of taking a power of attorney from the point of view of a bank is that the power can be made irrevocable and if it is given to secure a proprietary interest of the donee or the performance of an obligation owed to him, then so long as the obligation or interest continues the power will not be revoked by death, bankruptcy or mental incapacity of the donor. Such a situation could rise when a bank takes an equitable mortgage of a legal estate by receiving the title deeds. The deposit will be accompanied by a memorandum authorising the bank to sell the property in certain circumstances. Here the bank will have a proprietary interest in the land and so the power cannot be revoked.

Powers which have not been given by way of security will be revoked by the death or mental incapacity of the donor.

This situation has been improved by the *Enduring Powers of*

Attorney Act 1985. This provides that where an "enduring power" has been created it will not be revoked by the mental incapacity of the donor. The *Enduring Powers of Attorney (Prescribed Forms) Regulations 1986* specify the form that must be completed by the donor and the attorney.

If the attorney believes that the donor is becoming incapable he must apply for registration of the instrument creating the power to the Court of Protection. Before applying for registration he must give notice to certain relatives of the donor.

If the donor does eventually become incapable, the attorney may only act in accordance with the directions of the court until the instrument has been registered as mentioned above.

The timing of the creation of the enduring powers is of the greatest importance because a sane person may not be willing to execute the document and once he has become insane it is too late as the instrument could then be declared invalid.

In two cases *Re K* and *Re F* the court decided that it was sufficient if the donor understood the nature and effect of the power of attorney he or she was signing. It will not be necessary for the donor of the power to be able to manage his own affairs.

Duties of an Agent

The relationship between the principal and the agent, no matter how the relationship arose, is essentially one of trust (a fiduciary relationship).

1. The agent must obey the instructions given to him by his principal even if he thinks the instructions are wrong. Sometimes of course the principal may expect the agent to advise him and indeed this may be the reason he is employing an agent viz. to use his skill and care. The agent must not delegate his duty to another person unless such delegation has been agreed with the principal, is the custom of the trade or the delegation merely takes place in relation to purely administrative matters.
2. An agent must not allow his personal interests to come into conflict with those of the principal.

3. The agent must not make a secret profit or take a bribe from a third party. In *Reading v Att. Gen. (1951)* it was held that a sergeant in the British Army had misused his position by sitting on a lorry thereby giving the impression that it was a military convoy and so it was not inspected. He was ordered to repay the money he had received to the State.

4. If the agent accepts a secret commission or a bribe the following consequences may ensue:

    Salford Corporation v Lever (1891) Lever agreed to pay the Corporation's agent 1 shilling per ton if his tender for the supply of coal was accepted. When the bribe was discovered it was held that both the giver and the taker of the bribe could be sued and prosecuted under the *Prevention of Corruption Act 1906*. Also the agent could be dismissed without receiving his commission and the contract with the third party could be set aside. In that case it was held:

    a. The principal may dismiss him.
    b. He can recover the secret commission from the agent. If the commission has not been paid over to the agent, the principal may recover it from the person who promised the agent.
    c. Whether he has recovered the secret commission or not, the principal may still bring an action for damages against the person who gave the agent the bribe.
    d. He may refuse to pay the agent any commission or remuneration. If he has already paid it, he may recover it from the agent.
    e. The principal may repudiate the whole contract entered into by the agent whether the offer of a bribe did influence the agent's course of action or not.

5. The agent must not disclose any confidential information he has obtained through acting as agent. He must inform the principal of all matters relating to the agency when they come to his notice.

6. No delegation. This duty is often expressed by the latin maxim "delegatus non potest delegare." This is because the relationship between a principal and agent is a personal one. Where the agent's authority is coupled with a discretion (e.g. to inspect a picture, and if it is genuine, to buy it), delegation of such authority will be a breach of the confidence reposed in the agent.

Delegation is permissible in the following cases:

a. Where delegation was in the contemplation of the parties at the commencement of the agency.
b. Where the appointment of a sub-agent is necessary for the proper execution of his work.
c. If delegation becomes necessary as a result of a sudden emergency.
d. Where delegation is sanctioned by trade, custom or usage.
e. Where the work will not call for the exercise of any discretion by the sub-agent.
f. Delegation is also possible where part of the work requires special skill (e.g. solicitor to draft a conveyance of a house) and the agent does not have that skill.

Care and Skill
A paid agent is liable to the principal if he fails to do the work and as a result the principal suffers damage, as held in *Turpin v Bilton* (1843). A gratuitous agent is not liable for non-feasance.

However, once he commences the work he will be liable if he does not exercise appropriate care and skill: *Coggs v Bernard.* (1703).

A gratuitous agent must use the care and skill he will give to his own affairs. This means he must use such skill as he possesses. A paid agent must use the skill he claims to possess, or may be implied from his profession.

Rights of the Principal

The duties of the agent give corresponding rights to the principal. He may sue the agent for damages if he commits a breach of any of these duties.

Rights of the Agent

1. *Right of Re-imbursement.* Any reasonable expenses necessarily incurred by the agent in performing his duties must be repaid to him by his principal. This obligation may be enforced even where no amount has been fixed, by a quantum meruit.
2. *Set-off.* If the principal brings an action against the agent for breach of duty, the agent may exercise his right of setoff for any sums due to him either as commission or as indemnity for expenses incurred.
3. *Lien.* If the principal has failed to pay the agreed commission or an indemnity to the agent and the agent has any goods of the principal in his possession, then subject to certain conditions, the agent may exercise a lien on such goods and retain possession until the principal has honoured his obligation.
4. *Action for the Agreed Commission or Remuneration.* The agent is entitled to his commission after he has performed his agency.

Duties of the Principal

The rights of the agent impose corresponding duties on the principal: e.g., a duty to pay the agent the agreed commission and to indemnify the agent for any expenses incurred by him.

Termination of the agency

As the agency relationship is usually based upon agreement between the principal and agent then it follows that it may be terminated by mutual agreement. Apart from that however the principal may withdraw or revoke the authority of his agent; but if he does that he must remember to notify any third party with whom the agent may have had dealings, otherwise the principal might be liable if the agent contracts with them. Where the agent's authority is coupled with an interest then revocation is not possible, e.g. where the principal owes a debt to a person and authorises him to collect rents from houses he owns.

Furthermore the agency relationship may be terminated by operation of law. This means if a certain event occurs, such as the death or insanity of either principal or agent, or the bankruptcy of the principal then the agent's authority will be terminated. The point about this means of terminating the agency contract that should be borne in mind by the agent is that any of these events will take away the agent's authority whether or not he knows that the event has occurred. Consequently if the event occurs unknown to the agent he may be acting without authority and this will result in his being made liable for any contract he makes after the event has occurred.

In *Yonge v Toynbee (1910)* the principal became insane, unknown to his solicitors, who were acting for him in litigation. Because the solicitors took steps which resulted in the other party incurring expenses the court held that they were liable to reimburse the other party. The solicitors had acted without authority, although innocently, and thus were liable for breach of implied warranty of authority. This action is interesting because it means that when an agent notifies a party that he is an agent then the other party is entitled to assume that he has the authority he professes to have. If that turns out not to be so then the agent will be liable for breach of his warranty of authority.

Chapter Two

The Law of Partnership

Both partnerships and companies are business associations and if a sole trader decides to give up trading on his own then he can either form a partnership or a company. This would necessitate his joining with other people but that would be a normal step in the progression of a sole trader. Having started on his own he finds that, if his business is prospering, he will soon need more money. He can of course borrow money but there must be a limit to how much can be borrowed. However people may be prepared to supply the money if they, personally, can have some control over how the money is being used and for that situation to arise then a legal bond must be established. Both partnerships and companies are therefore different forms of legal relationships established for the purpose of running a business.

The *Partnership Act 1890* states that a partnership is "the relation which subsists between persons carrying on business in common with a view of profit". The legal term for a partnership is a "firm".

Notice that the *Partnership Act* speaks of "a relation which subsists". In other words if some people are carrying on business in common it may be that they are in partnership and do not realise that fact and accordingly the rules relating to such associations are contained in the Act of 1890.

From the definition above, three elements must exist before there can be a partnership:

1. there must be a business;
2. the business must be carried on in common;
3. it must be carried on with a view of profit.

The following relationships are therefore not partnerships;

1. Joint or part ownership of property does not of itself create a partnership.
2. Clubs and trade associations.
3. Companies registered under any of the *Companies Acts*, are not partnerships.
4. Barristers are not allowed to enter into partnerships.

No formalities are needed to form a partnership although there must be an agreement between the persons concerned to work in common. It may be that a number of persons are working together in a business with a view of profit and they know nothing of partnerships. Nevertheless a court may decide that they are legally in partnership and so the provisions of the *Partnership Act 1890* will apply. In particular Section 24 provides that:

1. all partners will share equally in the profits even though they have contributed different amounts;
2. no partner may receive any remuneration;
3. every general partner may take part in the management of the firm;
4. a partner is entitled to be indemnified by the firm in respect of payments made and liabilities incurred by him:
   a. In the ordinary and proper conduct of the business of the firm; or
   b. In or about anything necessarily done for the preservation of the business or partnership property.

Section 24 further provides that

1. No person may be introduced as a partner without the consent of all existing partners.
2. Any difference arising as to ordinary matters connected with the partnership may be decided by a majority of the partners.
3. No change may be made in the nature of the partnership business without the consent of all the existing partners.
4. Subject to any agreement between the partners, the partnership will be dissolved by the death of any partner.

It will be apparent that if these provisions were to apply then the partners would not always be particularly satisfied. Therefore it is more usual for a partnership agreement to be entered into called "Articles of Partnership" or if by deed, a "Deed of Partnership". In such an agreement the partners may agree anything they like and so it is usual, taking some of the previous points,

1. for the partners to agree that if one were to die his share of the partnership would be purchased by the surviving members;
2. the profits will be distributed pro rata to the amount of capital contributed by each of the partners;
3. the partners to receive an annual remuneration like any other employee.

The Firm Name

It sometimes happens that the partners carry on business under a name which is different from the names of the partners. This is known as the *firm name*.

Before the *Companies Act 1981*, it was necessary for the firm name to be registered under the *Registration of Business Names Act 1916*, however that Act was repealed and the provisions relating to business names have been consolidated in the *Business Names Act 1985*. The business name does not now need to be registered, but S.4 of that Act requires that publicity be given regarding the partners who are trading under the business name.

The methods of publicity are:

1. The name of each partner must be disclosed on all business letters, invoices and receipts.
2. The name and address of each partner must be displayed in any premises where the business is being carried on.
3. There must be disclosed, in relation to each partner, an address within Great Britain at which service of any document would be effective.

Failure to comply with the disclosure requirements is an offence punishable with a fine. Furthermore, if a firm using a business name has failed to comply with the disclosure requirements, and sues for breach of contract, the claim may be dismissed if the defendant can show:

1. That he has a claim against the firm arising out of the contract, which he is unable to pursue because of the plaintiff's non-compliance, or:
2. That he, the defendant, has suffered financial loss in connection with the contract, because of the plaintiff's non-compliance.

The court may however in such circumstances permit the proceedings to continue if satisfied that it would be "just and equitable" to do so.

Relationship of partners to third parties

An important feature of a partnership is that each partner is considered, in law, to be the agent of his fellow partner as regards the making of contracts which are made in the course of the partnership business (S.5). Thus every partner has authority to buy and sell goods commonly used in the partnership business; he can hire and fire staff; if it is a trading partnership (which is one which buys and sells goods as opposed to merely giving a service) then each partner has authority to issue negotiable instruments, to borrow money and pledge goods in the firm's name. Thus if a person is in a partnership (and remember he may not fully appreciate this fact) then he can be made liable for certain contracts made by a fellow partner. As far as the third party is concerned who has been dealing with the partnership it may well be important to have it established that a number of people are in partnership because then the list of defendants is extended and the plaintiff will have a better chance of getting his money.

So much for contracts, but the same reasoning applies as far as wrongful acts committed by a partner are concerned; his fellow partners will be held liable for these, provided of course they are committed in the course of the partnership business.

Relationship of partners between themselves

Between themselves the partners have rights and owe duties and these are set down in the articles of partnership as mentioned earlier, but also the contract of partnership is a contract of good faith in its operation. This means that there need not be the fullest disclosure when the contract is entered into, and so it is up to each partner to satisfy himself that he is doing the right thing by entering into partnership with his fellow partners (rather like marriage). However once the contract is made then there must be the fullest disclosure of all relevant matters concerning the partnership business. A partner may not make a secret profit and must render total account of his dealings. In the same vein a partner must not set himself up in competition with the partnership business.

At all times therefore every partner must conduct himself with good faith towards his fellow partners.

Section 25 provides that a majority of the partners cannot expel any partner without authority expressed in the Articles of Partnership.

Joint and Joint and several liability

In joint liability there is a single liability for the firm's contracts. Thus a creditor will have only one action – he may sue one partner or he may sue all the partners together – but he cannot do both. However under the *Civil Liability (Contribution) Act 1978* a creditor may sue the firm or each of the partners in the firm. This has always been the case where liability is joint and several. For that reason banks have always preferred joint and several liability. Even though the distinction between joint and joint and several liability has disappeared by virtue of the 1978 Act, banks still require liability to be joint and several because:

1. when a partner is bankrupt or dies the bank may proceed against his estate equally with his personal creditors.
2. if there is a debit balance on the partnership account the bank will obtain a right of combination in respect of a credit balance on the partner's personal account, since the partner is personally liable for the debt.

Retiring and New Partners' Liability

In the absence of any contrary agreement, a partner's liability for contracts or debts contracted while he was a partner does not cease upon his retirement. He remains liable for debts incurred whilst he was a member of the firm. The creditors may, however, agree to discharge him from his liabilities and agree to look to the new firm for payment by making a contract of novation which is a "new contract".

A valid contract of novation is usually effected by the introduction of an incoming partner who agrees to be liable together with the remaining partners for the retired partner's share of the debts.

Where the surviving partners do not intend to take on a new partner, the retiring partner's release by the creditors must be by deed.

An incoming partner is not liable for debts of the firm before he joined unless he is a party to a contract of novation.

Retiring Partner's Liability for Post-Retirement Debts

Section 36 of the *Partnership Act 1890* provides that a retiring partner may be liable for debts incurred after his retirement.

Creditors are divided into two classes:

1. Those who had dealt with the partnership before the retirement.
2. Those who did not deal with the partnership before the retirement.

The retiring partner is liable for new debts contracted with any creditor in group 1 unless the latter has received individual notice of his retirement.

If a creditor is aware of the retirement, the retiring partner will not be liable for post-retirement debts even if he has not given notice to the creditor.

With creditors in group 2 notice in the *London Gazette* is sufficient notice of retirement to the creditors.

If no Gazette notice is given a retiring partner will still not be liable for post-retirement debts to a creditor who did not know that he was a partner: *Tower Cabinet Co v Ingram (1949)*.

However if a partner has died and the firm's business is continued under the old name the continued use of that name or of the deceased partner's name shall not of itself make the deceased's personal representatives liable to partnership debts after his death. (S.14, S.36).

Dissolution of a Partnership

As we have seen, a partnership will usually come into existence because of the agreement of the persons who wish to join in partnership with one another. Thus it is quite logical for such a relationship, which came into being because of an agreement, to be terminated by agreement. On the other hand a partnership may be formed for a particular length of time or to perform some purpose. Obviously when the period of time has expired or the purpose has been achieved the partnership will be at an end. In addition the *Partnership Act* provides that a partnership will automatically be dissolved if one of the partners dies or becomes bankrupt. However the old partnership will not be dissolved if the partnership agreement provides for alternative arrangements to be made (e.g. the remaining partners to buy the share of the deceased or bankrupt partner). Thus any agreement with A, B and C will continue notwithstanding the death etc of A, if this has been agreed.

In the case of the death of a partner the deceased's estate will not normally be liable for debts incurred by the firm after his death and so it is essential that the account with the partnership is broken when the bank is notified of partner's death etc.

Apart from the above ways in which a partnership may be dissolved, it may be that the partners cannot agree between themselves. In that case an application may be made to the court to issue an order dissolving the partnership. This application must be based on one of the following grounds:

1. The insanity of one of the partners, under the *Mental Health Act 1983*.
2. Where a partner has become permanently incapable of carrying out his share of the partnership business.
3. When a partner wilfully and persistently commits a breach of the partnership agreement.
4. On the ground that the partnership can be carried on only at a loss, and there is no prospect of the firm making a profit.
5. When a partner has committed some act which will prejudicially affect the carrying on of the business. In *Carmichael v Evans (1904)* it was held that a conviction for dishonesty was sufficient reason for the dissolution of a firm of solicitors.
6. In circumstances that the court thinks just and equitable.

Public Notice of Dissolution
On dissolution every partner may publish a notice to this effect in the *London Gazette* and may compel the other partners to sign the notice. S.37.

Dissolution rescinds the power of the partners to act as agents for the firm, except in respect of:

1. transactions started but not completed; and
2. acts which are necessary to wind up the partnership affairs e.g., employing an accountant to prepare the final accounts. S.38

Partnership Property

This includes property originally brought into the partnership or was later acquired in the course of the partnership business or was bought with money belonging to the firm.

Naturally, upon the dissolution of the partnership it will be necessary to collect in the partnership property, liquidate it and distribute it. This will be done in the following order:

1. Creditors of the firm will be paid.
2. Partners will receive their loans to the firm if any.
3. Partners will receive their capital contributions.
4. Any surplus to be divided amongst the partners in the proportion in which profits are divisible.

If there are insufficient partnership assets to cover items 1, 2 and 3 then each partner must pay towards the deficiency in the proportion in which they shared profits.

If a partner, due to insolvency, is unable to contribute his equal share of the lost capital then the solvent partners are not liable to contribute it for him. In *Garner v Murray 1904* it was decided that each partner must contribute his share of the deficiency ignoring the share of the insolvent partner. Then the assets are distributed according to the rules mentioned earlier.

Bankruptcy of the Partnership
This must be distinguished from the bankruptcy of a partner which will result in the dissolution of the partnership unless the partners have agreed otherwise.

The *Insolvent Partnerships Order 1986* permits partnerships to be wound up as if they were unregistered companies and does not necessarily involve the bankruptcy of the partners.

Instead a creditor may present a bankruptcy petition against one of more of the partners; or petition for the winding up of the firm and the bankruptcy of the partners. *The Insolvent Partnerships Order 1986* provides that a creditor has three choices:

1. to wind up the partnership alone as if it were an unregistered company.
2. to make bankrupt the partners alone.
3. wind up the partnership and make bankrupt all the partners.

A petition for winding-up may be presented by a creditor or a partner on the following grounds:

1. the partnership has ceased to carry on its business.
2. the partnership is dissolved
3. the partnership is unable to pay its debts
4. it is just and equitable that the partnership be wound up.

A partnership is deemed unable to pay its debts if

1. a creditor who is owed £750 or more has demanded payment in writing and no payment has been made within three weeks or no security has been given.
2. notice of an action for debt has been served against a partner for a partnership debt and he has not paid within three weeks.
3. an execution against the partnership is unsatisfied.
4. the firm's liabilities exceed its assets.

Chapter Three

The Law of Companies

In addition to a partnership there is another form of business organisation called the registered company or limited company. It is called by these names because such a company is formed by registering certain documents with the Registrar of Companies and it is a limited company because the liability of its shareholders is limited.

A company is an artificial legal person. In other words it is a person in the eyes of the law and has rights and duties like any human person. This point was established in the famous case: *Salomon v Salomon & Co (1897)*

In that case Mr Salomon formed a company to take over his business of manufacturing shoes. The company paid Mr Salomon for his business partly in cash, partly in shares and partly by a charge over the company's assets. The company was wound up and its debts to creditors were in excess of its assets. Therefore the creditors claimed the assets of the company arguing that a person cannot owe money to himself and as Mr Salomon owned the company he and it were the same person. The court held that the company was a separate person from Mr Salomon who owned it.

However being artificial a company cannot be seen – it exists on paper. One can look at a factory manufacturing soap but one is not looking at Unilever plc or Lever Bros. plc but at a factory which happens to be owned by a person whose name is Unilever plc. One says one is going to do some shopping in Marks and Spencer. The shopping is being done in a shop owned by a single person called Marks and Spencer plc. How does one know that a company exists then? As a company exists only on paper – the Certificate of Incorporation is the document that brings a company into existence and this is proof of the company's existence. It is issued by the Registrar of Companies when he has examined the documents filed in his office by the promoters of the company.

The concept that a company exists as a single person on its own is the basis of company law. Together with the principle that the liability of the shareholders is limited to the amount due to be paid (if any) for their shares, they are the two main difference between a company and a partnership. As we have seen the partners contribute money to the assets of the partnership but if this is insufficient to pay the debts of the partnership then the partners must continue to provide more money, even if that means they are bankrupting themselves. In the case of a company the shareholders have contributed to the assets of the company but if this proves to be insufficient to pay the creditors of the company then the shareholders will lose their money in the company, but will not have to provide more money. The other difference is that the company is a person separate from the persons (the shareholders) who own it. A partnership is not a separate person but consists of the partners. As an illustration, it is often said that if all the partners of a partnership are in a room and a bomb explodes killing them all, that would be the end of the firm. But if all the shareholders of a company were killed in the same circumstances that would not be the end of the company. It would continue its existence, but with different shareholders of course.

The law relating to companies is contained mainly in the *Companies Act 1985*. This, in the main, is a consolidating Act.

Formation of a Company

The people who wish to form a company as a vehicle for running their business are called promoters. It is possible to buy a ready-made company or it may be decided to form a company from scratch. The procedure for this is to file with the Registrar of Companies certain documents – the most important being the Memorandum of Association and the Articles of Association.

The Memorandum of Association

By section 2 of the *Companies Act 1985* the memorandum of every company must state

1. the name of the company
2. whether the registered office of the company is to be situated in England and Wales or Scotland.
3. the objects of the company
4. in the case of a company having a share capital the memorandum must also state the amount of the share capital which the company proposes to be registered and the division of that capital into shares of a fixed amount.
5. also in the case of a company limited by shares there must be a statement that the liability of its members or shareholders is limited.

This document was of the greatest importance to outsiders dealing with the company because it contained the objects clause which stated the purposes for which the company had been formed and in so doing it established the powers of the company to enter into contracts. The rule was that a company could only enter into a valid and enforceable contract if it had power to do so. If any contract it made was outside its powers (ultra vires) then the contract was null and void. This principle was known as the "ultra vires doctrine" and was intended to protect investors in the company and those who were considering lending money to it. By consulting the objects clause then such people would know the permitted activities of the company.

However in practice this was not particularly helpful because the lawyers who drew up a company's documents usually made the objects so wide as to cover every possible activity that the company might have wished to enter into in the future. Nevertheless if a company entered into a contract and it was discovered that it lacked the power to enter into that particular contract then the contract would be void and the company could not be sued successfully. Since our entry into the European Economic Community we have had to modify our company law in certain areas to accord with Common Market practices.

The latest position is that the Companies Act 1989 has amended the Companies Act 1985. Section 108–112 of the 1989 Act has effectively abolished the "ultra vires" rule. These changes came into force on 4th February 1991. Section 35 of the 1985 Act (as amended) does away with the "ultra vires" rule.

Section 35A of the 1985 Act (as amended) relates to the power of directors to bind the company to acts within the power of the company.

Section 35B of the 1985 Act (as amended) provides that a party to a transaction with a company is not bound to enquire into the terms of the company's memorandum nor as to any limitation in the directors' powers.

Section 110 of the *Companies Act 1989* inserts a new *section 3A* into the *1985 Act* which allows a company to state that its objects are, "To carry on business as a general commercial company." A company which chooses this option in preference to a traditional objects clause will have power to carry on any trade or business and to do all things incidental or conducive thereto.

The Department of Trade and Industry has issued the following note:– **"Ultra Vires" reform – Companies Act 1989 (Sections 108–112)** The provisions of the 1985 Act which deal with the ultra vires doctrine and the authority of the board of directors are amended (the ultra vires doctrine is a common law rule which, in the absence of statutory provision, renders void acts by a company which are beyond its stated objects). The main features of the amended provisions are

1. the validity of a completed act of a company is not to be called into question on the grounds of lack of capacity by reason of anything in the company's memorandum of association;
2. in favour of a person dealing with the company in good faith, the power of the board of directors to bind the company or authorise others to do so is to be free of any limitation in the company's constitution;

3. a third party is to have no duty to enquire as to the capacity of a company or the authority of directors to bind the company;
4. transactions which are beyond the authority of the board of directors and to which directors or connected persons are a party are to be voidable in certain circumstances at the instance of the company;
5. if a company states that its object is to carry on business as a "general commercial company" it will have the object of carrying on any business or trade whatsoever, and will have the power to do whatever is incidental or conclusive to that object;
6. the provisions on capacity and authority are qualified in the case of charitable companies, so as to maintain current controls on charitable companies and to assist in the recovery of misappropriated charitable property. In order to prevent those provisions on charitable companies undermining the provisions affecting companies generally, charitable companies are required to disclose their charitable status in their official documents if the status is not apparent from their name.

Alteration of the Objects
A company may alter its objects by the passing of a special resolution to that effect.

After the resolution has been passed the company must wait for twenty-one days (before implementing the alteration) to see whether any members who oppose the alteration may apply to the court to have it set aside. An application to cancel the alteration will not be entertained by the court unless it is made by

1. at least 15 per cent of the members; or
2. the holders of at least 15 per cent of any debentures issued by the company.

The court may on such an application make an order confirming the alteration or may provide for the purchase by the company of the shares of any members of the company.

If the alteration is confirmed (i.e. the dissentients are overruled) the company must deliver to the Registrar a printed copy of the memorandum as altered.

Section 110 of the *Companies Act 1989* inserts a new *section 4* into the *Companies Act 1985*. This allows a company to alter its objects for any reason.

The Name of the Company
The name chosen must not be undesirable in the opinion of the Secretary of State for Trade and Industry. A name is undesirable if it is either:

1. too similar to the name of another company, or
2. misleading; e.g., the name suggests that the company has connections with a government department, a member of the royal family, a district or a country.

Once the Secretary of State has approved a name for the company, it must be painted or affixed on the business premises of the company, engraved on its seal, and mentioned on all business documents and negotiable instruments.

A company limited by guarantee may be allowed to dispense with the word "Limited" by the Secretary of State if the following conditions are satisfied: S.30.

1. the company is formed for promoting commerce, art, science, religion, charity or any other useful object;
2. its profits are to be devoted to the promotion of those objects; and
3. no part of its profits is to be distributed to the members in the form of dividends.

A company may alter its name provided the following procedure is adopted;

1. The company must pass a special resolution to effect the change, and,
2. obtain the written consent of the Secretary of State.

Once the alteration of the name has been made, the Registrar of Companies will issue an altered certificate of incorporation.

If a company has a trading name different from its registered name, the *Busines names Act 1985* will apply. The effect of this Act has been noted in the chapter on Partnerships.

Articles of Association

The other important document is the *Articles of Association*. This is of importance to the shareholders of the company because it contains their rights as to transfer of shares and payment of dividends. It also contains information regarding the holding of meetings, the appointment of the directors and their powers. Thus the articles are of importance to insiders. If a company does not wish to draw up its own articles then it may adopt the ready made set of articles known as Table A which is to be found in a statutory instrument called *The Companies (Tables A to F) Regulations 1985*. (S.1 1985 No 805 as amended by S.1 1985 No 1052).

In the case of a company limited by shares, its articles are not registered, Table A automatically applies to it.

The following are some of the matters which are provided for in a company's articles:

1. Calls on its shares.
2. The company's lien on its shares.
3. The transfer of shares.
4. The exercise of the borrowing powers of the company.
5. The delegation of the management of the company to the board of directors.
6. The voting rights of members.
7. The payment of dividends.
8. Variation of the members' rights.
9. The conduct of meetings.
10. The capitalisation of profits.
11. The use of the company's seal.

Effect of the Articles
When registered, the articles constitute a contract between the members and the company. This contract binds the members

to the company but only in their capacity as members. Hence if the articles confer on a member or any other person a right not shared by all the other members of the company, this cannot be enforced against the company.

In *Eley v Positive Assurance Co (1876)* a member was made a solicitor for life of a company by the articles of the company. When he was dismissed he sued the company but it was held that the contract in the articles should not be enforced by him as the right he sought to enforce was not a "membership right".

The members in their capacity as members are bound to the company: *Companies Act S.14*.

Alteration of the Articles
By Section 9 of the *Companies Act 1985* a company may alter its articles of association by a special resolution. Any alteration is as valid as if it was originally contained in the articles.

Directors

Mention has been made of the fact that the company is an artificial person and cannot be seen but only exists on paper. So the question will no doubt occur as to how can a company operate. The answer is through human agents called directors. The directors' powers are contained in the articles and so they operate and decide matters on behalf of the company, provided they have the necessary authority to act. Thus when one says, "The company has decided to buy X Co. plc" what that really means is that the directors have so decided. However when one considers who appoints the directors, then the answer is the shareholders in general meeting. Thus the shareholders own the company and they appoint the directors to run the company on their behalf. The directors are given certain powers to act without recourse to the shareholders but of course such powers may be curtailed or extended as the shareholders wish. The directors may only act on behalf of the company within the powers of the company and also within their own powers. These powers are set out in the Articles of Association. Certain matters may need the authority of the shareholders in general meeting e.g. the fixing of a dividend, the passing of the accounts or the appointment of the auditors.

As an agent is in a position of trust as regards his principal, so is a director as regards the company. A director must exercise his powers for the purpose for which they are conferred and for the benefit of the company and must not put himself in a position in which his duties to the company and his personal interests may conflict.

Some directors (called non executive directors) are appointed because of the contacts they can bring to the company. They might have been Cabinet Ministers, Trade Union leaders etc. Other directors perform some particular function within the company, such as Financial Director, Production Director etc. These latter are known as Managing directors or executive directors.

Article 70 of Table A states that "Subject to the provisions of the Act, the memorandum and the articles and to any directions given by special resolution, the business of the company shall be managed by the directors who may exercise all the powers of the company."

If a company has as its object "to carry on business as a general commercial company" then it will have the power to do whatever is incidental or conclusive to that object.

A person dealing with a company must ensure

1. The directors must have the necessary power to enter into any particular transaction on behalf of the company.
2. If any particular procedure has to be followed then the transaction must have been made according to that.

If a bank is contemplating lending money to a company it must ascertain the directors' powers to borrow money on behalf of the company by consulting the articles. In some cases the shareholders may desire to restrict the directors' borrowing powers.

It can happen that an act is intra vires the company but ultra vires the directors. In that case the unauthorised act of the directors may be ratified by the company.

However it may be that a bank should not consult the

Articles because once it does, it will have actual notice of any limitation on the powers of the directors. If the bank does not have actual notice then it may be protected by *Section 35A* of the *Companies Act 1985* (amended).

As regards any particular procedure that needs to be followed, the *rule in Turquand's case* may be of assistance.

The Rule in Turquand's Case

This rule reiterates the rule of agency that a person who deals with an agent will be able to bind the agent's principal provided the agent acted within the scope of his actual or apparent authority.

The rule merely extends it to the special circumstances of companies when the directors act as its agents.

Every person dealing with a company is deemed to know the contents of its public documents – i.e. the memorandum, articles and presumably copies of any special or extraordinary resolutions it may have passed. This is because copies of these documents must be filed with the Registrar of Companies and are therefore accessible and open to members of the public to inspect.

An outsider is, however, not entitled to insist on proof by the directors that the rules and procedures for the internal management of the company have been complied with before he contracts with them.

The rule in *Royal British Bank v Turquand* therefore states that a third party dealing with the agents of the company is entitled to assume that the agents have authority to bind the company with reference to the part of their authority which derives from the "indoor management" of the company. Hence if the directors need an ordinary resolution before they can do a certain act and they do it without the resolution being passed, since the third party cannot know whether it was passed or not, he is entitled to assume that it was passed.

The rule is subject to certain limitations such as if the third party knew or should have known of the irregularity.

Now that the ultra vires rule has been abolished then a company will be able to do anything that the directors wish. It will be unnecessary for an outsider to consult the memorandum. However, presumably the powers of the directors may be restricted by the articles but so long as the outsider has no actual notice of the contents of the articles then presumably he will be able to rely on the word of the directors and will be protected if he does so.

Although directors are agents of the company, they do have a greater number of restrictions placed upon them.

Personal Liability of Directors

It is the main purpose of forming a company to avoid liability attaching to its members of managers.

However there are exceptions to this rule.

1. *Guarantee.* A loan to a company (usually a small one) may be supported by a guarantee from a director.
2. A director may be liable for breach of warranty of authority.
3. *Promoters.* A person who contracts on behalf of a company before it is formed is liable on the contract.
4. *Bills of Exchange.* Where a director has failed to disclose that he was acting as agent of the company. He may be personally liable if he signs in his own name unless he uses "For" or "per pro" or "for and on behalf of" or he signs "as agent for the company".

    If he signs a cheque in his own name but the company's name is printed on the cheque and there is an account number this may indicate that liability is attached to the holder of that account, so that if it is the company's account, the company alone is liable. *Bondina Ltd v Rollaway Shower Blinds Ltd (1986)*.
5. If the membership of a company falls below two and the company continues in business for more than six months after that, the remaining member is jointly and severally liable with the company for its debts (*S.24 Companies Act 1985*).
6. *Fraudulent and wrongful trading.* A feature of the new

insolvency legislation has been the attempt to ensure that any liability for fraud or wrongful transactions may be placed upon the directors of a company and that they should not be allowed to shelter behind the corporate façade. Directors may be civilly or criminally liable for fraudulent trading (*Section 213 Insolvency Act 1986*) if it can be shown, in a winding up of a company, that the business of the company was carried on with intent to defraud the creditors of the company.

In *Re William C Leitch Brothers Ltd (1932)* it was held to be fraudulent to continue to trade when the directors must have known there was no reasonable prospect of the company being able to pay its debts.

It is sometimes difficult to prove the necessary "fraudulent intent" on the part of the directors.

Therefore S.214 of the *Insolvency Act 1986* makes a director liable where a company is in insolvent liquidation and the directors should have realised that the company had no prospect of avoiding liquidation. This is known as wrongful trading.

Note that liability for wrongful trading (not fraudulent trading) may attach to "shadow directors". These are persons in accordance with whose directions the company is accustomed to act. A bank therefore could on occasions, be classified as a shadow director. It must be careful to give advice only and not instructions.

Section 212 of the Insolvency Act 1986 makes a director liable for misfeasance and breach of duty to the company.

Apart from the *Insolvency Act*, eight months earlier the *Company Directors Disqualification Act 1986* was passed. This Act consolidated the law relating to disqualification orders contained in the *Companies Act 1985* and the *Insolvency Act 1985*.

Under this Act a director may be disqualified if

1. he has been convicted of an indictable offence in connection with the management or liquidation of a company.
2. he has persistently been in default in delivering any document to the Registrar.

3. he has failed to comply with any provision of the Act and in the 5 years up to that conviction has been convicted of 3 or more similar offences. The director may be disqualified for up to 15 years.

A register of disqualified orders will be kept by the Secretary of State.

Meetings

The business of the company is transacted by means of passing resolutions at meetings. The meeting must be properly called and constituted according to the rules contained in the Articles of Association and according to the general law relating to meetings. For example, all persons who have a right to attend a meeting must be notified that one is to take place. Such persons may have to be given a minimum length of notice to attend. Also there must be a quorum present at the meeting, which means there must be a minimum number present in order for a valid resolution to be passed. Sometimes it is also necessary that the members constituting a quorum must have no personal interest in the matters being discussed or at least must have disclosed any interests they might have.

When a bank lends money to a company and takes security from it, it will require a certified copy of the resolution which authorises the charge. If a quorum was not present or if it was an invalid quorum because one of its number was an interested party then it would follow that any resolution passed would itself be invalid.

A bank therefore must be on its guard and if it knows that the meeting was invalid then it must reject any resolution made by such a meeting. This situation arose in *Victors Ltd v Lingard (1927)* in which the directors of the company personally guaranteed the company's overdraft with the bank. Later the directors in meeting resolved that the company should issue debentures to the bank as additional security. The articles of the company provided that no director should vote in connection with any matter in which he was personally interested.

In the subsequent case Romer J held that by agreeing to the issue of debentures by the company the directors were thereby relieving themselves of their personal liability for the overdraft and so were interested parties.

To avoid any difficulty which might arise as a result of a similar situation the bank should examine the articles to see how many directors must form a quorum and whether it must be a disinterested quorum. The bank may also rely on the Rule of Turquand's case and Section 35 of the *Companies Act 1985*.

If the ultra vires doctrine is abolished in the near future then a bank will be safe so long as it does not have actual notice that a director is exceeding his ostensible authority.

Every company must hold once a year a General Meeting of shareholders at which the accounts of the company are presented by the directors, who may have to submit to questioning from the shareholders. At this Annual General Meeting, of which the shareholders must receive 21 days notice, they appoint or re-appoint the directors and the auditors. They also confirm, or not as the case may be, the dividend proposed by the directors to be distributed. Every company must hold its first General Meeting – the statutory meeting – within six weeks of its formation.

Apart from the annual Meeting, the directors may, either of their own accord or because they have been so required by members of the company holding not less than one-tenth of the paid-up capital of the company – call on Extraordinary General Meeting of shareholders who must be given 14 days notice. At these meetings proposals are made and if accepted resolutions are passed. If the subject matter of the resolution is not particularly important, then it may be passed by an ordinary majority. However, if the matter is important, e.g., changing the name of the company or modifying the details of the objects clause of the Memorandum – then such a resolution must be a special resolution. Therefore it must be passed by a majority of 75% of those who attend and vote at the meeting. The same majority is required to pass an extraordinary resolution. If it is desired to propose a special resolution then 21 days notice must be given to those persons entitled to attend.

Capital

The share capital of a company goes under a number of different names. First there is the *Authorised Capital* or *Nominal Capital*. This is the capital stated in the Memorandum of Association and which the company is authorised to issue. It may not, at least initially, issue all its authorised capital and so the capital that has been issued is quite reasonably called *Issued Capital* or *Allotted Capital*. If some shares are issued only partly paid then the amount the shareholders have actually paid for their shares is called the *Paid Up Capital*. It is not so common nowadays for a company to issue partly paid shares.

Preference Shares

The capital is divided usually into two main classes, preference shares and ordinary shares. The preference shares, as their name implies, give the holder of such shares preference over other shareholders in the payment of dividends and also in the re-payment of capital in the event of the company being wound up. Preference shareholders receive a fixed dividend from any profits set aside by the directors for distribution. The dividend never varies and so such shares are usually considered solid and dependable and suitable for trustee investments. Preference shareholders are also usually given a preference as to return of capital in a winding-up. When the company is a going concern, the following presumptions apply to preference shares:

1. They confer a right to a cumulative dividend, this means that if no dividend is declared in any particular year, the arrears of dividend must be carried forward from year to year until they are all paid, before the ordinary shareholders can receive any dividends.
2. They are non-participating. This means they do not confer any right to participate in the profits of the company after the ordinary shareholders have been paid a dividend.

40 The Law of Companies

Redeemable Preference Shares

A company may, however, issue preference shares which from their inception are redeemable, either at a fixed date or after a certain period of time at the option of the company.

Sections 159 and 160 of the *Companies Act 1985* lay down conditions to be fulfilled before a company may redeem redeemable preference shares. Basically these conditions seek to maintain the capital of the company. For example, the redemption must be made out of profits, and only shares which are fully paid may be redeemed.

Ordinary Shares

These normally carry the residue of profits available for distribution as dividend after the preference shareholders, if any, have been paid their fixed dividend. *Ordinary Shares* are sometimes called the risk capital. This is because the dividend paid to the ordinary shareholders varies accord-ing to how well or badly the company has performed during the year. After the preference dividend has been paid then the residue is distributed to the ordinary share-holders and of course the amount will depend on the performance of the company.

In a winding up, if preference shares have priority as to return of capital, the ordinary shares will be entitled to the surplus assets, unless there are deferred shares. Hence ordinary shares are sometimes called the equity share capital of the company because they take what is left (the equity). Also the ordinary shareholders have a vote at the Annual General Meeting of the company and so the power to control the company rests with them.

These are the two main types of capital, preference or ordinary. There are other types of shares but these are not so common.

By issuing shares a company acquires money for its activities. However by issuing shares to the people who contribute money the company is acquiring more shareholders and consequently the control of its existing shareholders is being weakened. An alternative method of acquiring money is for the company to borrow it and in that case it will issue debentures to those people who lend it money. A debenture is a document which is evidence of a debt. The point about debentures is that the holders of these are not members of the company and do not have the same control over the company as do the shareholders. Instead of dividends, debenture holders receive interest on their holdings. However, like shares, debentures may be transferred on the Stock Exchange.

Running a Company's bank account

If the bank's customer is a company there are certain matters which must be considered.

1. The bank must see the certificate of incorporation because this document establishes the existence of the company.
2. The bank must examine the company's memorandum of association in order to ascertain the powers of the company. In addition the articles of association must be examined to ascertain the power of the directors to borrow money for the company.

Once the ultra vires rule has been abolished then presumably it will no longer be necessary for a bank to examine the above mentioned documents. A bank will be able to assume that the company has power to do anything it wants so long as it is not aware of any restriction on the company's authority, or on the authority of the directors.

3. If a company wishes to borrow money the bank must ensure

1. the company has power to borrow. This will be implied in the case of a trading company but is usually stated in the objects clause of the memorandum.
2. the loan is to be used for an intra vires purpose. *Re Introductions Ltd (1969)*
3. the directors have the authority to borrow the money on behalf of the company.

4. The bank will wish to see a resolution of the board of directors appointing the bank as the bankers of the company.

At this time the persons with signing powers will be designated in the mandate given to the bank.

5. If the company is a public company the bank will require to see the certificate to commence business.

6. When the account has been opened a bank must take the same care in paying company cheques as it does in the case of an individual. In collecting the proceeds of a cheque the amount must only be credited to the account of the company. Collecting the proceeds of a cheque payable to a company for the account of a third party is an unusual transaction and inquiries should be made. If the practice is likely to become commonplace then an authority authorising such collections should be taken from the company concerned.

7. In the same way that a loan to a company will be void if it is to be used for an ultra vires purpose a bank may also be in difficulties if it lends money to a company which is to be used for an illegal purpose and this purpose was known or should have been known to the bank. It may be that the bank could be held liable as a constructive trustee if it knowingly pays out money for the purpose of the loan.

An example would be when the company proposes to lend money to a director. The rules relating to loans to directors were strengthened following major scandals in the 1970s. *Sections 330–342* of the *Companies Act 1985* govern such a transaction and make such a loan illegal if made to a director or to a "connected person", i.e.

1. directors' families.
2. companies in which the director owns over one fifth of the equity.
3. the trustee of a trust whose beneficiaries include the director or members of the classes referred to above.
4. a partner of the director or any person in 1, 2, or 3 above.

In addition to loans purely and simply, other transactions, are also caught by the prohibitive section such as
– quasi loan which includes the provision of credit card facilities as where the company is the cardholder and the card is used by the director.

– a credit transaction where goods or services are provided on the undertaking that payment will be made later e.g. hire purchase terms.

– and back to back arrangements where company X lends to the directors of company Y on the understanding that company Y will lend to the directors of company X.

Sections 332–338 provide certain exceptions to the above prohibitions. The overall effect is: To allow all loans up to £2,500 for each director. To allow credit transactions if they are on normal commercial terms. To exempt loans to cover expenses incurred by a director if the transaction has the approval of the general meeting, subject to a maximum of £10,000 for directors of public companies. To allow quasi loans up to £1,000 if the terms require payment within 2 months. To allow credit transactions or the making of guarantees up to £5,000.

Money lending companies may make loans or quasi loans to directors on normal commercial terms subject to a maximum of £50,000. The terms may be more favourable if intended for house purchase or improvement.

Recognised banks can lend to their directors without limit provided the loans are on normal commercial terms. However the £50,000 limit applies if the loan is for house purchase or improvement.

8. A public company is not permitted to give financial assistance to anyone for the purpose of purchasing shares in the company. *Section 151.*

Exceptions would be if the loan is part of a larger transaction and not merely to purchase shares e.g.

1. the distribution of lawful dividends.
2. the allotment of bonus shares.
3. reductions of capital confirmed by the Court.
4. provision of money to allow employees to buy shares.
5. lending money is part of the company's business.

The importance to a bank of the points mentioned in 7 and 8 is that the bank may become involved if it lends money to the company for either of these purposes. It may become involved because it may be that the bank will be considered a constructive trustee if it knows or should have known that the company's funds held by the bank were being used for an illegal purpose. If that is so the bank may have to compensate the company for the illegal payments the directors have ordered it to make.

9. *Shadow Directors*

Section 251 of the *Insolvency Act 1986* defines a shadow director as "a person in accordance with whose directions or instructions the company is accustomed to act".

Thus the definition could apply to a number of persons such as

1. an Administrative Receiver under a bank debenture who continues to trade with the company during the receivership.
2. a parent company which exercises control over a subsidiary.
3. also it may be that in a liquidation of a company a bank could be held to have been giving instructions. It will be up to the manager concerned to ensure that he is merely advising and not directing or instructing.

Chapter Four

Borrowing by a Company

As was mentioned earlier, a company may sometimes need to borrow money. A power to borrow money will presumably be implied into the objects clause of every company registered with the "general trading" object. The directors are the persons who will actually arrange the loan on behalf of the company and so they too must have the necessary power to act. Sometimes the shareholders may wish to restrict their borrowing powers to a certain maximum amount.

Now that the doctrine of ultra vires has been abolished a company will have implied power to borrow and to give security for the loan but the authority of the directors will still have to be considered. This, no doubt, may continue to be restricted if so desired, but such restrictions will not affect persons dealing with the company unless they are aware of them.

The same principles apply to securities given by companies as apply to securities given by individuals. Some must be by deed e.g. a legal mortgage and in that case the company's seal must be affixed. If the document may merely be signed, the person signing on behalf of the company must be authorised by resolution of the board of directors.

An important requirement as far as charges given by companies are concerned is that *Section 398 of the Companies Act 1985* provides that the prescribed particulars of the charge together with the instrument (if any) by which the charge is created or evidenced must be delivered or received by the Registrar of Companies in Cardiff for registration within 21 days after the date of the charge's creation. Particulars may be delivered by any one interested in the charge. The company no longer receives a certificate. Instead the Registrar sends a copy of the particulars and a note of the date to the company, the chargee and any other interested person.

Examples of changes include:

1. A charge securing any issue of debentures.
2. A charge on land.
3. A floating charge on the undertaking or property of the company.
4. A charge on goodwill, patent or trade mark.

A banker who proposes to lend to a limited company should therefore inspect the register before doing so to see whether any prior charges exist on the company's property.

Even though it is the duty of the company to register the charge, where the company defaults, the creditor himself may register it and recover from the company any fees paid by him.

Certain charges are not required to be registered:

1. where a company mortgages shares or assigns a life policy or pledges goods.
2. where a negotiable instrument is given to secure the payment of any book debts of a company.
3. where an unpaid vendor's lien exists.

S.399 of the *Companies Act 1985*, as amended by S.95 of the *Companies Act 1989* provides that if particulars are not delivered within 21 days the charge is void as against:

1. an administrator or liquidator; or
2. any person who for value acquires an interest in or right over any property subject to the charge. Where the relevant event (for 1, beginning of insolvency proceedings or for 2, the acquisition of the right or interest) occurs after the creation of the charge.

New S.400 of the *Companies Act 1985* provides that where particulars are delivered more than 21 days after creation the charge is not void where the relevant event occurs after the particulars are delivered. It is therefore no longer necessary to obtain court approval to register out of time.

However the charge will be void as against an administrator/

liquidator if at the date of delivery of the particulars the company is unable to pay its debts (as defined by S.123 of the *Insolvency Act 1986*); or becomes unable to do so as a result of the charge and insolvency proceedings begin with the relevant period (i.e. beginning with the date particulars are delivered – 6 months in the case of fixed charges, 1 year if a floating charge but extended to 2 years if in favour of a connected person).

S.401 of the *Company Act 1985* as amended by S.96 of the *Companies Act 1989* provides that where the registered particulars are incomplete or inaccurate, further particulars signed on behalf of the company and chargee may be delivered at any time.

Debentures

Section 744 of the Companies Act 1985 provides that a debenture includes debenture stock, bonds or any other securities of a company, whether constituting a charge on the assets of the company or not.

More usually a debenture is considered to be evidence of a loan and a certificate will be issued to the creditor.

A debenture created by a company in favour of a bank will usually give a fixed charge over certain assets of the company and a floating charge over the remainder of the assets.

Fixed and floating charge

A fixed charge may be a legal or an equitable mortgage of some fixed or specified assets of the company. The effect of this is that the assets may not be sold or destroyed by the company otherwise the security on which the mortgagee is relying would be affected. If certain assets such as raw materials or finished stock were to be the subject of a fixed charge then they could not be used in the manufacturing process or sold. Consequently a floating charge was devised which would float over certain assets, not fastening on to them until certain events occurred which would have the effect of crystallising the floating charge. The assets which are subject to the floating charge may be used in any way the company desires, even to the extent that they are used up entirely.

A floating charge will crystalise or become fixed if the company:

1. defaults in payment of interest or capital or commits some breach of another term of the debenture and the mortgagee takes some step such as the appointment of a receiver.
2. goes into liquidation.
3. ceases to carry on business.

Often a company will borrow money from more than one person and in that case the interests of the creditors are represented by a trustee whose powers are stated in the trust deed. If any breach of convenant occurs then a receiver can be appointed.

Debentures are similar to shares in that they can be transferred on the Stock Exchange. However in the case of a debenture the holder

1. is a creditor and not a member of the company
2. he receives interest and not dividends
3. he has no voting rights
4. in a winding-up a debenture holder is treated according to whether the debenture is secured or unsecured.
5. a debenture may be repayable at a future date or may be irredeemable.
6. debentures may be issued at a discount whereas shares may not as a rule be issued at a discount.
7. a company may purchase its own debentures but it may only purchase its own shares in certain circumstances.

Debentures may be registered or issued to bearer. They may be secured or unsecured in which case they are called mortgage debentures or naked debentures.

If a bank lends money to a corporate customer it will use its own debenture form and the following are some typical clauses to be found therein.

Bank debenture form

The following clauses are usually contained in the bank's debenture form.

1. ───────────────────────────────

    The Company hereby covenants to pay to the Bank on demand the sum of One pound (£1) and to pay and discharge on demand all monies obligations and liabilities which may now or at any time hereafter may be or become due owing or incurred by the Company to the Bank on any account (whether solely or jointly with any other person and whether as principal or surety) present or future actual or contingent of the Company to the Bank together with interest and other bank charges so that interest shall be calculated and compounded in accordance with the practice of the Bank from time to time as well after as before any demand made or judgment obtained hereunder.

    ───────────────────────────────

    The company agrees to repay all liabilities present, future actual or contingent together with expenses.

2. ───────────────────────────────

    The Company as beneficial owner and to the intent that the security created shall rank as a continuing security hereby charges with the payment or discharge of all monies obligations and liabilities hereby convenanted to be paid or discharged (together with all costs and expenses howsoever incurred by the Bank in connection with this Mortgage Debenture on a full indemnity basis):

    a. by way of legal mortgage any property referred to in the Schedule hereto (the legally mortgaged property) and/or the proceeds of sale thereof

    b. by way of specific equitable charge all estates or

interests in any freehold and leasehold property (except the legally mortgaged property) now and at any time during the continuance of this security belonging to or charged to the Company (the equitably charged property) and/or the proceeds of sale thereof

c. by way of specific charge all stocks shares and/or other securities now and at any time during the continuance of this security belonging to the Company in any of its subsidiary companies or any other company and all dividends and other rights in relation thereto

d. by way of specific charge all book debts and other debts now and from time to time due or owing to the Company

e. by way of specific charge its goodwill and the benefit of any licences.

f. by way of floating security its undertaking and all its property assets and rights whatsoever and wheresoever present and/or future including those for the time being charged by way of specific charge pursuant to the foregoing paragraphs if and to the extent that such charges as aforesaid shall fail as specific charges but without prejudice to any such specific charges as shall continue to be effective.

As continuing security the company creates a fixed charge over freehold and leasehold property, plant and machinery, stocks and shares etc. It also creates a floating charge over other property not subject to a fixed charge.

3.

With reference to the property assets and rights subject to the floating charge:

a. the Company shall not be at liberty without the consent in writing of the bank to:

      i. create any mortgage or charge ranking in priority to or pari passu with that charge and/or

      ii. sell the whole or except in the ordinary course of business any part of the Company's undertaking

  b. the Company agrees to effect and maintain such insurances as are normally maintained by prudent companies carrying on similar businesses

  c. the Bank may by notice to the Company convert the floating charge into a specific charge as regards any assets specified in the notice which the Bank shall consider to be in danger of being seized or sold under any form of distress or execution levied or threatened and may appoint a receiver thereof.

The company agrees not to create any mortgage charge or lien on the property, to rank in priority to the floating charge.

4.

With reference to the legally mortgaged property and the equitably charged property the Company agrees:

  a. to keep it in a good state of repair and condition and insured against such risks and in such office and for such amounts as the Bank may require or approve and that failure to do so will entitle the Bank to do so at the expense of the Company and as agent of the Company without hereby becoming a mortgagee in possession

  b. that the statutory power of leasing and/or accepting surrenders of leases conferred on mortgagors shall not be exercised by the Company without the consent in writing of the Bank but the Bank may grant or accept surrenders of leases without restriction

c. not to part with the possession of it or any part thereof nor confer upon any person firm company or body whatsoever any licence right or interest to occupy it or any part thereof without the consent in writing of the Bank.

To keep insured the property charged.

5.

Immediately upon or at any time after the presentation of a petition applying for an administration order to be made in relation to the Company or at any time after this security shall otherwise have become enforceable the Bank may by writing under the hand of any area director or manager of the Bank appoint any person (or persons) to be an administrative receiver (the Administrative Receiver) of the property hereby charged. Where two or more persons are appointed to be an Administrative Receiver the Bank will in the appointment declare whether any act required or authorised to be done by such Administrative Receivers is to be done by all or any one or more of such Administrative Receivers for the time being holding office. Any Administrative Receiver shall be the agent of the Company and the Company shall be solely responsible for his acts or defaults and for his remuneration and any Administrative Receiver shall have all the powers of an administrative receiver specified in Schedule 1 of the Insolvency Act 1986 or any statutory modification or re-enactment thereof.

The bank may appoint a receiver.

6.

Section 103 of the Law of Property Act 1925 (the 1925 Act) shall not apply to this security which shall immediately become enforceable and the power of sale and other powers conferred by section 101 of the

1925 Act as varied or extended by this security shall be immediately exercisable at any time after notice demanding payment of any moneys hereby secured shall have been served by the Bank on the Company.

Section 103 (power of sale) and Section 93 (consolidation) of the Law of Property Act 1925, shall not apply.

7.

The Company shall from time to time supply to the Bank such accounts or other information concerning the assets liabilities and affairs of the Company its subsidiary or associated companies as the Bank may require.

The company will send to the bank copies of its trading account and Balance Sheet.

Floating Charge

The characteristics of a floating charge are set out in *Re. Yorkshire Woolcombers Association (1903)*.

1. It is a charge on a class of assets of a company present and future.
2. The class of assets is constantly changing from time to time.
3. The company may deal with the assets in any way that it wishes, until the holder of the charge takes some step to enforce it.

Useful though a floating charge is it should never be taken without the addition of a fixed charge. The floating charge is only appropriate for certain fluctuating assets. The disadvantages of a floating charge are:

1. Because the company may continue to deal with the assets which are subject to a floating charge it may be that when the mortgagee seeks to enforce the charge there will be no assets left. To minimise this risk a bank may ask for statements of assets from the company from time to time.

2. In the winding up of the company its preferential creditors e.g. the Inland Revenue will have priority over creditors holding a floating charge. Also creditors other than preferential may obtain priority over a creditor holding floating charge such as a landlord levying distress for rent or the sheriff seizing goods to satisfy a judgment.

3. On the same point concerning priority of creditors it may be that a supplier has sold goods to the company and has included in the contract of sale a "Romalpa" clause. This is the name given to the clause that was examined by the court in *Aluminium Industrie Vaasen B.V. v Romalpa Aluminium Ltd (1976)*. The case concerned the sale of aluminium foil by a Dutch company to an English company. The seller had inserted a clause to the effect that the ownership of the foil should remain with the seller, that the product of the goods should be held by the buyer as "producing owner" and that it should be stored separately from other stock on the supplier's behalf as "surety" for the remainder of the price. Also that the products might be sold by the buyers as agents for the sellers.

When the buyer became insolvent it was held that the seller could assume ownership of the goods in the hands of the buyer thus defeating the receiver.

It seems therefore that if the goods sold remain identifiable then the seller may assert his ownership. However if the goods sold are mixed with other goods so that the original goods lose their identity then problems may arise. In *Borden (UK) Ltd v Scottish Timber Products Ltd (1981)* the original goods became mixed with others and there was no provision in the contract for ownership in the mixed product remaining with the original sller. Consequently the attempt by the seller to retain ownership of the goods he had sold, failed.

In *Clough Mill Ltd v Martin (1985)* the court considered the matter obiter and came to the conclusion that the retention of ownership clause (Ramalpa clause) would be effective in relation to unmixed goods. If it had been intended that a charge be created over the goods sold that now form part of the mixed goods then this must have been registered.

It does seem therefore that the retention of ownership clause will be effective, if drawn correctly, in the case of unmixed goods provided such a clause provides for separate accountability for the proceeds in the event of a re-sale by the original buyer. There are considerable difficulties in the case of mixed goods.

Avoidance of a floating charge

4.   *Section 245 of Insolvency Act 1986* provides that – "where a company is being wound up a floating charge on its property created within 12 months of the commencement of the winding up is invalid (unless it is proved that the company, immediately after the creation of the charge, was solvent), except to the amount of any cash paid to the company at the time of or subsequently to the creation of, and in consideration for, the charge, together with interest on that account."

In this connection the rule in Clayton's case may operate in favour of the bank, because money paid into a company's account after the charge has been created will be linked with any debt outstanding when the charge was made. Therefore if the amount paid into the account after the charge was created, equals the debt the charge was intended to secure, the amount paid in will cancel the debt outstanding when the charge was made and the charge will be valid to secure loans made after the charge was created. *Re Yeovil Glove Co Ltd (1965)* which approved *Re Thomas Mortimer Ltd (1925)*.

If the charge was created in favour of a person connected with the company then a floating charge created within 2 years of the commencement of a winding up will be invalid whether or not the company was solvent.

Any charge made by a company within 6 months before commencement of a winding up (2 years, if a person connected with the company) is void if it is a preference of any of the company's creditors or within 2 years if it is a transaction at an undervalue.

5.   As a floating charge is an equitable charge, if the company which has given the charge later executes a fixed mortgage or charge over assets comprised in the floating charge then the latter fixed charge may take priority over the floating charge.

56 *Borrowing by a Company*

This situation may be avoided by the bank's inserting a clause into its debenture form to the effect:

"The company covenants not to create any mortgage or charge to rank in priority to or pari passu with the floating charge."

In order to make this restriction binding on possible later chargees the restrictive clause must be stated in Form 395 when registering the debentures with the Registrar of Companies.

A typical debenture form

The Royal Bank of Scotland plc

Debenture
Secs 1

Date: 19

Definitions

Company:

whose registered office is at

Bank: The Royal Bank of Scotland plc

Interest: Interest at the rate stipulated by the Bank from time to time or in the absence of a stipulation the rate of   % per annum above the Bank's fluctuating Base Rate

Property: The whole and any part of the undertaking property and assets of the Company charged by Clause 1

Registered Land: Description of Property   Land Registry Title Number

Company's Obligations: All the Company's liabilities to the Bank of any kind (whether present or future actual or contingent and whether incurred alone or jointly with another) including banking charges and commission

Expenses: All expenses (on a full indemnity basis) incurred by the Bank or any Receiver at any time in connection with the Property or the Company's Obligations or in taking perfecting enforcing or exercising any power under this deed with Interest from the date they are incurred

Charge

1 The Company covenants to discharge on demand the Company's Obligations together with Interest to the date of discharge and Expenses and as a continuing security for such discharge and as beneficial owner charges to the Bank:—

1.1 By way of legal mortgage all the freehold and leasehold property now vested in or charged to the Company including any Registered Land

1.2 By way of fixed charge all estates or interests in any freehold and leasehold property now and in the future vested in or charged to the Company except the property charged by Clause 1.1

1.3 By way of fixed charge all the plant machinery and fixtures and fittings furniture equipment implements and utensils now and in the future belonging to the Company

1.4 By way of fixed charge all the goodwill and uncalled capital of the Company present and future

1.5 By way of fixed charge all stocks shares and other securities now and in the future belonging to the Company

1.6 By way of fixed charge all intellectual property rights choses in action and claims now and in the future belonging to the Company

1.7 By way of fixed charge all book debts and other debts (including any funds standing to the credit of the Company from time to time on any account with the Bank or any other bank or financial institution or organisation) now and in the future owing to the Company

1.8 By way of floating charge all the undertaking and all property assets and rights of the Company present and future not subject to a fixed charge under this deed

Restrictions

2 The Company will not without the previous written consent of the Bank:—

2.1 Create or permit to arise any mortgage charge or lien on the Property and the Company requests the Chief Land Registrar to enter a restriction on the Register of any Registered Land that except under an order of the Registrar no disposition by the proprietor of the land is to be registered without the consent of the registered proprietor of this deed

2.2 Dispose of the Property charged by Clauses 1.1 to 1.7 inclusive

2.3 Deal with the Company's book debts and other debts otherwise than by collecting them in the ordinary course of the Company's business and in particular the Company will not realise its book debts and other debts by means of block discounting factoring or the like

2.4 Dispose of the Property charged by Clause 1.8 other than in the ordinary course of business

2.5 Grant or accept a surrender of any lease or licence of or part with or share possession or occupation of its freehold and leasehold property or any part of it

Insurance

3.1 The Company will keep comprehensively insured to the Bank's reasonable satisfaction all of the Property which is of an insurable nature for its full reinstatement cost and in default the Bank may effect such insurance and for that purpose may enter the Property (without becoming liable to account as mortgagee in possession)

3.2 The Company will hold in trust for the Bank all money received under any insurance of the Property and at the Bank's option will apply the same in making good the relevant loss or damage or in or towards discharge of the Company's Obligations Interest and Expenses

Deeds Securities and Debts

4.1 The Company will from time to time deposit with the Bank all deeds documents of title and insurance policies relating to the Property

4.2 The Company will pay into the Company's account with the Bank (or such other account as the Bank may specify from time to time) all money which the Company may receive in respect of the Company's book debts and other debts

Repair

5 The Company will keep the Property charged by Clauses 1.1 to 1.3 inclusive in good condition and in default the Bank may enter and effect repairs (without becoming liable to account as mortgagee in possession)

Notice of Crystallisation

6 The Bank may by written notice to the Company convert the floating charge into a fixed charge as regards any of the Property specified in the notice

Powers of the Bank

7.1 The Bank may without restriction grant or accept surrenders of leases of the Company's freehold and leasehold property or any part of it

7.2 Section 103 of the Law of Property Act 1925 shall not apply and the Bank may exercise its power of sale and other powers under that or any other Act or this deed at any time after the date of this deed

7.3 The Bank may under the hand of any official or manager or under seal appoint or remove a Receiver or Receivers of the Property and may fix and pay the fees of a Receiver but any Receiver shall be deemed to be the agent of the Company and the Company shall be solely responsible for the Receiver's acts defaults and remuneration

7.4 All or any of the powers conferred on a Receiver by Clause 8 may be exercised by the Bank without first appointing a Receiver or notwithstanding any appointment

7.5 The Bank will not be liable to account to the Company as mortgagee in possession for any money not actually received by the Bank

7.6 Section 93(1) of the Law of Property Act 1925 shall not apply to this deed

7.7 The Bank may at any time (both before and after demand) set-off or appropriate any credit balance on any account of the Company with the Bank (whether or not such balance is due to the Company) in discharge of the whole or any part of the Company's Obligations.

Receivers

8.1 Any Receiver appointed by the Bank shall be a Receiver and Manager and shall (in addition to all powers conferred on him by law) have the following powers which in the case of Joint Receivers may be exercised jointly or severally:—

8.1.1 To take possession of and generally manage the Property and any business of the Company

8.1.2 To carry out on any freehold or leasehold property of the Company any new works or complete any unfinished works of building reconstruction maintenance furnishing or equipment

8.1.3 To purchase or acquire any land and purchase acquire or grant any interest in or right over land

8.1.4 To sell charge or otherwise deal with and dispose of the Property without restriction

8.1.5 To lease surrender or accept surrenders of leases of any freehold or leasehold property of the Company without restriction

8.1.6 To carry into effect and complete any transaction by executing deeds or documents in the name of or on behalf of the Company

8.1.7 To take continue or defend any proceedings and enter into any arrangement or compromise

8.1.8 To insure the Property and any works and effect indemnity insurance or other similar insurance and obtain bonds and give indemnities and security to any bondsmen

8.1.9 To call up any uncalled capital of the Company with all the powers conferred by the Articles of Association of the Company in relation to calls

8.1.10 To employ advisers consultants managers agents workmen and others

8.1.11 To purchase materials tools equipment goods or supplies

8.1.12 To borrow any money and secure the payment of any money in priority to the Company's Obligations for the purpose of the exercise of any of his powers

8.1.13 To do any other acts which the Receiver may consider to be incidental or conducive to any of his powers or to the realisation of the Property

8.2 A Receiver shall apply all money he receives first in repayment of all money borrowed by him and his expenses and liabilities and in payment of his fees and secondly towards the remaining matters specified in Section 109(8) of the Law of Property Act 1925

Power of Attorney

9 The Company hereby irrevocably appoints the Bank and any Receiver severally to be the Attorney of the Company (with full power of substitution and delegation) in the Company's name and on the Company's behalf and as the Company's act and deed to sign or execute all deeds instruments and documents which may be required by the Bank or any Receiver pursuant to this deed or the exercise of any of their powers

Appropriation

10.1 Subject to Clause 10.2 the Bank may appropriate all payments received for the account of the Company in reduction of any part of the Company's Obligations Interest and Expenses as the Bank decides

10.2 The Bank may open a new account or accounts upon the Bank receiving actual or constructive notice of any charge or interest affecting the Property and whether or not the Bank opens any such account no payment received by the Bank for the account of the Company after receiving such notice shall (if followed by any payment out of or debit to the Company's account) be appropriated towards or have the effect of discharging any part of the Company's Obligations outstanding at the time of receiving such notice

Information

11 The Company will send to the Bank not later than 6 months after the close of each financial year of the Company a Balance Sheet Profit and Loss Account and Trading Account showing the true position of the affairs of the Company and its subsidiaries (if any) duly signed by the Auditors of the Company and also from time to time furnish to the Bank such other information regarding the assets and liabilities of the Company and its subsidiaries (if any) as the Bank may reasonably require

Preservation of other Security and Rights and Further Assurance

12.1 This deed is in addition to all other security present or future held by the Bank for the Company's Obligations and shall not merge with or prejudice such other security or any contractual or legal rights of the Bank

12.2 The Company will at its own cost at the Bank's request execute any deed or document and take any action required by the Bank to perfect this security or further to secure on the Property the Company's Obligations

Memorandum and Articles of Association

13 The Company certifies that this deed does not contravene the Company's Memorandum and Articles of Association

Notices

14.1 Any notice or demand by the Bank may be served personally on any director or the secretary of the Company or may be sent by post or telex or delivered to the Company at the above address or the Company's address last known to the Bank

14.2 A notice or demand by the Bank by post shall be deemed served on the day after posting

14.3 A notice or demand by the Bank by telex shall be deemed served at the time of sending

Governing Law

15 This deed shall be governed by and construed in accordance with the laws of England

Interpretation

16.1 The expressions 'Company' and 'Bank' where the context admits include their respective successors in title and assigns

16.2 Interest will be calculated both before and after demand or judgment on a daily basis and compounded quarterly on such days as the Bank may select but after a demand Interest will also be calculated on the Company's Obligations together with accrued Interest as at the date of the demand

16.3 References to the Property include any part of it

16.4 Each of the provisions of this deed shall be severable and distinct from one another and if one or more of such provisions is invalid or unenforceable the remaining provisions shall not in any way be affected

In Witness whereof this deed has been duly executed

The Common Seal of the Company was
affixed in the presence of:—

Director _____

Secretary _____

pursuant to Section 401 (2) of the Companies Act 1985

I hereby certify that a Mortgage or Charge dated the
and created by

for securing all moneys now due or hereafter to become
due or from time to time accruing due from the Company
to The Royal Bank of Scotland plc on any account whatsoever
was registered pursuant to Chapter I of Part XII of the
Companies Act 1985 on the

Given under my hand at the Companies Registration Office
Cardiff the

An authorised officer

The Royal Bank of Scotland plc

Debenture

Date:

Branch:

Granted by:

---

named Company the undertaking and other property and
assets charged by the within written Debenture

Signed Sealed and Delivered for and on behalf of
The Royal Bank of Scotland plc by
a duly authorised Attorney

(SEAL)

Date _____ 19 ____

20320 (6/88)

Chapter Five

Arbitration

Where a contract is made between two parties in the course of a business, it is becoming increasingly more common for the parties to agree that any dispute shall be resolved by arbitration.

> "All disputes,, differences or questions between the parties to the Contract with respect to any matter or thing arising out of or relating to the Contract shall be referred to the arbitration of two persons, one to be appointed by X and one by the Contractor or their Umpire. . . ."

Such contracts, providing as they do, that any disputes shall be solved extra-judicially are perfectly valid. Indeed if one party disregards such a clause the court may stop the action and in effect will compel the party to go to arbitration – *Arbitration Act 1950* S4(1).

In this connection a distinction must be made between a domestic arbitration agreement and a non-domestic arbitration agreement. A *domestic agreement* is one in which the parties are UK citizens or UK companies. In this case a stay of proceedings may only be granted if the matter in question is within the scope of the arbitration agreement and the applicant has taken no steps in the court proceedings (S4(1)). Also he must have been ready to do everything necessary for the proper conduct of the arbitration and there must be no good reason why the dispute should not be referred to arbitration. The same principles will apply when the parties have agreed on an exclusive jurisdiction clause and not an arbitration clause.

A cargo of turpentine was loaded at a Russian port into a

German vessel. The bills of lading were held by an English company which claimed that the turpentine was contaminated in transit and brought an action against the German vessel in the English courts. The owners of the German vessel applied for a stay on the ground that the bills of lading provided that all the disputes should be judged in the USSR **Held**, that the stay should be refused because the dispute had little connection with the USSR. None of the parties had Soviet nationality and virtually all the witnesses and other evidence were to be found in England; *The Fehmarn (1957)*.

> Egyptian Spring potatoes were carried in the El Amria, a ship owned by an Egyptian shipping company, from Alexandria to Liverpool. The bill of lading provided that any disputes should be decided in the country where the carrier had his principal place of business, i.e. in Egypt. The plaintiffs, who were the cargo owners, alleged that the cargo was found to be in a deteriorated condition when unloaded. They brought an action in the English courts against the defendant shipowners, claiming damages for breach of contract and for negligence. The defendants alleged that the deterioration of the cargo had occurred as the result of the unreasonably slow discharge and applied for a stay of proceedings in the English courts on the ground that the parties had agreed that the dispute was to be decided by the Egyptian courts. **Held**, the application for a stay of proceedings should be refused and the case should be allowed to proceed in the English courts. The issues raised between the parties relating to the alleged slow discharge solely concerned events which occurred in England and since the plaintiffs had issued a writ against the Mersey Docks and Harbour Co. it would be a matter of great convenience if that action could be tried at the same time as this action. Further, the most important evidence was in England. There were therefore strong reasons for refusing a stay of the English

proceedings: *Arata Potato Co Ltd v Egyptian Navigation Co. The El Amria (1980)*.

In the case of a *non domestic arbitration* the court *must* order a stay of proceedings unless it is satisfied that the arbitration agreement is null and void or incapable of being performed or that there is not in fact any dispute between the parties with regard to the matters agreed to be referred to arbitration. *Arbitration Act 1975 S1(1)*.

In 1970 the plaintiffs Nova, an English company, entered into a partnership agreement with the defendants Kammgarn, a German company, whereby the plaintiffs were to supply the defendants with knitting machines. The contract contained an arbitration clause and there was also a separate arbitration agreement. In 1972 the plaintiffs sold 12 machines to the defendants and received 24 bills of exchange for a total of £173,558. The first six of these bills of exchange were honoured by the defendants but the others were not paid on the ground, as the defendants alleged, of fraud. The defendants commenced arbitration proceedings in Germany and the plaintiffs issued a writ in the English courts for service out of the jurisdiction claiming payment of the outstanding bills of exchange. The defendants applied for a stay of the court proceedings. One of the issues was whether the arbitration agreement extended to the claims of the plaintiffs for payment of the outstanding bills of exchange. If this question had to be answered in the affirmative, the court was bound by section 1(1) of the Arbitration Act 1975 to grant a stay of court proceedings. Held, however, the arbitration agreement did not extend to claims made under the bills of exchange and the application for a stay of court proceedings on the bills of exchange should be dismissed: *Nova (Jersey) Knit Ltd v Kammgarn Spinnerei GmbH (1977)*.

Judicial Review
The court may still retain some control over the resolution of the dispute and may grant leave to appeal from a decision of an arbitrator on a point of law. However this leave will only be given sparingly and in particular a party to the dispute must have informed the arbitrator before the award was made that a reasoned reward was requested or that there was some special reason why the arbitrator was not notified.

The appeal may be brought to the High Court if the parties consent or by leave of the court. The court will only give leave if it considers that the determination of the question of law could substantially affect the right of one or more of the parties to the arbitration agreement.

Arbitration Act 1979 S(3) and (4)
Usually leave will only be granted in a "one-off" contract. This is a contract of a single occurrence and not made on standard contract forms.

> The owners of the Nema chartered her to the charterers for seven consecutive voyages to Sorel in Canada. Sorel was at the St Lawrence River and was icebound for many months of the year. After one round voyage the Nema arrived back at Sorel but was unable to load owing to a strike. The owners, who were permitted by the terms of the charter-party to take the Nema on one transatlantic voyage, took her to Spain. The main issue between the parties was whether, as the charterers claimed, the Nema was bound to proceed from Spain to Sorel and wait there until either the strike ended and she could load or the open water season ended and loading was made impossible. Or whether, as the owners contended, their obligations to make the Nema available for the outstanding voyages had ended by frustration. The parties agreed on arbitration by a single arbitrator who decided that the whole charter-party, as far as not performed, was frustrated. On appeal to the court, Robert Goff, J gave leave for judicial review of the arbitration award and held that the charter-party was not frustrated, but his decision was reversed by the

Court of Appeal. The charterers then appealed to the House of Lords. Held, (i) Robert Goff J should not have granted leave to appeal from the decision of the arbitrator nor should leave have been given to appeal to the Court of Appeal; and (ii) the arbitrator rightly decided that the whole charter-party, as far as not performed, was frustrated: *Pioneer Shipping Ltd v BTP Tioxide Ltd (The Nema) (1982)*.

Appeals may also lie to the Court of Appeal with leave of the High Court or Court of Appeal.

Exclusion agreement
The parties may sometimes exclude a judicial review, and so the effect will be that there will be no appeal to the High Court on a point of law.

In *domestic arbitrations* the parties may exclude a judicial review by an exclusion agreement if the agreement was made after the commencement of the arbitration proceedings. S3(6). In *non-domestic arbitrations* the parties may enter into an exclusion agreement before or after the commencement of the arbitration proceedings. S4(1).

Where the dispute is concerned with a claim falling within the Admiralty jurisdiction of the High Court (i.e. concerning shipping), a dispute arising out of a contract of insurance or out of a commodity contract then the exclusion clause will be admitted after the commencement of the arbitration or if the contact is governed other than by the law of England and Wales.

The Arbitration Agreement
The main reasons why the parties may insist on an arbitration clause in their agreement are

1. The procedure is quicker than going to an established court of law.
2. Consequently the dispute can be resolved more cheaply.
3. The arbitration proceedings can be conducted out of the glare of publicity.

4. The arbitrator will usually be someone who is qualified in the technical aspects of the matter in dispute.

Every agreement is assumed to include the following provisions unless a contrary consideration is expressed.

1. Reference is to a single arbitrator.
2. If there is reference to two arbitrators they may appoint an umpire at any time after they themselves have been appointed.
3. If the arbitrators have informed the umpire in writing that they cannot agree, he may act.
4. The parties to the arbitration proceedings must allow themselves to be examined under oath and must produce all relevant documents.
5. Witnesses must also be examined on oath.
6. The award when made by the arbitrator will be final and binding on the parties.
7. The arbitrator can order specific performance of any contract, except one relating to land.
8. An interim award may be made.
9. Costs are in the discretion of the arbitrator and he can award costs to be paid by either party.
10. Where the reference is to a single arbitrator or an umpire, and the parties do not agree or the arbitrator or umpire dies or refuses to act, any party may serve notice on the other to make an appointment and if not made within 7 days the court will appoint.

> The mv Tanais was under charter for a voyage between Canada and Italy. The charter-party provided, inter alia, for "arbitration to be settled in London". A dispute arose between the ship-owners and the charterers and the shipowners requested the charterers to agree on the arbitrator, but the latter refused to co-operate. Held, that the dispute should be settled by arbitration and an arbitrator be appointed by the court: *Tritonia Shipping Inc v South Nelson Forest Product Corpn (1966)*.

11. A similar situation will arise when a third party e.g. a chamber of commerce or the president of a professional association fails or declines to appoint an arbitrator. After 7 days the court may appoint.

The award
1. Must be certain and follow the agreement.
2. If a contract contains an arbitration clause and a claim is made in negligence (a tort) then, provided it is connected with the contract, it is within the jurisdiction of the arbitrator.

> Charterers thought that they had a claim for damages against the shipowners who had stopped the discharge of goods from the ship. In pursuance of their claim, the charterers arrested the ship. The shipowners claimed that the arrest was wrongful and demanded damages. The charter-party contained an arbitration clause and the arbitractors decided the claim for damages for wrongful arrest in favour of the shipowners. *Held*, (1) the claim for damages for wrongful arrest of the ship was founded in tort, (2) the arbitrators had jurisdiction to dispose of the claim as the arrest of the ship was only the sequel to the claim of the charterers and so closely connected with the alleged breach of charter-party that it was within the scope of the arbitration: *Astro Vencedor Compania Naviera SA of Panama v Mabanaft GmbH; The Damianos (1971)*

3. The award must be final, legal, reasonable and possible.
4. It must be reasoned if so requested by a party.

Arbitration, as described above, has existed for a very long time. It was devised to avoid the expense and slow pace of a court action, and principally because arbitration proceedings are held in private. This last point is important if the parties are companies in the public eye or partners in dispute.

However arbitration is very similar to litigation. In each case the solution is imposed by an arbitrator or judge and is binding on the parties.

Arbitration has now overspilled into the legal arena and there is provision for arbitrators in the courts. The *Courts and Legal Services Act 1990* and the *Supreme Court Act 1981* provide for judges of the Commercial Court and Official Referees to act as arbitrators. Also the rules of evidence will apply in such proceedings and the parties must state their case in writing, similar to a pleading in the High Court.

In these cases, of course, it is up to the parties as to whether they wish to use the arbitration procedure. There is no compulsion.

However in a small claim (under £1000) heard in the County Court the District Judge will act as an arbitrator instead of as a judge.

A different form of arbitration is Alternative Dispute Resolution known as ADR. This, like, arbitration, can only take place by agreement between the parties. The main feature of this system of solving disputes is that a decision will not be imposed by a judge or an arbitrator but will be reached by the parties themselves.

Alternative Dispute Resolution
ADR was initiated in the USA over ten years ago and is intended to overcome some of the disadvantages of going to court.

There is nothing new in the idea because it has been realised by lawyers that it is usually preferable to settle out of court. The risks of allowing a dispute to be decided by a judge are obvious and the expenses can be sometimes be considerable. Also if a dispute can be resolved by agreement between the parties then each party will consider that he has won whereas if the case is decided by a judge then there will be a loser and a victor.

The parties who have been in dispute can resolve their differences and then carry on business in the future on a friendly basis. ADR consists of mediation or conciliation and this may take the form of oral hearings in the presence of both parties or maybe documents only are submitted. Usually the mediator will see one side in one room and after listening to their grievances will see the other side in another room. Eventually some common ground may be reached which will form the basis of a compromise. In this way a great deal of money may be saved compared with the costs of going to court.

A more formal type of mediation is the Structured Settlement Procedure which is organised on the lines of a trial. In this case management representatives of each party are given the facts as viewed by both sides. Then, with the assistance of a neutral adviser, they enter into negotiations to solve the dispute.

If each party is intent on sticking to his strict legal rights then the ADR will probably not be a success. What is essential is that both sides should be prepared to discuss the question of compromise.

If ADR is not successful then litigation may follow. This will not be prejudiced by the use of ADR because any evidence arising from the ADR procedure will be confidential and without prejudice and may not be disclosed in later litigation. Sometimes ADR may be used after litigation has commenced. In that case the court action will be suspended to permit the meditation method to be given a chance to solve the dispute.

At the end of the day the question is whether the parties want a solution imposed by a court with its attendant expense and publicity or are do they want to try to solve the dispute themselves, with the help of a mediator.

Part 2

Relationships

Relationships in a commercial context must necessarily mean that the parties have entered into a contract and especially a contract for the sale of goods.

Consequently we now consider in Part 2, the rules relating to contracts and the protection of the consumer.

In addition a person may have acquired a monopoly over the right to manufacture some product; or have acquired a trade name by which his products are known; or may wish to acquire some compensation in the event that his goods are damaged, stolen or destroyed.

These topics are considered under Patents, Trade marks and Insurance.

Chapter Six

Formation of a Contract

The law is concerned with relationships between parties. In business the most common relationship is the contractual one, because obviously business consists of buying and selling goods and an important contract is that for the sale or purchase of something. Apart from that, organisations employ people and so the contract of employment is an important subject in business law.

In ordinary everyday life contracts are important because in addition to buying and selling goods and land and employment contracts, a person is entering into contract to travel on a train or bus, to purchase insurance cover for his life or his home and contents, or to enter into a contract of hire in respect of a car or a television set.

A contract may be expressed or implied. An expressed contract will arise when the parties consciously and intentionally enter into an agreement. An implied contract is one which can be assumed to exist because of the surrounding circumstances.

All these situations give rise to contractual relationships and so we must consider some aspects of contracts. It is probably only right that it should be generally agreed that if A promises to do something for B then B should be able to hold him to his promise and to recover compensation from A if A fails to do what he has promised to do. Therefore a contract is usually described as a legally binding agreement. A legally binding agreement is one which can be enforced in a court of law, thus A can sue B if he does not perform his part of the agreement or conversely B can sue A.

Before the plaintiff can successfully sue the defendant in an action for breach of contract the plaintiff must be able to prove to the satisfaction of the court that indeed there was in the first place a contract. In order to do that reference must be made to some essentials of a contract. The main essentials of a contract are the intention of the parties that their agreement shall be legally binding, the agreement between the parties and consideration which must be provided by the plaintiff.

Essentials of a Contract

Intention

It was stated earlier that a contract is described as a legally binding agreement. It follows therefore that there may be agreements that are not legally binding. Whether or not an agreement is legally binding – in other words whether or not a legal action can be brought in respect of it – may depend on

1. The intention of the parties.
2. An Act of Parliament.
3. Whether or not it is a social or domestic agreement.

The parties themselves may agree that an agreement reached between them shall not have any legal repercussions. This is usually effected by inserting an "honour clause" in the agreement. An example would be where a person completes a football pool coupon and signs at the bottom. The printed words at the bottom of the coupon usually contain the words "This transaction shall be binding in honour only". It follows therefore that if some difficulty arises in regard to the football pool coupon no legal action can be brought in respect of it. In addition large companies can sometimes agree that their agreements shall not have any legal force, so that in the event of a disagreement no legal action will be brought by either party. In *Rose and Frank Company v Crompton and Brothers Ltd (1923)* the Court of Appeal held that the agreement between the parties was not a binding contract because the parties had expressed an intention not to create legal relations. In the contract these words appeared "This arrangement is not entered into, nor is this memorandum written, as a formal or legal agreement, and shall not be subject to legal jurisdiction in the Law Courts either of the United States or England; that it is only a definite expression and record of the purpose and intention of the three parties concerned, to which they each honourably pledge themselves with the fullest confidence based on past business with each other; that it will be carried through by each of the three parties with mutual loyalty and friendly co-operation".

It is quite common where the parties are in business for them to agree that in the event of a dispute this shall be resolved by recourse to arbitration rather than to a court of law.

Some Acts of Parliament decide whether a particular agreement shall be legally binding or not. An example is the *Law Reform (Miscellaneous Provisions) Act 1970* in which Section 1 provides that an agreement between two persons to marry one another shall not under the Law of England and Wales have effect as a contract giving rise to legal rights and no action shall lie in England and Wales for breach of such an agreement, whatever the law applicable to the agreement. Thus it is no longer possible as it was before 1970 for a party who has entered into an areement to marry and who has been jilted, to sue the other party.

Finally there are a number of social and domestic agreements; these agreements are made by parties who have never given any thought to taking legal action if their agreement should not be complied with. Examples would be a "car pool" agreement between neighbours, an invitation to dinner, meeting a person outside a bingo hall or an agreement between a husband and wife whereby the husband agrees to pay a certain sum of money weekly to the wife for housekeeping. In *Balfour v Balfour 1919* the House of Lords held that an agreement between a husband and wife "is not a contract because the parties did not intend that it should be attended by legal consequences". Of course that will not preclude a wife from claiming against her husband if she is not adequately maintained by him; nor does it preclude a husband and wife from entering into a binding contract in certain circumstances.

So the first essential requirement of a binding agreement is that the parties must intend their agreement to be carried out and would expect legal consequences if it were not.

The second essential is the agreement itself.

The Agreement

The courts, in practice, are not usually concerned with the manner in which an agreement was entered into by the parties. They are only interested in whether or not the parties were in agreement. However an agreement may be analysed by considering its two constituent parts – the offer and the acceptance of that offer. Sometimes it is not clear who made the offer and who accepted it. In *Simpkins v Pays (1955)* Sellers J held binding an agreement between A, a paying boarder at B's house, B and B's grand-daughter C. They entered a fashion competition in a Sunday newspaper each week, each filling in one line, but the entry was sent in B's name. Sellers J. found that there was an agreement that, whichever line won, all should share equally and that A was entitled to receive one third of the prize from B.

Offer

The offer itself must be certain, it must be notified to the party to whom it was made (the offeree) although an offer may be made to no one person in particular (as in the reward cases).

Offer to the world at large
Carlill v Carbolic Smoke Ball Co (1893) QB. The defendants who sold the medical preparation "The Carbolic Smoke Ball" inserted in the Pall Mall Gazette an advertisement to the effect that £100 would be paid to anyone contracting influenza after having used the ball three times daily for two weeks. They also stated that £1,000 had been deposited at the Alliance Bank in Regent Street as evidence of their good faith. Mrs Carlill used the ball as directed and then found she had contracted influenza. She sued the manufacturers, claiming the £100.

The case is important because it established:–

1. An offer may be made not to a particular person but to the world at large.
2. It was intended to be binding because the defendants had deposited a sum of money at the bank.

3. Mrs Carlill had accepted the offer by complying with its terms.
4. Mrs Carlill had provided consideration by using the smoke ball and this conferred a benefit on the manufacturers because their sales would be increased.

Invitation to Treat

An offer must be distinguished from situations in which it may appear that an offer is being made, e.g. the display of goods in a shop window or on the shelves of a supermarket are not offers. They are invitations for the public to make offers for them (invitations to treat).

Pharmaceutical Society of Great Britain v Boots (1953) QB. A sale of goods occurs when an agreement is made between the seller and the buyer. Therefore if the seller makes the offer the sale is concluded when the buyer accepts or vice versa. This case hinged on whether or not the display of goods on the shelves of a supermarket constituted offers. If they were offers the offer could be said to have been accepted on each occasion when the customer took the article from the shelf and a sale would be made several times within the supermarket. The court decided that the display of goods on the shelves is only an offer to treat or an invitation to the public to make an offer for the goods. Therefore the sale takes place once only, when the customer proffers his money for the goods to the girl at the cash desk and she accepts the money.

Fisher v Bell (1961) QB decided a similar point in relation to goods on display in a shop window. It is the customer who offers to buy the goods and he may offer whatever he wishes for the goods. It is, of course up to the shopkeeper as to whether or not to accept the customer's offer.

The supply of information or a statement of intention e.g. to hold an auction sale, are not offers. *Harris v Nickerson (1873) QB.* The defendant, an auctioneer, advertised in the London papers that certain articles would be sold by him at Bury St Edmonds on a certain day. Harris went to the sale but the articles he was interested in bidding for were not put up for sale. He sued the auctioneer to recover compensation for two days' loss of time.

He failed, because it was held that there was no contract between the parties as Nickerson had merely stated his intention to sell certain articles and there was no offer capable of being accepted.

Notification of an offer
The offeree must know that the offer has been made, because you cannot accept an offer if you do not know that it has been made.

1. A has lost his watch and advertises in the local paper "Anyone finding my watch and returning it to me will receive £10." B reads the advertisement, finds and returns the watch and can now force A to give him the reward.
2. A has lost his watch and advertises in the same way as in 1. B does not read the advertisement but nevertheless finds and returns the watch. Later finding out about the reward offer he asks A, who refuses to give him the £10. B can do nothing – there was no contract.

Revocation of an Offer

An offer can be revoked at any time before it has been accepted. Thus the offeror can change his mind after making his offer but he must notify his cancellation of the offer to the offeree. If the offeror has promised to keep open the offer for a period of time and provided the offeree has given consideration for his promise then the offer cannot be revoked. This is known as buying an option. To post a letter of acceptance is a sufficient act of acceptance, but for revocation of an offer to be effective it must reach the offeree. In *Byrne v Van Tienhoven (1882)*. T posted a letter in Cardiff on October 1st offering to sell B some tin plate. On October 8th T posted a letter revoking his offer. On October 11th B received a letter containing T's offer and immediately telegraphed his acceptance. On October 20th B received T's letter of revocation. The court held that a contract had been made when B accepted the offer and the revocation took effect on October 20th which was too late.

As regards notification of revocation of an offer, in some cases the question may arise as to whether or not the offer has in fact been validly revoked. For example, if a notice of revocation has been delivered to the last known address of the offeree that would probably be effective if he had moved without informing the offeror of his new address. When an offer is made by public advertisement, a revocation will probably be sufficient if it is published in such a way that it is likely to come to the attention of those persons who saw the original advertisement.

Lapse

An offer may come to an end by lapse of time. Obviously if the offeror when he made the offer stated that it had to be accepted within a stated period of time, then it follows that if the offer was not accepted within that period then the offer would lapse. If no time was stated by the offeror then the offer will lapse at the end of a reasonable time and what is reasonable will depend on circumstances, in particular probably the general market conditions in which the offer was made. In *Ramsgate Victoria Hotel Company v Montefiore (1866)* M offered in June to buy shares from the Hotel company. In November, the company allotted shares to M, who refused to take them, contending that his offer had lapsed. It was held that the offer had indeed lapsed through passage of time as acceptance had not been made within a reasonable period of time from the date of the offer.

The Companies Act 1985 now applies.

Death of Offeror or Offeree

On the death either of the offeror or the offeree before acceptance again the offer will usually lapse. The situation may be different if there is a continuing contract as in the case where A has made a continuing offer to B to guarantee loans to be made by B to C. In that case if A dies unknown to B who makes a further loan to C then B might well be prejudiced if in fact A's death terminated the offer. Note that we are only considering the effect of death on the offer. If the offer has been accepted then a contract would exist between the parties and if either party then died after the contract had come in existence then probably the contract will be unaffected. This of course would not be so if a contract required personal services e.g. a person has agreed to sing or to give a concert at a theatre.

Rejection

It should always be remembered that the offeree may of course reject any offer made to him. If he does so then rejection is considered to put an end to the offer and the effect of this is that the offeree cannot subsequently change his mind and accept the offer. In this connection a counter offer is rather similar to a rejection and this will be mentioned when we deal with acceptance.

Acceptance

The basic rule is that an offer must be accepted exactly as it stands and the acceptance must be completely in accordance with the terms of the offer.

Counter Offer

If the person to whom the offer was addressed (offeree) accepts the offer subject to certain conditions, or if the acceptance is not exactly in accordance with the terms of the offer, then there will be no valid acceptance. This is known as a counter offer, and the effect of that is to destroy the original offer so that it is not possible for the original offeree (who made the counter offer) to change his mind and accept the original offer.

Hyde v Wrench (1840). Wrench offered to sell his farm to Hyde for £1,000. Hyde made a counter offer of £950, which Wrench refused. Hyde then changed his mind and wrote that he would accept the original offer of £1,000 made by Wrench. The court held there was no contract because the counter offer by Hyde had destroyed the offer made by Wrench and it was not possible for Hyde, later, to accept that offer.

Notification of Acceptance

The basic rule is that an acceptance must be brought to the

notice of the offeror. If the words of acceptance are drowned by an aircraft flying overhead or if the telephone crackles so that the offeror does not hear or is not aware that the offeree has accepted his offer then there will be no agreement. An exception to the rule that an acceptance must be notified to the offeror occurs in what are called the postal cases.

Postal Acceptance

It is only reasonable that the offeror should be notified by the other party that he has accepted; but if the postal system is used then the offer is deemed to have been accepted when the letter of acceptance is posted. If the letter of acceptance never reaches the offeror there is still a valid contract in existence.

Household Fire Insurance Co v Grant (1879). In a majority verdict the court decided that an offer is accepted when the letter of acceptance is posted even though, as in this case, the letter of acceptance did not reach the offeror. The view was that the Post Office is the common agent of both the offeror and the offeree. The moral of the story is – if you make an offer by post to someone, make sure that he does not intend to accept your offer if you are contemplating making the same offer to another person. The onus is placed upon the offeror. This decision was made purely on the grounds of expediency. Students often wonder how the posting of the letter of acceptance can be proved. There are many ways in which this may be done but quite simply if the posting cannot be proved then there is no point in going to court. Every litigant in any court action must be able to prove his case to the satisfaction of the court. If he thinks he cannot do so then he should be advised to save his money.

A court may rely on the word alone of the witness – if there is some corroborative evidence then he may, more readily, be believed. The burden of proof is that the court must be satisfied "on the balance of probabilities" – not as in a Criminal Court – "beyond all reasonable doubt".

Note that although an acceptance will be effective when the letter of acceptance is posted a revocation of an offer will not be made merely by posting it but will only be effective when the offeree receives the notice of revocation.

Method of acceptance prescribed by offeror

When the offeror makes his offer he may state the manner in which the acceptance must be made e.g. by letter or telex. The offeree can then accept only in that way as presumably the offeror has made the requirement for his own protection. An offer may stipulate that it can be accepted by silence as in *Felthouse v Bindley (1862)*. In that case the plaintiff wished to buy a horse belonging to his nephew and wrote to him stating "I will offer you £X for the horse and if I hear no more from you then I shall consider that the horse is mine." The nephew did not reply to the letter but instead he sold the horse and the action was brought by the plaintiff claiming that he had a contract with the nephew. He was unsuccessful as the court held that there was no valid contract for the sale of the horse. There must be some positive action taken by the offeree in order to make a valid acceptance and it is not possible, or indeed fair, for the offeror to attempt to force an acceptance from the offeree.

Once an offer has been validly made and the offeree has made an effective acceptance there can be said to be an enforceable agreement between the parties.

Thus a valid agreement is one which the parties intend should be legally binding. However, there is one other element which is peculiar to systems of law based on the English common law, that is:

Consideration

This has been defined by Pollock as "the price for which a promise is bought". Again it does not usually cause the courts much difficulty in establishing that consideration is present because it is the element of exchange in a bargain. Only when a person has made a gift to another person will there be no consideration. If there is no consideration then if the party who has made the promise breaks his promise (breach of contract) then the other party will not be able to sue successfully as he gave no consideration in return for the promise of the other. This is known as a bare promise and is not enforceable in English law, but may be enforced under French law. A says to

B, "I will give you my car on Friday." Presumably B will be happy to receive the car, so they are in agreement. However, if A breaks his promise and fails to give B his car, then B can do nothing about it. He, B, has given no consideration in return for A's promise.

There is no good reason why a person who makes a promise to another should not have to pay compensation to the other if he breaks his promise, but that is not the case in English law. However, there is an additional body of rules called Equity which are occasionally brought into use by the judge, purely at his discretion. If it can be shown that to keep strictly according to the letter of the law would result in injustice the judge may diverge slightly from the strict letter of the law. Thus if A makes B a promise and B acts upon this promise and does some act he would not have done if he had not relied on A's promise then A may be barred (estopped) from going back on his promise notwithstanding that B gave no consideration. This is known as the rule in the High Trees Case and is an example of a rule of equity being brought into operation.

Sometimes the rule is called "equitable or promissory estoppel?", and was first stated in *Central London Property Trust v High Trees House (1947)*. In 1937 C let to H a block of flats for ninety-nine years at £2,500 a year. In 1940, owing to war, very few flats were let and C agreed to reduce the rent to £1,250. In 1945, C sued for arrears of rent at the rate of £2,500. *Held*, as the agreement for the reduction of rent had been acted upon, C could not claim the full rent, but that it was only operative during the conditions which had given rise to it. As the flats had been fully let in 1945 the full rent was payable from then. It means that the promisor is estopped or prevented from going back on his word. It is looked upon as a slight inroad into the doctrine of consideration, but it does not in any way do away with that doctrine. In *Combe v Combe* it was called "a shield rather than a sword".

Combe v Combe (1951) KB. After divorce proceedings the husband and wife entered into an agreement by which the husband promised to pay to the wife £100 per annum. The husband failed to do this and the wife sued him. In the High Court the wife was successful because although the wife had given no consideration for the husband's promise the judge followed the principle in the High Trees case. However, on Appeal Denning LJ, who was responsible for the principle in the High Trees case when he was in the High Court, stated that it does not do away with the need for consideration in English law. It may only be used to prevent a party from insisting on his strict legal rights, when it would be unjust to allow him to enforce them, having regard to the dealings which had taken place between the parties. The principle may not be used on which to base an action but only as a defence.

However, apart from these exceptional cases a contract must have consideration and a party will not be able to successfully sue in respect of a broken promise unless he can prove that in return for the promise, he provided consideration.

Form of consideration
Consideration will usually take the form of the payment of a sum of money or the doing of some act. However, as was mentioned earlier, a right is a valuable thing because it can be enforced in a court of law. Consequently if a person has promised to pay a sum of money or to do an act, that will be acceptable as consideration, because the person to whom the promise was made has a right to sue the promisor if he breaks his promise.

Thus if A says to B, "Do you wish to buy my car for £500?" and B says "Yes," there is a valid enforceable contract. Nothing is required to be in writing. A has promised to give B his car and B has promised to give A £500. That's all that is needed. Of course it would be preferable if there were some witnesses, because A or B might deny what they said. On the other hand, both parties could go to court without witnesses and leave it to the judge to decide which party he chooses to believe. The promise of each of the parties will be consideration.

Consideration must be real but need not be adequate
Consideration must be real but need not be commensurate to the value of what the other party has done or promised to do. The courts will never enquire as to whether any consideration is adequate in relation to the value of the subject matter of the contract. This merely reiterates the principle of freedom of contract. If A wishes to sell his £500 car for £1 that is A's

business. Provided B has paid a £1 or has promised to pay him that sum, there will be a valid contract, because B has provided consideration in return for A's promise to sell him his car.

On the other hand the consideration must be real and in the opinion of the court of some value. In *White v Bluett (1853)* a son's promise to stop being a nuisance to his Father was held to be not good consideration. However, in *Chappell v Nestlé and Company (1959)* some empty chocolate wrappers sent to the chocolate company by the public were held by the court to be valuable consideration.

It must be something more than the person to whom the original promise was made has already promised to do.
Stilk v Myrick (1809) The crew of a ship sailing to the Baltic and back to London had entered into an agreement to sail on the round trip and to receive payment a the rate of £5 per month. During the voyage two of the crew deserted and so the captain promised to share the wages of the deserters amongst the crew remaining on board ship. When the voyage was completed the captain failed to pay the extra amount he had promised, and in court it was settled that he was not liable on his promise because no consideration had been given in return for it. The crew who remained on board ship had done nothing more than they were already bound to do by the terms of their contract. If they could have proved that they had done extra work (which they could not do in this case) that would have been consideration for the promise of the captain.

Payment of a smaller sum
Payment of a smaller sum will not discharge liability to pay a larger unless the smaller sum was paid earlier than the agreement required or in a different form of place from that originally intended. This point arises where A has lent B £100 and B repays £75. A then says to B, "I will release you from payment of the balance." A therefore has made a promise to B but cannot be held to that promise because B has not given any consideration. However if the loan of £100 was for a period of three weeks and B repays £75 in two weeks then he would be providing consideration because he would be conferring a

benefit on A by letting him have some of the debt earlier than was necessary. Now A will not be able to go back on his promise. Also the High Trees principle could apply here if B can show that in reliance on A's promise not to sue him for the balance of the £100, he, B, did something he would not have done if A had not made to him that promise.

Consideration must not be past
Past consideration occurs when it has been given or executed before the promise is made. Thus if X gives Y £500 and Y promises to go to London to transact some business for X – this is executed consideration since the promise to go to London is given at the time the £500 is handed over.

If Y without any arrangement with X goes to London and transacts some business for X. When he returns X promises to pay Y £500 for what he has accomplished in London. This is past consideration because Y has provided his services (consideration) before X has agreed to accept and pay for them.

In this chapter we have been looking at the main essentials of a contract. It must be remembered that a contract is an agreement and that an agreement takes place in the minds of the parties. It may be necessary to have some evidence that an agreement has been reached, but in most cases written evidence is not needed. Also the agreement may take place without the contract being performed. Of course it will have to be performed but that may be some time after the agreement (or contract) has been made.

We have seen that a legally binding contract will only exist if;

1. the parties intend their agreement to have legal effect
2. the parties are in agreement
3. there is consideration present provided by the party who seeks to enforce the contract (plaintiff).

Formation of a Contract

A number of people believe, quite wrongly, that a contract must be made in writing and be signed by the party making it. This is an understandable mistake because a very large number of contracts are in writing. But the reason for that is because it is sometimes more convenient to have a written record of the terms of the contract rather than because the law requires it so. In fact a contract may be made by word of mouth or even by implication – as when a passenger steps on to a bus and thus enters into a contract with the bus company.

The law therefore only requires a contract to be in writing in a small number of cases. For example, a share transfer, a hire purchase agreement, a bill of exchange (i.e. a cheque) or a contract for the purchase or sale of land.

As regards the last example the law has recently been changed by the *Law of Property (Miscellaneous Provisions) Act 1989*. It provides

1. A deed may be written on any substance, not only paper or parchment.
2. If an individual is executing the deed there is no need for a seal to be used although the document itself must state that it is a deed.

    Companies will presumably still have to use their seals.
3. Two witnesses are required to attest the parties signatures.
4. The contract for the sale of land must incorporate all the terms agreed by the parties together with all the signatures of the parties.

Invalidating factors

It can be said that a contract (a legally binding agreement) cannot exist unless all three requirements are present. However the converse does not hold good because sometimes even though the three essentials are present there may still not be a legally binding contract because some other invalidating factor might prevent a contract coming into existence.

For example, force might be used to get one of the parties to agree; the parties might be in mistake; one party might deceive the other; the contract might be for an illegal purpose. In all these cases even though the three essentials might be present, the contract would be either void or voidable because of these additional invalidating factors.

Chapter Seven
Mistake, Misrepresentation and Illegality

Mistake

The first of these invalidating factors is mistake. In this case the effect of mistake will be to destroy the basis of the agreement. A mistake which does not do that will of course have no effect on the contract.

When buying goods a person may buy the wrong size or colour or later find that he could have bought the same article at a cheaper price. He could say that he has made a mistake, but legally he can do nothing about it. However, if the existence of certain mistakes means that there never was a true agreement because the minds of the parties were not together, then the contract will be void. Agreement takes place in the minds of the parties and so if one party is thinking of one thing and the other is thinking of something quite different then their minds are not at one – there is no agreement (consensus).

If the mistake is of a fundamental nature it is called an operative mistake and its effect will be to render a contract void. A void contract is one which is without legal effect. It is a complete nullity in law and confers no rights on either party.

The following are examples of operative mistakes.

1. *Mistake as to the identity of the subject matter of the contract*
   The parties may be mistaken as to the identity of the subject matter of the contract or even as to whether it exists or not.
   Raffles v Wichelhaus (1864) Exchequer It so happened there were two ships both named Peerless. What caused the difficulty was that both of them were leaving Bombay at around the same time. The defendant entered into an agreement to buy cotton "ex Peerless" and he was

thinking of the ship that left Bombay in October. The plaintiff agreed to sell cotton "ex Peerless" and he had in mind the ship that left Bombay in December. The court held there was no binding contract because of the operative mistake. The parties were not thinking of the same thing.

If both parties believe the subject matter of the contract to be in existence, but in fact at the time when the contract is made it is non existent, there is no contract. In *Scott v Coulson (1903)* G agreed to assign to H a policy of assurance upon the life of L. Unknown to either L had died before the agreement was made. *Held* no contract.

In *Bell v Lever Brothers Ltd (1932)* B and S were employed by L under agreements for a fixed time. Later L paid B and S £50,000 to be discharged from these agreements. B and S had been making secret profits, which would have entitled L to dismiss them without notice, but this was unknown to L at the time the £50,000 was paid. There was no evidence of fraud on the part of B and S. The court held L could not recover the £50,000. There was no mistake on either side as to the contracts which were being released. The fact that L could have obtained the release on much cheaper terms did not, in the absence of fraud or breach of warranty, render the contract void.

The general rule is that if a person makes a mistake as to the offer of the other party to the contract, the contract is never the less binding upon him. In *Smith v Hughes (1871)* Blackburn J. stated "If, whatever a man's intentions may be, he so conducts himself that a reasonable man may believe that he was assenting to the terms proposed by the other party, and that other party upon that belief enters into the contract with him, the man thus conducting himself would be equally bound as if he had intended to agree to the other parties' terms". In *Smith v Hughes* S sold H a quantity of oats, a sample of which S had shown H. The oats were new oats but H who had inspected the sample erroneously thought that he was buying old ones.

The price was high for new oats but oats were very scarce at that season. *Held* H's mistake was irrelevant unless S positively knew that H wanted to buy old oats only.

If, in *Smith v Hughes* S had *known* that H had made a mistake in accepting his offer, there would have been no contract. In *Scriven Brothers and Company v Hindley and Company (1930)* an auctioneer was selling tow and hemp. A lot of tow was put up for sale and M was under the impression that it was hemp and made a bid for it. The bid was extravagant for tow, but reasonable for hemp. From the price bid the auctioneer knew that the bidder was made under a mistake. The court held that there was no contract.

2. *Mistake as to identity of the other party contracted with*

A party may be mistaken as to the identity of the other party to the agreement. This mistake can only arise if the parties are apart and are in correspondence. If the parties are contracting face to face then they cannot be mistaken as to the person with whom they intend to make the contract. In other words, the identity of the other contracting party is irrelevant.

Cundy v Lindsay (1878) AC. In this case the rogue wrote to Messrs Lindsays in Belfast and acquired some handkerchiefs by means of forging the name of a reputable merchant with whom Lindsays had previously done business. The rogue disposed of the handkerchiefs to Cundy and Lindsays tried to recover them back. The case hinged on the point as to whether the right of ownership of the goods had passed to the rogue. If he had acquired the right of ownership or title to the handkerchiefs then he would have been able to pass this on to Cundy, who would then have been able to retain possession of the goods because he would have been the owner.

However, the court held that the contract between the rogue and Lindsays was void on the grounds of mistake and so the right of ownership never left Lindsays. Consequently they were able to recover possession of the handkerchiefs from Cundy because they had remained owners of the goods.

We shall consider the sale of goods later. It should be remembered that when a person "buys goods" he is in fact in law wishing to acquire the title or right of ownership in the goods. If the seller has the right of ownership and the contract between him and the buyer is valid – then the seller's title will pass to the buyer and he will become the owner of the goods. In *Cundy v Lindsay* the contract of sale between the rogue and Lindsays was void and so the rogue did not acquire title to the handkerchiefs. Consequently the rogue did not become the owner of the handkerchiefs and when he sold them to Cundy he could not pass right of ownership on to Cundy. Therefore Lindsay was entitled to have the goods returned to him.

In *Cundy v Lindsay* the parties were in correspondence and some distance apart. Consequently Lindsays only had the signature on the letter to help to identify the person with whom they intended to make the contract. In the next case the parties were face to face – *Lewis v Averay (1971) AC*.

Again Lewis was mistaken as to the identity of the other party. Lewis thought he was dealing with a film star called Richard Greene, and gave possession of the car to the rogue, who disposed of it to Averay. If Lewis was to be successful in recovering possession of his car then, as in *Cundy v Lindsay*, he would have to prove that his title to the car had never left him. However the court held that the contract between Lewis and the rogue was not void for mistake because Lewis had made no mistake "as to the person with whom he intended to make the contract of sale". The identity of the rogue was not material. Consequently the rogue acquired a title to the car; but because of the deception the contract between the rogue and Lewis was voidable. This meant that Lewis could escape liability under the contract, provided he took steps to avoid the contract before a third party became involved. To avoid a contract which is voidable the other party should be notified of the intention to avoid liability under the contract, and if that is impossible then the police or the Automobile Association, in the case of a car, should be notified. *Car and Universal Finance Co Ltd v Caldwell (1965)*. If such steps are taken before the goods are transferred to the third party then the contract will have been avoided. However, in this case the rogue acquired a voidable title to the car and he passed this to a third person, Averay, before Lewis took steps to avoid the contract. Lewis therefore could not recover his car.

3. *Mistake as to the type of written contract signed*

If a person has made a mistake as to the contents of the contract then, if he has signed it, he cannot escape liability under it. That is the basic rule regarding signing contracts. The well known advice is to make sure you read the small print before you sign a contract and indeed that is very good advice. Whether you have read the contents of the contract or not or whether you haven't fully understood the contract matters not. Quite simply if you have signed it you are bound by it.

However, a written contract may be avoided after a person has signed it if he can prove that he was mistaken as to the type of contract that he was signing and that when he signed he was not negligent.

Saunders v Anglia Building Society (1970) is the leading case on this point. It provides that a person who has made a mistake as to the type of contract he has signed may be able to have it set aside if he was not negligent when he signed it. In practice, it would seem that the person who signs a contract different in nature from the one he thought he was signing, must have been deceived by the other party. It would not be possible for that to happen unless there had been fraud present. In the Saunders case an old lady, Mrs Gallie, wished to transfer her house to her nephew. A friend of the nephew called Lee persuaded her to sign a document to transfer in his (Lee's) favour. The court held that Mrs Gallie had not signed a contract radically different from the one she thought she was signing and also she had been negligent. Although she did not succeed, the case is important for the guide-lines it sets out.

Rectification

If the parties were in agreement on all important terms but by mistake wrote them down wrongly, rectification of the written document may be ordered. To obtain rectification it must be proved:

1. there was complete agreement between the parties on all the important terms.
2. the agreement continued unchanged until it was reduced into writing and
3. the writing did not express what the parties had already agreed.

It will be noticed that here there has been a mistake not as to the contract itself but a mistake as to what was written down and so a document will normally only be rectified if both parties have made a mistake as to its contents. For example, if an oral agreement were made for the sale of peas and a written document recorded a sale of beans, the written document could be rectified by the substitution of "peas" for "beans". If the written document does accurately record the previous agreement then it cannot be rectified on the grounds that the previous agreement was itself made under some mistake. Equity does not rectify contracts but only documents. *Mackenzie v Coulson (1869)*.

Misrepresentation

When parties are considering entering into a contract with each other then invariably statements will be made by each of them. These statements are called representations. For example, if A is attempting to sell a motor car to B then A will probably say "It's an excellent vehicle" or "It's a good runner" or "It has only done 10,000 miles". All these statements are representations and are perfectly in order unless a representation happens to be a false statement. In that case it is called a misrepresentation.

A misrepresentation is defined as "a false statement of material fact made by a party to the contract or his agent which induces the other party to enter into the contract".

The important points of this definition are:

1. *The false statement must be of fact not opinion*
   A fact is usually said to be capable of proof. An opinion on the other hand is usually so vague as to have no legal effect at all. These are constantly used in advertising.

   In *Bisset v Wilkinson (1927)* Bisset said the land he was selling was large enough to support 2,000 sheep. The court held this was merely his opinion.

   Or again "This car is a good runner" or "This car will last you a life time" are statements of opinion. On the other hand "This car has travelled 10,000 miles" is a statement of fact.

2. *The false statement must have been made by a party to the contract*
   This means that only if the statement was made by a person who intended to be a party to the contract can any false statement be called a misrepresentation. If for example the false statement was made by a person who is not a party to the contract then it would not be misrepresentation. The person who made the false statement may never the less still be liable in law. In *Hedley Byrne and Company Ltd v Heller and Partners Ltd (1964)* A was induced to enter into a contract with B because he relied on a statement made by C. This was not misrepresentation but never the less the court held that it would be possible for C to be liable for the false statement he had made. This is known as a negligent mis-statement. This principle was established in the Hedley Byrne case and in that case it was held that it may be possible for C to be made liable for his false statement if it can be shown that C made the statement negligently and knew that the person

to whom he was making the statement was going to rely upon it.

3. *The false statement must have been relied upon by the other party*
If A makes a false statement intending to deceive B but B takes no notice of the statement and makes his own investigations before deciding to enter into the contract then B cannot later claim that he has been deceived by the false statement of A.

In *Horsfall v Thomas (1862)* the seller of a gun filled in a crack in the barrel with the intention of deceiving the purchaser into thinking that the gun was in good condition. However the purchaser agreed to buy the gun without examining it. The court held that he could not claim to have been deceived. This then is the definition of a misrepresentation. It will be apparent that a misrepresentation may be made by a person intending to deceive, or it may be made by a person innocently, who does not know that the statement he is making is false. Never the less the other party will still have been deceived. The distinction between the various types of misrepresentation is of some importance. There are three types of misrepresentation:

a. *Innocent misrepresentation* This arises where the person making the statement does not know that it is untrue.
b. *Innocent but negligent misrepresentation* In this case the person who makes the statement does not know that the statement is untrue but should have checked up before making the statement. In this sense he may be said to have been negligent.
c. *Fraudulent misrepresentation* In this case the person making the statement knows that he is making a false statement and intends to deceive the other party.

In all these cases the person hearing or receiving the false statement has been deceived but the importance of the distinction between the various types of misrepresentation hinges on whether damages may be awarded. At one time damages could only be awarded for fraudulent misrepresentation. In the case of fraudulent misrepresentation it has always been possible for the person who has been deceived to bring a civil action based on fraud. Such an action is available without reference to any contract.

As regards negligent misrepresentation it had also been possible since *Hedley Byrne and Company Limited v Heller and Partners Limited* for an action to be brought based upon the wrongful act, again irrespective of contract. However, the *Misrepresentation Act 1967 Section 2(1)* provides that damages are payable "where a person has entered into a contract after a misrepresentation has been made to him by another party". Thus an action since 1967 may be brought for negligent misrepresentation based on contract. It is always true to say that if a choice exists as to whether to sue in contract or in tort it will usually be easier to bring an action based on contract. In the case of negligent misrepresentation all that the plaintiff has to show is the existence of a contract after the misrepresentation has been made. The other party, the defendant, is assumed to have been negligent unless he can prove to the contrary.

In the case of a wholly innocent misrepresentation the party misled has no right to damages but the judge has a discretion to award them.

Disclosure of Material Facts

The general rule is that mere silence is not a misrepresentation. A party is not usually obliged to disclose all material facts to the other party, even if he knows that the other party is ignorant of some important fact.

In contracts for the sale of goods this rule is called "caveat emptor", which means "let the buyer beware". However as we shall see when we consider the law relating to the sale of goods the caveat emptor principle has been modified.

In the following cases a party is under a duty to disclose all material facts unasked.

1. When in the course of negotiations, a party has made a

representation of fact which was true when made but before the contract has been made becomes untrue to his knowledge, then the person who made the statement is under a duty to correct the statement he originally made.

In negotiating the sale of a medical practice in January, X represented the takings to be at the rate of £2000 a year. In May, when the contract was signed, the takings had, due to the illness of X, fallen to £5 a week.

Held the contract could be rescinded owing to X's failure to disclose the fall in the takings *With v O'Flanagan (1936)*.

2. If part only of a series of facts is disclosed, and the undisclosed part so modifies the part disclosed as to render it, by itself substantially untrue, there is a duty to disclose the full facts.

3. A latent defect may not merely affect the value of the subject matter of the contract but also cause further loss or injury to the buyer. In this case the seller may be liable in negligence for failing to warn the buyer of the existence of the defect if he knows that it does exist.

In *Hurley v Dyke (1979)* the defendant was a garage owner who sold a three-wheeler car by auction on terms that it was sold "as seen and with all its faults and without warranty". The vehicle was resold by the purchaser to a person named Clay and eight days later it crashed because of corrosion in the chassis, injuring the plaintiff passenger.

The plaintiff's claim failed because the defendant had given warning to the purchaser and had no knowledge of the specific defect.

The point was not taken but it would appear that if the defendant had known of the defect he might have been in breach of duty.

4. Contracts of utmost good faith.

These are sometimes referred to as "contracts uberrimae fidei" and they are the main exception to the rule that silence does not amount to misrepresentation. In these contracts, one party has full knowledge of all material facts and so a duty is imposed on him to make full disclosure to the other party.

Examples are:
a. contracts of insurance
b. contracts of family arrangement
c. certain contracts for the sale of land
d. contracts of suretyship and partnership in their operation.

Contracts of insurance are the most important contracts in this category and in *London Assurance v Mansel (1879)* M, in reply to questions which asked whether any previous proposals had been turned down by any other insurance company answered negatively. In fact several other offices had declined his proposals. *Held* there had been a material failure to disclose, and the policy could be set aside.

Rescission

Rescission means the cancellation of a contract. It enables an innocent party to recover any property transferred under a contract or any payment made in advance, whilst at the same time he must restore any property he obtained under the contract. Rescission may be obtained by application to the court or by giving notice to the other party.

Rescission is known as an equitable remedy. This means that it is within the discretion of the court whether or not to grant the remedy.

Some factors which will be taken into account by the court in deciding whether or not to rescind the contract are as follows:

1. The judge may declare the contract to continue to exist and award damages in lieu of rescission.
2. If the deceived party, with knowledge of the misrepresentation, takes a benefit under the contract or in some other way affirms it, then the contract may not be rescinded.
3. If the parties cannot be restored to their original positions. In *Lagunas Nitrate Company v Lagunas Syndicate (1899)* – L Syndicate sold Nitrate Works to the Lagunas Nitrate

Company under a contract which contained misleading particulars. The company sued for rescission of the contract. *Held* Owing to alteration of the property consequent on its being worked by the company, the position of the parties had been so changed that they could not be restored to their original positions, and therefore the contract could not be rescinded.

4. If a third party has acquired for value, rights under the contract. If A obtains goods from B by fraud and pawns them with C, B will not normally be able to rescind the contract on learning of the fraud so as to be able to recover the goods from C – *Phillips v Brooks (1919)*.
5. The fact that the contract has been performed does not deprive the deceived party of his right to rescind.

As was stated above a contract may be rescinded either by the deceived party applying to the court for rescission or by his notifying the other party that he intends to rescind the contract. It is in fact sufficient if the deceived party does all that he can in the circumstances to rescind the contract even though he has been unable to get in touch with the person who made the false statement. In *Car and Universal Finance Company Limited v Caldwell (1965)* the facts were – on January 12th 1960 C, the owner of a Jaguar car was persuaded to sell and deliver the car to a rogue who gave C a car of much lower value than the Jag. The next morning C ascertained that the cheque was worthless and at once asked the police and the Automobile Association to recover his car. The rogue sold the car to a person who did not acquire it in good faith and only on January 15th was the car acquired by a purchaser in good faith. It passed through several hands and eventually was acquired by the Car and Universal Finance Company Limited which acted in good faith. The court held that while normally the rescission of a voidable contract must be communicated to the other contracting party, that was not necessary if, as in the present case, the other party by deliberately absconding put it out of the power of the rescinding party to communicate. Consequently C had rescinded the contract when he notified the police and the Automobile Association.

Duress

The essential of any agreement is the valid consent of each of the parties and so it follows that if consent has been obtained by improper use of pressure then there will be no valid agreement. If consent is obtained by actual or threatened violence which puts the other party in fear for his life or physical well being then the contract may be set aside. Such a situation rarely happens in practice. However, in recent years the notion of economic duress has gradually become accepted by the English courts. In *Pao On v Lau Yiu Long (1979)* Lord Scarman stated "There is nothing contrary to principle in recognising economic duress as a factor which may render the contract voidable, provided always that the basis of such recognition is that it must always amount to a coercion of will, which vitiates consent."

In *Atlas Express Limited v Kafco (Importers and Distributors Limited) (1989)* the facts are – K were basketware importers and had a contract to supply 800 Woolworths Stores. Needing a carrier to transport their products K entered into a contract with A whereby A agreed to carry the cartons at £1.10 each; the contract to run from October 10th 1986 to May 31st 1987. Some weeks later A realised it had under priced the job and realised that if K failed to deliver as agreed with Woolworths K would lose its business and be sued. A took advantage of the situation by getting one of its drivers to deliver to K an updated agreement and informed K that he would not carry away any goods unless K signed the agreement. Unable to arrange alternative transport K signed the agreement under protest.

K now refused to pay A's invoices and when sued by A, one of its defences was economic duress. This defence succeeded on the grounds that K's apparent consent to the new agreement was vitiated by A's threat to withdraw transport facilities, so that the new agreement had been secured unlawfully.

Undue Influence

This is another form of unlawful pressure and falls outside the originally narrow common law definition of duress. In this case the act of coercion need not be unlawful but there must be present some form of exploitation by one party over a weaker party. In addition there is a presumption that in certain relationships undue influence does exist. Such relationships are those between parent and child, doctor and patient, solicitor and client, trustee and beneficiary but not between husband and wife, nor between banker and customer. The mere existence of such a relationship is not, on its own, a ground for relief. The party seeking to set the transaction aside on the ground of undue influence must show that it was unfair and that he, the innocent party, was put at a disadvantage. The other party for his part may protect himself by showing that there was independent and professional advice given before the transaction was entered into. At one time it was always the practice of a bank which is entering into a contract with a young lady to get her to agree that she had taken independent legal advice before signing the agreement. However since the sex discrimination legislation this matter has to be treated very carefully.

Illegality

A contract may be illegal by Statute or at Common Law. A Statute may expressly prohibit a certain act such as traders agreeing between themselves the price at which goods may be resold. Such an agreement would be contrary to the *Resale Prices Act 1976*. Another example is the *Life Assurance Act 1774* which provides that "No insurance shall be made by a person on the life of another in which he has no insurable interest." Contracts which contravene this prohibition have been held to be illegal. Obviously a contract for the deliberate commission of a crime would be illegal; also if a contract is capable of being performed in an unlawful way then again it would be unenforceable.

Contracts contrary to Public Policy

In addition to the above contracts certain contracts have been declared by the courts over the years to be contrary to public policy. In such cases the judges have refused to enforce certain contracts on the grounds that to do so would be harmful to society. Examples would be:

1. a contract damaging the administration of justice (e.g. stifling a prosecution). In a somewhat similar vein, if any person interferes with the course of justice by giving aid to a litigant without good reason or by agreeing to share the proceeds of an action with one of the parties, then such an agreement shall be void.
2. a contract to defraud the Revenue. In *Miller v Karlinski (1945)* a contract was considered which provided that one of the parties could include in his expense account the amount of the income tax he was due to pay. It was decided that this was a fraud upon the Revenue and so was declared illegal.
3. a contract tending to promote sexual immorality. In the well known case of *Pearce v Brooks (1866)* the defendant was a prostitute and she had hired a carriage in which to ply her trade. The court held that the supplier of the carriage could not succeed in an action against her for the money he was owed as he knew of the use to which the carriage was to be put and that was an illegal contract.
4. a contract damaging to the institution of marriage. Contracts which could damage the institution of marriage would be a marriage brokage contract (marriage bureau), or a contract for possible separation of husband and wife in the future.
5. a contract to oust the jurisdiction of the courts.

All these contracts have been held by the courts to be contrary to public policy and therefore harmful to society.

Restraint of Trade
Finally the last large group of contracts are contracts in restraint of trade. Such a contract in restraint of trade will often arise in an employment contract when the employee agrees, on leaving his present employer not to work for a competitor for a certain period of time. Such a contract will only be enforced by the courts if it is reasonable as regards

a. the type of employment. In other words the employee must have been in a position where he could damage his former employers' interests if he went to work for a competitor.
b. the area of restraint, and
c. the period of the restraint.

Points (b) and (c) are usually taken together so that a restraint covering a wide area for a short period may be allowed, as may a restraint covering a narrow area for a long period.

In *Fitch v Dewes (1921)* a solicitor's clerk agreed not to set up as a solicitor, for the rest of his life, within seven miles of Tamworth Town Hall. This agreement was upheld by the court.

Restraints may arise in other situations such as when a vendor of a business is asked to agree not to set up a similar business in competition with the business he has just sold. Otherwise the seller might set up in a business nearby and attract all his old customers away from the buyer.

As was stated above every restraint is presumed void unless it can be proved otherwise. It can be proved valid if it can be shown to be reasonable in the interests of both parties and in the interests of the public at large. The courts are more likely to permit a restraint clause to operate if it is contained in an agreement between the vendor of a business and the purchaser. In such a case the parties will be business men and therefore presumably capable of taking care of themselves. In the *Nordenfelt case (1894)* an inventor and manufacturer of munitions sold his business to a company and agreed not to engage in munitions business, or in any other business liable to compete in any way with that for the time being carried out by the company, in any part of the world, for the next 25 years. The House of Lords decided that the munitions restraint was valid not withstanding the time and extent because in fact it concerned a world-wide business. The second restriction, covering competition with any other activity of the company was held to be too wide and therefore void.

Agreements to Fix Prices or Regulate Supplies

Such contracts are nowadays governed by statute. In particular the *Restrictive Trade Practices Act (1976)* requires that such agreements affecting goods or services must be registered with the Director General of Fair Trading. These agreements are presumed void unless the parties can prove to the Restrictive Practices Court that the agreement is beneficial and in the public interest.

Restrictive trading agreements may also now be invalid in English Law if they contravene article 85 of the Treaty of Rome. This provides that all agreements between firms which may affect trade between member States and which operate to prevent, restrict or distort competition within the Common Market shall be automatically void unless specifically exempted by the Community authorities.

An agreement may be void under the Treaty or specifically exempt under the Treaty and at the same time fall with the *Restrictive Trade Practices Act 1976*. The Act deals with this possibility so as to give effect to the general policy that Community principles governing restrictive trade practices should, where they apply, prevail over the domestic rules.

Effects of Illegality

The law relating to the enforcement of illegal contracts is complex but the basic rule is that a guilty party cannot enforce the contract while an innocent party may be able to do so.

When one party repents of the illegal purpose before carrying it out, the court may allow him a remedy. However his repentance must be genuine.

Finally, if the ownership of goods passes as the result of a illegal contract then the original owner cannot reclaim them once they have been delivered. However he may be able to claim damages for the tort of conversion if the other party is equally at fault.

Chapter Eight
Terms of the Contract

Every contract contains terms or stipulations. Usually these are expressly stated in the contract. However sometimes terms are implied into a contract. Such terms may be implied by fact, by law or by custom.

By fact
As regards terms implied by fact, these are terms which the court decides that partners must have intended to include. At one time the test was "would an officious bystander have assumed that the parties would have intended to include some term". Now the courts seem to insist that the implication must be obvious to both parties.

By law
The best example of terms implied by law is the operation of the *Sale of Goods Act 1979*. That act implies terms into every contract for the sale of goods, primarily that the goods should not be defective.

By custom
Finally when parties have traded in a particular market for a period of time they will be assumed to go along with any custom of the market. Thus in *Smith v Wilson (1832)* it was proved that by local custom when a sale of 1000 rabbits took place this meant 1200 rabbits. Everyone surely has heard of "a baker's dozen" i.e. 13.

Standard terms
It is now common practice in some areas for one party to present to the other certain terms usually set out in printed

form. The advantages of this system are obvious as it avoids the necessity of establishing the terms of the contract each time an agreement is reached. In this way a standard pattern of dealing is set up. Such standard terms are to be found in railway tickets, insurance contracts and contracts between suppliers of goods and services and the purchasers of these. When there is a business document given by one party and received by the other as the document containing the terms of the contract, the offeror is under no obligation to call the offeree's attention to all the terms of the document, unless the terms are printed in such a manner or are in such position as to mislead a reasonably careful business man.

> R ordered four lots of timber from N's traveller. The traveller left a sold note setting out the sale and containing a clause "Goods are sold subject to their being on hand and at liberty when the order reaches the head office." N did not deliver the timber, and, on being sued by R, pleaded the clause set out above. R did not know of the clause and had not read it. Held, R was bound by the clause, unless it was so printed that from its position in the document and the size of the type an ordinary careful business man, reading the document with reasonable care, might miss it: *Roe v RA Naylor Ltd (1971)*

When the offeree has signified his acceptance by signing a document presented by the offeror, the offeree cannot plead ignorance of the terms of the offer, in the absence of fraud or misrepresentation, even if he is in fact ignorant of them.

> The proprietress of a cafe bought an automatic cigarette vending machine from the defendants. She signed a document which contained a number of clauses in small print, amongst them a clause excluding "any express or implied condition statement or warranty, statutory or otherwise, not stated therein." She refused to pay the price on the ground that the machine did not work and contended inter alia, that she was not bound by the

exclusion clause as she had not read it. Held, the clause was binding on her: *L'Estrange v F Graucob Ltd (1934)*

If the contractual document is signed as a result of the offeree's oral misrepresentation of one of its terms, the offeree will not be able to rely on that term.

> C took a dress to D to be cleaned and was asked to sign a receipt which contained, among other terms, a clause, "This article is accepted on condition that the company is not liable for any damage howsoever arising." C asked why she had to sign and was told that D would not accept liability for damage to beads or sequins. She then signed. The dress was returned stained. Held, D could not rely on the clause, because C's signature was obtained by misrepresentation of the effect of the document: *Curtis v Chemical Cleaning & Dyeing Co (1951)*

Similarly, if at the time when the contract is made a person gives an oral promise which cannot be reconciled with a term in the printed contract, the oral promise takes priority over the printed clause.

> M left his car in N's garage. Contrary to the rules of the garage, the car attendant who took the car over told M he must not lock the car. M informed the attendant that there was valuable property in the car and the attendant promised to lock the car after he had moved it. By the terms of the ticket which the attendant gave M, N, excluded responsibility for the loss of contents of the car. A suitcase containing valuables was stolen from the car. Held, N was liable. Though the attendant had no actual authority to promise to lock the car, he had ostensible authority to make a statement concerning the safety of the car and its contents. The printed exclusion clause was repugnant to the express oral promise and could not be relied upon by N: *Mendelsohn v Normand Ltd (1979)*

Where printed conditions in a contract are repugnant to a binding oral promise they do not provide exemption from liability for breach of that promise: *J Evans & Son (Portsmouth) Ltd v Andrea Merzario Ltd (1976)*.

"Battle of Forms"
In business transactions a contract may be entered into by each party exchanging a printed form of contract with the other party. It should never be forgotten that if one receives a printed form and there is a clause with which one does not agree then this may be altered or deleted. It is only what actually appears on the form, which is eventually signed, that in fact is binding on the parties.

The situation just described where each party sends the other a printed form of contract containing standard clauses is sometimes referred to as the "battle of forms". The leading case on this point is *Butler Machine Tool Co Ltd v Ex-Cell-o Corporation (England) Ltd (1979)*.

In that case the plaintiffs quoted to the defendants a price for a machine tool and their quotation was stated to be subject to the seller's standard terms which included a price variation clause. In addition the quotation made it clear that their standard terms and conditions should prevail over any terms contained in the buyers' order.

The buyers ordered the product and their printed order was on the buyers' standard terms which did not include a price variation clause. The buyers' order form stated in a tear-off slip – "We accept your order on the Terms and Conditions stated thereon." This was intended to be signed by the sellers and this was duly signed and returned to the buyers – a covering letter stated that this order was accepted in accordance with the original quotation.

When the sellers delivered the product they relied on the price variation clause in their standard terms and asked for a price increase of nearly £3,000. The buyers argued that their terms applied and these made no provision for a price increase.

When the case came before the Court of Appeal that

court held that the plaintiff sellers' quotation was an offer – Ex-Cell-O's order was a counter offer and the return of the acknowledgement slip by Butler amounted to an acceptance of the counter offer. Therefore the contract was made on the terms put forward to Ex-Cell-O.

It could be argued that by accepting the offer from Butler, Ex-Cell-O had agreed to the terms of that offer. However it could also be argued that Ex-Cell-O had not accepted the offer on the same terms as the offer and so had in fact rejected the offer.

What is certain is that this situation is fraught with difficulties and maybe the courts will have no choice but to adopt the established solution, *Hyde v Wrench 1840*.

In order to avoid such difficulties the party must ensure that, when exchanging forms containing standard terms, each party must study closely the other party's form to make sure that new terms to the agreement have not been introduced.

Exclusion or Exemption Clauses

Amongst these standard terms is often to be found a clause which seeks to exempt or restrict the liability of the party who inserted the clause.

For such exemption clauses to be valid and enforceable at common law the courts have laid down certain principles e.g.

1. The existence of such a clause must be brought to the attention of the other party. It matters not whether he has read it, but at least he must know that the clause exists. Thus the holder of a ticket should be notified on the ticket that "the conditions of contract are obtainable on request . . ."
2. Such exemption clauses or references to them must be contained in "a contractual document and not in a mere voucher or receipt.
Chapelton v Barry UDC (1940)

> C hired a chair from the council, paid for it and was given a ticket which he put in his pocket unread. The

chair collapsed and C was injured. The ticket had a clause that the council were not to be liable for accidents or damage. Held, this was not binding on C.

Thornton v Shoe Lane Parking Ltd (1971)

Mr Thornton wished to park his car in a multistory automatic car park belonging to the defendants. A traffic light at the entrance of the car park showed red. A ticket was extruded from a machine. When Mr Thornton took the ticket the light turned green and the car was taken up. When Mr Thornton collected the car, an accident occurred and he was injured. The defendants pleaded that the ticket contained a notice in small print that it was issued "subject to the conditions of issue as displayed on the premises," and that these conditions, displayed inside the garage, contained a clause exempting the defendant from liability for personal injury. Mr Thornton had not read the small print. Held, the exempting clause in the conditions did not protect the defendants. 1. Lord Denning MR held that the contract was concluded when Mr Thornton positioned his car at the appointed place and the light turned green, and the ticket was only a receipt which could not alter the terms of the contract; 2. all three judges of the Court of appeal agreed that the defendants had failed sufficiently to bring to the notice of Mr Thornton the limitation of liability:

3. Finally the clause must be notified to the other party either before or at the time the contract is made. When the guest at an hotel read the notice, which was affixed to his bedroom door, after he had booked in to the hotel – the court held it was ineffective.

Olley v Marlborough Court Ltd (1949)

The plaintiff and her husband took a room in a residential hotel owned by the defendants. At the reception desk they were asked to pay a week in advance. They did so and went to their bedroom in which a notice was displayed stating that the proprietors did not hold themselves responsible for the loss or theft of articles unless handed to the manageress for safe keeping. Owing to the negligence of the defendants' personnel, a stranger gained entrance into the hotel and stole articles from the plaintiff's room when she was absent. Held, the defendants were liable. The contract was concluded at the reception desk and the terms of the notice in the bedroom were not incorporated in it.

In 1977 Parliament passed *The Unfair Contract Terms Act* and this had a considerable effect on the effectiveness of exemption clauses. The Act applies to the following types of contract:

1. contracts for the sale of goods
2. contracts of hire purchase
3. other contracts under which possession or ownership of goods passes.
4. contracts for the supply of goods and services to which the *Supply of Goods and Services Act 1982* applies.

It does not apply to other types of contract e.g. contracts of insurance. The prohibitions and qualifications which the Act provides, apply only to business liability, i.e., liability arising in the course of a business.

Any clause in a contract excluding or restricting liability for death or personal injury resulting from negligence is absolutely void s.2(1).

In the case of other loss or damage then such terms that exclude or restrict liability must satisfy "the requirement of reasonableness" otherwise it will be void. The Act seeks to protect private persons. In other words the contract must be between a person in business and another person who is not in business (who deals as a consumer).

Terms of the Contract

Dealing as a consumer
A party is dealing as a consumer if

1. the goods are of a type ordinarily supplied for private use or consumption and
2. the seller sells them in the course of his business to someone who is not buying or holding himself out as buying in the course of a business.

> The seller, a boat builder, contracted to build a boat for a Mr Atkinson. The contract of sale contained an exclusion clause claiming to exclude the seller's liability for breach of the implied terms as to merchantable quality and fitness for the purpose. Subsequently, before delivery, a limited company, Rasbora Ltd, was substituted as buyer in place of Mr Atkinson. This was done by way of novation, i.e. an extinguishing of the original contract between the seller and Rasbora Ltd. Rasbora Ltd was a company incorporated in Jersey. It was wholly owned by Mr Atkinson and had been formed by him for the purpose of buying the boat and with the intention that the boat was to be used only by Mr Atkinson and his friends; there was no intention to hire out the boat. Shortly after it was delivered, the boat caught fire and sank. Held, the seller was liable for breach of the implied term as to merchantable quality. The exclusion clause was totally ineffective

a. because the contract with Rasbora Ltd (like the earlier one with Mr Atkinson) was a consumer deal and, alternatively,
b. because the exclusion clause, claiming to exclude the whole liability in respect of merchantable quality and fitness for the purpose, did not satisfy the requirement of reasonableness; *Rasbora Ltd v JCL Marine Ltd (1977)*.

A supplier of goods cannot escape his responsibility for selling goods which are unmerchantable or which do not correspond with a sample or description.

Terms of the Contract 113

Producers can also be made liable for "defective" products if they cause death, personal injury or damage to property under the *Consumer Protection Act 1987* and again this liability cannot be excluded by contract.

If the parties are not a business man and a consumer but the contract lies between one business man and another then there may be an exclusion or restriction of liability for breach of contract but only if such exclusion is "reasonable". In deciding the meaning of reasonable the Act states that the term must be fair and reasonable having regard to all the circumstances, e.g.

a. the relative strength of the bargaining positions of the parties, taking into account alternative means by which the customer's requirements could have been met;
b. whether the customer received any inducement to agree to the exclusion clause or had an opportunity of entering a similar contract with other persons without having to agree to a similar clause;
c. whether the customer knew, or ought reasonably to have known, of the clause;
d. where the clause excludes or restricts a liability if some condition is not complied with, whether it was reasonable at the time of the contract to expect that compliance with that condition would be practicable; or
e. whether the goods were manufactured, processed or adapted to the special order of the customer.

A contract on standard written terms provided for the sale of seed potatoes by potato merchants to farmers. One clause in the contract purported to exclude liability if the buyers had not given notice of any defects within three days of delivery. Another clause purported to restrict the sellers' liability for any consequential loss, limiting that liability to the amount of the contract price. After the potatoes had been planted and had come up, they proved to have been infected with a virus. Held, the clause excluding liability unless notice of the defect was notified within three days of delivery was unreasonable (see guideline d. above). The other clause, however, had been in use for many years with the approval of the negotiating bodies repesenting potato merchants and farmers and its terms restricting the seller's liability to the contract price were reasonable: *R W Green Ltd v Cade Bros Farmers (1978)*.

The plaintiffs, farmers, ordered 30lb of cabbage seed from the sellers. The seed arrived together with invoices which included a clause excluding all liability for any loss or damage and limiting the sellers' liability to an obligation to replace the seed or repay the price. The price of the seed was £192. The farmers planted the seed which was not the seed contracted for and which produced a useless crop, causing the farmers a loss of over £61,000. In defence to a claim for that loss, the sellers sought to rely upon the exclusion clause. Held, the clause did not satisfy the requirement of reasonableness. Judgment was for the farmers; *George Mitchell (Chesterhall) Ltd v Finney Lock Seeds Ltd (1983)*. (Note that the statutory test applied in this case and in Green v Cade, above, was the test laid down in the earlier Supply of Goods (Implied Terms) Act 1973 which was whether it was fair and reasonable to allow the defendants to rely on the exclusion clause. This has now been replaced by the test quoted on p. 113 ante, laid down in the Unfair Contract Terms Act 1977, i.e. was the clause a fair and reasonable one to be included in the contract?).

Clauses merely limiting liability are, as far as the requirement of reasonableness is concerned, generally judged by less exacting standards than exclusion of liability or indemnity clauses (*Ailsa Craig Fishing Co Ltd v Malvern Fishing Co Ltd (1983)*.

The Act does not apply to contracts of insurance or to any contract relating to the transfer of an interest in land.

Certain contracts such as those relating to the international carriage of goods and persons are governed by international conventions which make void any attempt further to reduce liability by contract.

Chapter Nine
Discharge of a Contract

One does not refer to a contract as merely being performed but of its being discharged. This is because when the contract was originally made by the parties then the rights and duties already referred to were set up. Consequently when those rights and duties have been extinguished then the contract can be said to have been discharged. Performance is merely one, albeit the most obvious, method of discharge.

If A and B have entered into a contract then rights and duties have been created between them. A has rights against B and B owes duties to A and vice versa, B has rights against A and A owes duties to B. If both A and B do what they have promised to do under the contract then the contract is at an end. Of course if only A performs his duties then B no longer will be able to enforce his rights against A but naturally A will still retain his rights against B and may enforce them in a court of law if he wishes.

The methods of discharge are:

1. *Performance*
A contract may be said to have been discharged when each party has completely performed his duties under the contract. The operative word is "completely" and so it follows that if a party has only partially performed his part of the contract then he will not have discharged his duties under it and so the other party will likewise be relieved of his obligations.

If each party has performed his part of the contract then the contract is discharged, but the performance of each party must be complete and exactly in accordance with the terms of the contract. If the contract is an entire contract and the party only performs half of it then he is not entitled to any payment at all.

116 Discharge of a Contract

If A has two large lawns and he agrees to pay a jobbing gardener £10 if he mows the two lawns then he does not have to pay anything at all if the gardener only mows one lawn and then leaves the job. On the other hand sometimes it is agreed between the parties that the contract should be split up into sections and then the situation is that as each instalment is completed the other party is obliged to pay for that instalment. Building contracts are often arranged in this way, otherwise the builder would have to await payment until the job was completed and this might entail a large outlay of capital by the builder unless the work was split up into instalments. This is known as a severable or divisible contract. In addition, it may be agreed between the parties that the payment shall be made in stages so as to encourage the completion of the contract. The supplier of goods may receive payment partly in advance of completion provided the work is being done according to schedule.

However sometimes it is difficult to be certain when a contract has been completely performed. This may be the case in contracts of service. So in order to avoid the possibility of one party evading his liabilities by claiming that the contract has not been completely performed, the doctrine of substantial performance has been created. Thus if the contract is performed as well as a reasonable man would expect then the court will state that the contract has been performed, with possibly some adjustment to the actual price paid.

In *Hoenig v Isaac (1952) C.A.* the plaintiff agreed to redecorate the defendant's flat for £750. The defendant paid £400 but complained that the contract had not been carried out to his satisfaction. The Court of Appeal held that the plaintiff had substantially performed his part of the contract and that he was entitled to his price less an amount to cover the defects.

Performance very often calls for the payment of money and when this is the case then the following will apply:

1. The exact money must be tendered and the party making payment has no right to any change if he tenders a sum larger than is called for by the agreement. In practice it

would be unthinkable that a shopkeeper who wanted to stay in business would refuse to give change to a customer. However, the legal position is that he is not required to do so. In fact it is on that particular point that certain transport operators are enabled to run their services and state that "no change will be given".
2. Payment by cheque is at the discretion of the payee and in any case is only a conditional payment. This means that if the cheque turns out to be worthless then the payer still has an obligation to pay the amount agreed. The statement sometimes encountered "No cheques accepted here, not even good ones" says it all. It is up to the payee to decide whether or not he wishes to be paid by cheque.
3. If cash is paid the rules of legal tender will apply. This means that only cash in the following denominations may be tendered in payment of a debt:

Notes of any amount
Gold coins of any amount
50p coins up to £10
Silver/cupro-nickel coins of 20p or less up to £5
Bronze coins up to 20p

Legal tender is intended to avoid the situation where A owes B money but is reluctant to pay – eventually he agrees to pay (say £5) and A goes along to B and hands over 500 pennies and says "Here is the money I owe you." Legally there has been no payment because it was not in legal tender and B can sue A for non payment.

In practice, a creditor would probably be so pleased to receive payment in any form, that he would not insist on legal tender.

2. *Agreement*
A contract comes into existence because of an agreement between the parties so it must follow that it can also be discharged by agreement. Thus A and B enter into some agreement. A wants to change his mind and not carry out his terms of the contract. Of course if he does this unilaterally then

he will be in breach of contract to B. However, if A approaches B and states that he would like to be released from his liabilities under the contract then B might agree. In that case the contract is discharged. In effect B has promised not to sue A if he does not perform his part of the contract and the consideration for this promise is A's promise not to sue B.

Of course if A has actually performed his part of the agreement but wants to release B from his obligations then to make such an arrangement legally binding, B would have to provide some fresh consideration in return for A's promise not to sue him. This is technically known as "accord and satisfaction", which is the equivalent of "agreement and consideration".

Note that in the case of discharge by agreement, the contract is at an end but neither party has performed what he has promised to do under the contract.

After an agreement is reached between A and B, A then agrees with B not to carry on with the contract. In effect A is saying "I promise not to enforce the agreement against you if you promise not to enforce the agreement against me." This amounts to mutual promises which is good consideration.

If A has performed his part of the contract and then promises to release B from his obligations then B must supply fresh consideration to support A's promise not to sue him. Either that or a deed of release signed by A, because an agreement contained in a deed does not require consideration.

3. *Frustration*

Sometimes, after a contract has been made, something occurs to make the contract impossible to perform. What effect does this situation have on the parties? As always it will depend on the particular facts of the case. If one party has given his absolute undertaking that something will be done by a certain time then probably he will be liable for breach if he is unable to do what he has promised to do. However, if whatever happens to prevent the contract from being performed

a. has not been caused by either party
b. could not have been foreseen

c. and its effect is to destroy the basis of the contract

then the courts will probably state that the contract has been frustrated. If that happens then the contract will have been discharged and neither party will have any liability under it.

Taylor v Caldwell (1863) Caldwell had agreed that Taylor could use "The Surrey Gardens and Music Hall" on four named days for the purpose of holding concerts there. Just before the time for the performance of the contract, the Music Hall was destroyed by fire.

Taylor wanted compensation from somebody so he sued Caldwell. On the other hand, the fire was not due to the negligence of Caldwell. The court held that as the Hall had ceased to exist, without fault of either party, both parties must be excused from performance of their contract.

The courts will not readily say that a contract has been frustrated because by doing so they are taking away the rights of each party to sue the other and to get compensation. A frustrating event will arise without any warning and it may be that each party loses his right to sue the other. What happens if one party has incurred some expenses before the frustrating event occurred, or has promised to pay a sum to the other? Until 1943 the position was unsatisfactory but in that year the *Law Reform (Frustrated Contracts) Act* was passed and since then the position is:

1. Money due but not in fact paid ceases to be payable.
2. A party who has incurred expenses may be awarded compensation.
3. A party who has gained a benefit may be requested to pay a just sum for that.

In practice, and to avoid the necessity of having to go to court for a decision on the liability of the parties to a contract which has become impossible to perform, an appropriate clause may be inserted in the contract. This is called a "force majeure" clause and its purpose is to deal with the situation where a contract becomes impossible to perform because of the happening of some event outside the control of the parties. Events such

120 Discharge of a Contract

as strikes, accidents to machinery, delays in delivery and changes in government policy are often included in such clauses, and a party is asked to suspend or cancel the operation of that contract if one of these events has occurred.

4. *Breach*
A breach of contract will occur if one party

a. fails to perform his part of the contract by the agreed date
b. makes it impossible for himself to perform the contract
c. repudiates his liabilities under the contract.

It will be seen that b and c may occur before the date fixed for performance of the contract. In that case an action may be brought immediately and there is no need to wait until the date fixed for performance. This is known as "anticipatory breach".

Hochster v De La Tour (1853) is a case usually remembered as it concerns a travel agency who decided to employ a person as a courier in the summer; the appointment having been made earlier in the year. Soon after the appointment the travel agency wrote saying it would no longer require the services of the courier in the summer. Did the courier have to wait until the date fixed for performance of the contract before he could sue or could he sue immediately he knew the other party had repudiated his liabilities? The answer, said the court, was that he could sue immediately.

It is up to the party concerned whether he wishes to look upon a breach as a breach of a fundamental term or condition and thus treat the contract as discharged and in addition may claim damages, or whether he is happy to look upon the breach as a minor matter and is willing to sue for damages for breach of a warranty rather than to treat the contract as discharged.

The difference between a condition and a warranty is illustrated in *Bettini v Gye (1876)* in which an Italian opera singer had agreed to undertake a tour in this country on certain dates and also to arrive in this country six days before the start of the tour. He did turn up for the tour but not the required number of days prior to the commencement. The organiser tried to escape liability under the contract claiming that the singer had broken the contract. He was not successful as the court held that the singer had broken a minor term of the contract (a warranty) and was liable in damages in respect of that. He had not broken a condition which is a major term of the contract and one on which the contract hinges.

As regards the time when a contract must be performed, this is often not agreed between the parties. It is usually said that "time is not of the essence of the contract". On the other hand there is no reason why it should not be so. If the time of performance is not agreed when the contract is made then the contract must be performed within a reasonable time. Either party may make the time of performance important and if so the contract must contain an appropriate clause to ensure that it is performed by a certain time or during a specific period. If the contract is not performed by that agreed time then the defaulting party will be in breach of contract.

If a time of performance is agreed between the parties then normally a party who fails to perform on the due date will be in breach of contract, because the time of performance will then be a condition of the contract.

Sometimes a party may make time of the essence by giving notice to the party who has delayed performance, that he must complete his part of the agreement within a reasonable specified time, otherwise he will treat the contract as broken.

Rickards (Charles) Ltd v Oppenheim (1950)
Oppenheim purchased a Rolls Royce chassis with a body built on it from Rickards – the delivery was to be by March 20th.

The delivery date passed and Oppenheim pressed for delivery. Eventually Oppenheim notified Rickards in June that he would not accept delivery after July 25th. The car was still not delivered so Oppenheim bought another one.

Rickards offered to deliver the car in October but Oppenheim refused. Rickards sued for the price. The court held that Oppenheim had waived the original time for delivery but was entitled, by giving reasonable notice, again to make time the essence of the contract.

Remedies

When two parties have entered into a contract and one of them has broken his part of the bargain then it is only natural that the other should seek compensation. This is called damages in law and takes the form of a money payment. It is a common law remedy which means that it is the usual remedy which will be awarded by the courts and the successful party in any action has a right to damages.

When one considers the losses for which compensation might be claimed one is immediately involved with the topic of remoteness. In other words the law seeks to restrict the losses for which damages are awarded to those losses which arise naturally as a result of the breach of contract. Other losses which are too far removed from the breach cannot be eligible for compensation. The rule relating to this matter is the rule stated in the case *Hadley v Baxendale (1854)*. In that case a miller delivered the broken shaft of his mill to a carrier with instructions to take it to a manufacturer to be repaired. The carrier took an unreasonable length of time to transport the shaft and so the mill was out of use for longer than it should have been. The court held the carrier was liable for negligent performance of his contract; but when it came to the assessment of damages it held the carrier was not liable for loss of profits during the delay. The carrier, in the opinion of the court could not have known, and was not informed, that the miller had only one shaft.

The problem of remoteness also arises in areas other than that of the damages for breach of contract. It arises in tort – "for what harm will the defendant be liable?" Basically only those injuries or those damages which he should reasonably have foreseen would be likely to result from his acts. Also in criminal law where it is spoken of as causation. If one person stabs another and then the friends of the victim carry him to the medical aid centre and drop him twice on the way, were they responsible for the victim's death or was the person who stabbed him in the first place?

In contract the matter of remoteness is only concerned with

establishing the harm for which the defendant may have to compensate the plaintiff.

Basically the rule is that the plaintiff in a breach of contract action will be awarded compensation for any loss which the defendant knew or should have known was likely to result from his breach of contract. The rule has been confirmed notably in *Czarnikow Ltd v Koufos (1969)* also called *The Heron II*. In a case in which a ship is concerned, the report of the case is often referred to by the name of the ship. In that case the ship was the Heron II and its owner had agreed to transport a cargo of sugar from Constanza to Basrah. The sugar reached the destination later than it should have done owing to the fault of the shipowner. The owners of the sugar sustained a loss because the price of the sugar had dropped. The court held that the shipowner must pay the loss of profit to the charterer because he must have known that the sugar was to be sold.

In *Victoria Laundries v Newman Industries Ltd (1949)* a manufacturer of boilers was late in delivering a boiler to the laundry. Consequently he was sued for loss of profits that the laundry would have earned if they had received the boiler on time. The plaintiff was not able to recover damages in respect of another contract to dye materials, made by the laundry with a Government Department, and of which the boiler makers had no knowledge.

Damages may be either liquidated or unliquidated. A liquidated sum is a fixed or ascertainable sum. One speaks of the liquidation of a company when its assets are sold and converted into cash. In bankruptcy proceedings a liquidated sum may be claimed or proved but not if it still has to become fixed, in which case it is a contingent liability. Liquidated damages are those damages which the parties have agreed, when they made their contract, should be paid by the defaulting party to the other in the event of the contract being broken. Liquidated damages are frequently encountered in building contracts or in contracts for the charter of a ship. In these contracts the parties agree that in the event of, say, the builder failing to complete the building by the agreed date, he will pay to the other party £X for each week or part of a week he is late in finishing the building. If the other party's actual loss is more than the amount agreed to be paid then he can only recover the liquidated sum and not the actual loss.

In *Cellulose Acetate Silk Co v Widnes Foundry (1933)* Widnes Foundry agreed to erect a plant for Cellulose Acetate Silk by a certain date and also agreed to pay £20 for every week they took beyond that date. They were 30 weeks late, and Cellulose Acetate Silk claimed £5,850, their actual loss from the delay. Held – Widnes Foundry had only agreed to pay £20 a week for delay and was not liable for more.

On the other hand if the sum agreed to be paid is held by the court to be excessive by reference to the actual loss, then the agreed amount may be classified as a penalty and not liquidated damages and will not be payable. The courts will not enforce payment of an agreed sum if they consider that the payment of this money has been held over the head of the other party (in terrorem). This was the case where an actor agreed to pay a large sum of money if he broke any of the rules of the theatre where he was appearing. Those rules contained some minor matters such as smoking in dressing rooms and so the court considered the amount to be paid was in the nature of a penalty and not true liquidated damages.

Kemble v Farren (1829) Farren agreed to act at Kemble's theatre and to conform to all the regulations of the theatre. Each agreed to pay £1,000 as liquidated damages. Farren broke the contract and damages were assessed at £750. Held – The sum of £1,000 was a penalty because it was payable even if Farren had broken any of the most minor regulations of the theatre.

Unliquidated damages on the other hand are to be assessed by the court and the plaintiff must plead special damages which are those losses he can quantify himself such as loss of earnings, damage to his car etc. He should also claim general damages which are awarded in the discretion of the court.

There are other principles which the courts will apply when deciding the question of damages, such as . . .

Mitigation

The injured party must do what he reasonably can in order to reduce the amount of loss he is suffering. He must "not sit around in the sun". *Brace v Calder (1895)* Brace had a contract of employment with a partnership for a period of two years. After six months the partnership was dissolved and although Brace was offered employment by two of the remaining partners, he declined. Held – Brace was wrongfully dismissed but should have attempted to find alternative employment.

Compensation not Punishment

Damages are not of course subject to the income tax laws but nevertheless the effect of these laws should be taken into account when assessing the damages to be awarded. In *B.T.C. v Gourley (1956)* the plaintiff's estimated future earnings amounted to £37,000. However it was pointed out that such earnings, if actually paid, would have had tax deducted from them. The House of Lords decided that the damages should also be reduced because of the tax element and Mr Gourley received £6,000. In this context taxation is intended to refer to income tax. In another context it should be remembered that taxation is the name given to the procedure where the party to litigation has his costs examined by the District Judge in the County Court or the Taxing master in the High Court to see which costs may be allowed and which may be disregarded. This was a tort case but the same principles apply as in contract. This point also illustrates the fact that a plaintiff must not be allowed to make a profit. The purpose of awarding damages is to attempt to put the plaintiff back into the same position as he would have been in had the contract been performed. Damages are intended as compensation and not as punishment. Incidentally the party who benefitted from this decision was B.T.C. because the damages they had to pay were considerably reduced.

This point also arises when there is a contract for the sale of goods and the contract goes off. If there is a market for the goods then if the seller is in default the buyer can go and buy similar goods and can only claim damages for the difference between the contract price and the market price. Likewise if the buyer is in default then the amount of damages depends on whether or not the seller can easily sell the goods. If he can, then he may not deserve compensation. If there is no market for the goods then the seller will have lost a sale and will be able to recover the profit he would have made if the sale had gone through.

W. L. Thompson Ltd v Robinson Gunmakers Ltd (1955) The defendants bought a Standard "Vanguard" motor car from the plaintiffs and then refused to accept it. The seller's profit would have been £61. As the supply of this particular vehicle exceeded the demand the sellers could not re-sell it and so lost their profit. They succeeded in recovering the whole loss of profit.

Charter v Sullivan (1957) The defendant bought a Hillman Minx motor car from the plaintiff. The latter's profit would have been £97.15s. When sued for non-acceptance the defendant was only ordered to pay nominal damages because it was proved that the seller could sell as many Hillman Minx cars as he could obtain. Therefore he had not incurred any appreciable loss.

Difficulty of Assessing Damages

Sometimes it may be difficult for the judge to estimate the amount of damages he should award; however this should not deter him. In *Chaplin v Hicks (1911)* Hicks advertised a beauty competition, by which readers of some newspapers were to select 50 girls and from them Hicks would select 12 for whom he would provide theatrical bookings. Chaplin was one of the 50 but owing to Hicks' breach of contract, she was not present when the final selection was made. *Held* –Although it was problematic whether she would have been one of the 12 selected and although it was difficult to assess damages, Chaplin was entitled to have damages assessed. Also it is permissible for a sum to be awarded in respect of nervous shock suffered or the effect of loss of status following demotion in employment or loss of enjoyment in a holiday.

This then is damages – the common law remedy for breach of contract.

Other remedies are said to be equitable and they are:

Specific Performance

This is not available as of right to a plaintiff and is only awarded at the discretion of the judge. Where it is awarded the court will order the defaulting party to carry out his promise under the contract. In sale of goods contracts it will only be ordered when the subject matter of the contract is unique and very special such as a painting or some collector's item. The remedy is most commonly awarded in a contract for sale of land. Every piece of land is of itself totally unique. Specific performance will never be awarded when damages are an available remedy and never in a contract of employment.

Injunction

This is an order of the court ordering a person not to do some act or occasionally, in a mandatory injunction, ordering him to do some act. The order is more common in tort actions – ordering a person to cease trespassing for example. In a contract of employment a person will not be ordered to work for somebody (this would be tantamount to slavery) but if a person has promised to work for one person and not for any other person then he or she can be restrained from working for anyone other than the original employer with whom the agreement was made and which the employee is contemplating breaking. The film actress Bette Davies figured (in her real name) in *Warner Bros. Pictures Inc. v Nelson (1937)*. She attempted to escape from the, apparently, iniquitous studio system whereby film stars were bound to one studio for extensive periods of time.

Rescission

A more specialised remedy is rescission, which is available

Discharge of a Contract

when one party has been deceived by the other or has been subjected to duress or undue influence. In cases of this sort the party at a disadvantage, because of deception or coercion, can apply to the court to have his contract rescinded. Whether or not the court will order rescission will depend on:

1. whether or not the injured party has affirmed the contract. For example, if a person finds out that he has been tricked and deceived but nevertheless does nothing about it and allows the contract to stand, he cannot later ask the law to rescind the contract.
2. whether it is possible for the parties to be put back into the position they would have been in before the contract was made. *Lagunas Nitrate Co. v Lagunas Syndicate (1899)*. The syndicate sold a nitrate works to the company and the contract of sale contained some misleading statements. The company sued for rescission. *Held* – Because the company had worked the property the parties could not be restored to their original positions and so the contract could not be rescinded.
3. whether or not a third party's rights would be affected by rescission of the original contract. *Lewis v Averay (1972)* Lewis was deceived by a rogue into handing over to him his motor car. The rogue sold the car to Averay and Lewis tried to get his car back again. *Held* –Lewis had been deceived but the court not rescind the contract between Lewis and the rogue because a third party (Averay) had become involved. However, if Lewis had taken steps to avoid the contract with the rogue before Averay had bought the car then Lewis would have been entitled to recover his car.

In *Car and Universal Finance Co. Ltd. v Caldwell (1965)* it was held that normally the rescission of a voidable contract must be communicated to the other contracting party but that was not necessary if the other party deliberately absconds. Rescission can be accomplished by getting in touch with the police or (in the case of a car) the Automobile Association.

Chapter Ten
The Law Relating to the Sale of Goods

In recent years "consumerism" has become very prominently to the fore. Most shoppers know that if goods are defective they probably have a right to their money back. Most shopkeepers also appreciate this fact. However, there is nothing new in this situation. It has certainly existed, in statute form, since the *Sale of Goods Act 1893*. It was one thing to have the law on your side, but it was another thing, and a more expensive thing, to put it into motion. Consequently it was only when the small claims procedure in the County Court became available that people began to consider the possibility of taking legal action.

It may now be quite widely appreciated that purchasers have their rights and consequently that sellers owe them duties, but we shall have to look at the current Act – *Sale of Goods Act 1979* – to fully appreciate the extent of these rights and duties.

First of all one must understand that a sale is a contract and if we remember what has been already written about a contract, we will understand that it is merely an agreement between two parties. In this case an agreement between the seller and the buyer. An agreement takes place in the minds of both parties and so if A says to B "Do you want my car for £2,500?" and B says "Yes", that is a contract of sale. There is an agreement between seller and purchaser. They both intend their agreement to be legally binding and B's consideration for A's promise to let him have his car is his promise to pay £2,500. On the other hand A's consideration to support B's promise to pay him £2,500 is his promise to give B his car. There is no need for anything in writing but of course both A and B might be in a happier position if they had witnesses to back them up that a contract had in fact been made.

It is perfectly possible for one party to sue another without the

130 The Law Relating to the Sale of Goods

help of witnesses but that means that it is up to the court to decide which party to believe. This is within the power of the court and judges are usually quite adept in deciding which party is telling the truth. In the case of business contracts very often one party or the other wishes to put certain terms of his own into the contract. Therefore it is more convenient for a contract which may be quite complicated to be in writing, even though legally this may not be necessary.

Once the contract has been made, what do the parties have to do as far as performing their side of the bargain is concerned? Obviously, B must pay A £2,500. What about A? Equally obviously A must hand the car over to B. However the physical fact of A handing the car to B tends to confuse the situation because although more often than not that is in fact what will happen, the important thing to remember is that what A is selling and what B is buying is A's ownership in the car. Sometimes ownership is called property or title.

The *Sale of Goods Act 1979 Section 2(1)* states "a contract of sale is a contract whereby the seller transfers, or agrees to transfer, the property in goods to the buyer for a money consideration called the price." Thus if goods are given in exchange for goods, that is not a sale – it is barter or exchange. However, part exchange where a person hands over his car to a dealer together with a sum of money in exchange for a car that the dealer is selling, is a contract of sale.

Ownership and Possession

At this point a distinction must be made between ownership and possession. Possession is said to be a matter of fact, ownership a matter of law. It is a fact that I have this book, this car or these golf clubs in my possession. Am I the owner of them? I may be, but if called upon to prove my ownership I might be in difficulties. In that case I would be thrown back upon the phrase "possession is nine tenths of the law". In other words if I have some personal property in my possession there is a presumption that I own it unless the true owner can prove his ownership of the thing. But returning to the book, the car and the golf clubs. I might have borrowed the book from the library, I might have hired the car and I might have stolen the golf clubs. In all these cases I would have the things in my possession but in all cases I would be the owner of none of them.

Property in the Goods

To return to the example of B's buying A's car. In legal terms B is buying A's right of ownership in the car. If he acquires ownership then this will give him a right to possession of the car also. But it may be that B merely wants to own the car so that he can resell it and does not necessarily want possession of it. Again, only the owner of a thing can sell it because what the buyer is buying is the right of ownership and if a person has not got ownership in a thing, he cannot sell it. There is a Latin phrase which describes this situation and it is "Nemo dat quod non habet" this means that no-one can give what he has not got. There are some exceptions to this rule and we will consider these later.

If B wanted to resell the car he would have to have ownership himself first, but he would not necessarily want possession of it. Indeed, say B was a wholesaler and instead of 1 car was buying 100 cars, he might immediately resell them to dealers and probably would arrange for the cars to go directly from the manufacturer to the dealers and so would not, himself, wish to acquire possession of them. Thus we can say that a contract of sale is an agreement to transfer the ownership in goods to the buyer. If one were to say "I am going to buy the right of ownership in a pair of shoes on Saturday," one's friends would be rather surprised but that is legally what would be happening. One would also probably acquire possession as well but not necessarily in all cases.

Goods

So much for the meaning of "sale" in the phrase "Sale of Goods". The meaning of goods is defined in the Act as "including all personal chattels other than things in action and money". In other words goods includes anything that is not land.

Supply of Goods and Services Act 1982

A distinction must be made between a contract for the sale of goods and one for the sale of services. Sometimes there may be a mixed contract. For example when a lady buys a hair dye from a chemist, she is buying goods; when she goes to a hairdresser just for hair-styling that is a contract for services. However if she has her hair dyed that would be a mixture of sale of goods and services.

Whether or not a person has any complaint about the service he has paid for is another matter. In fact the *Supply of Goods and Services Act 1982* covers the situation where there is exchange or barter and also when a person is carrying out some repairs or is for example painting a house. In the latter case the contract is predominantly one for the provision of services but there may be the sale of the paint also.

Sometimes the goods part of the contract is so insignificant that it is swamped by the services or skill element. As when one's portrait is painted by a well known artist. The finished work is on canvas and consists of paint and may have a frame but predominantly one is paying for the skill of the artist. But to buy a reproduction painting from a shop, that is a contract for the sale of goods.

That then is the meaning of the term "Sale of Goods". What is the purpose of the *Sale of Goods Act 1979*? Basically it is to:

1. protect the purchaser of goods.
2. to set out rules for determining when the ownership of the goods passes from the seller to the buyer.
3. to lay down some remedies available to the seller if he does not get his money and to the buyer if he does not get the goods.

Protection of the Purchaser

The basic principles of the law of contract were settled many years ago when laissez-faire was the prevailing philosophy. Consequently it followed that parties to a contract were permitted to enter into any type of agreement they wished, provided it was legal. Nobody was going to interfere with them and likewise they had to stand on their own feet. Thus if the contract turned out to be disadvantageous to them they had only themselves to blame. This was called "freedom of contract".

Over the years gradually the picture has changed as the courts and Parliament have slowly attempted to protect the weaker party; to ensure that no party should profit from his own wrongdoing or bad faith; and to bring the concept of reasonableness into consideration as affecting exclusion clauses. *Unfair Contract Terms Act 1977.*

This new approach has also been evident in the contract for the sale of goods. The principle used to be exclusively – Caveat Emptor – "let the buyer beware". Translated, this meant and sometimes still does – the buyer does not have to enter into his contract to buy the goods; nobody is forcing him, and if he has any doubts he should not agree to buy. However, once he has agreed to buy, if it turns out that he regrets his decision, there is nothing he could do about it.

This principle still applies in many contracts and also to the contract for the sale of goods except that some protection has been given to the consumer in certain circumstances. So if a person buys goods from another, not in the course of trade, and the goods prove to be defective there is nothing that can be done. However if the seller sold the goods in the course of a business then the buyer will have his remedies against him.

It can be seen therefore that this protection only applies when a seller is selling the goods in the course of a business. The carrying on of a profession or the activities of a Government department or a Local Authority are all regarded as businesses. At one time the seller had to be in the business of selling the goods; now it is sufficient if he is in a business and sells the goods.

Terms of a Contract

Every contract will contain some terms which are normally put in by the parties themselves. One obvious term is the price. These terms will be binding as long as both parties agree to them and anything can be put into a contract so long as it is legal.

The terms or stipulations in a contract may be either conditions or warranties.

Conditions

A condition is a representation of fact which is vital to the existence of the contract, a representation on the truth of which the existence of the contract may depend. Conditions go to the root of the contract and it is reasonable to suppose that if the buyer had known it to be untrue he would not have contracted at all.

Warranties

The other type of term or stipulation in a contract is called a warranty. This is an agreement with reference to the goods forming the subject matter of the contract of sale but collateral to the main purpose of such a contract. It relates to a matter of subsidiary importance and does not go to the root of the contract.

It is important to distinguish between a condition and a warranty because the remedies available are different in each case. As a condition is fundamental to the contract then it follows that the party breaking it is in effect attempting to substitute something different in kind from the performance which the contract contemplated. To compel him to take the goods and merely to attempt to compensate him by damages would be, in substance, to force on him a different contract from that which he actually made. So the law gives to a party injured by a breach of condition a right to rescind the contract altogether. Rescission, however is not the only remedy open to him. He may if he wishes waive the condition, or he may treat its breach as a breach of warranty giving rise to an action for damages and not as a ground for repudiating the contract. *Sale of Goods Act 1979 Section 11(2)*.

On the other hand a warranty is not so serious as a condition and since a warranty does not affect the foundation of the contract but is collateral to its main purpose, then a breach of warranty gives rise to a claim for damages but not to a right to reject the goods and treat the contract as repudiated. *Section 11(3)*.

Some terms or stipulations are implied into a contract. These terms may not be known to the parties who probably know nothing about the law. One term, which happens to be a condition, is that the goods shall be of merchantable quality, i.e. that the goods shall be reasonably fit for the purposes for which they are normally used. So the contract would read, if it were to be written down and A is writing, "I agree to sell you B my car £2,500 and it is a condition of this contract that the car shall be of merchantable quality". Of course this is not written down and is not expressed by A who may know nothing of the Sale of Goods Act. Nevertheless, if the car proves not to be of merchantable quality then A the seller will be in breach of a condition and B the purchaser will have his rights against A. One other point is that A must have sold the car in the course of a business, so this provision would not apply to a private sale.

Implied Conditions

Condition No. 1
Section 12 of the Act provides that there is "an implied condition on the part of the seller that in the case of a sale, he has a right to sell the goods, and in the case of an agreement to sell, he will have such a right at the time when th property is to pass."

It should be noticed that since the implied stipulation that the seller has a right to sell the goods is a condition, the breach of it entitles the buyer to recover the whole of the price he has paid for the goods, as upon a total failure of the consideration.

In *Rowland v Divall (1923)* R bought a motor car from D and used it for four months. D was not the owner of the car and so R in due course had to return the car to the rightful owner. R now sued D for the total purchase price he had paid to D. *Held*: R was allowed to cover in full not withstanding the fact that he had the use of the car for four months.

Section 12 also includes two warranties i.e. that the goods are free from encumbrance (such as a mortgage) and that the buyer will enjoy quiet possession of the goods. These warranties sometimes overlap with condition in Section 12 but sometimes they are important as in *Microbeads A. G. v Vinhurst Road Markings Ltd (1975)*. In that case after the sale a third party obtained a patent which interfered with the buyer's right to use the machines (i.e. with his quiet possession). There had been no breach of the condition in Section 12 because the seller had had the right to sell. However the buyer was entitled to recover damages for breach of the warranty in Section 12.

Condition No. 2
Section 13 provides that "where there is a contract for the sale of goods by description there is an implied condition that the goods shall correspond with the description".

This condition will apply where goods are ordered through a catalogue or where some article is ordered from manufacturers through a dealer. In these cases the goods will always be sold by description. Even if the purchaser sees the goods and chooses them they can still be sold by description and a customer is entitled to expect that the goods he chooses from the shelf of a supermarket will correspond to the description on the tin or packet.

The word description can of course apply to a variety of matters concerning the goods. Description can refer to the quantity, to the weight, to the ingredients and even packaging has been held to be part of the description. In *Re Moore & Company and Landauer & Company (1921)* the buyer described in the contract how he wished the consignment of canned fruit to be packed. He specified that he wanted 3,100 cases of Australian canned fruits, the cases to contain 30 tins each.

When the goods were delivered, the total quantity was delivered but about half the cases contained 24 tins and the remainder 30 tins. There was no difference in market value between goods packed 24 tins and goods packed 30 tins to the case. *Held*: that as the goods delivered did not correspond with the description with those ordered then the buyer could reject the whole.

As stated above goods will be sold by description if the buyer does not see them; but they may also be sold by description if he does see them. In *Beale v Taylor (1967)* a buyer inspected a car described in an advertisement as "a 1961 model". After buying it he discovered that the car had been cannibalised and consisted of half a 1961 model and half of an earlier car. *Held*: the seller was liable under Section 13 because the buyer had relied to some extent on the description.

In *Harlingdon and Leinster Enterprises Ltd v Christopher Hull Fine Art Ltd (1990)* the purchaser had bought a painting which the seller said was by a German expressionist painter called Münter. However the purchaser did not rely on the description because he relied on his own inspection instead. This situation was known to the seller and the purchaser. The Court of Appeal decided therefore that the purchaser could not complain when it turned out that the painting was not by Münter since he, the purchaser, did not rely upon the statement by the seller but used his own judgment and assessment. The court decided that as there had been no connection between the description and the sale – in other words the buyer had not relied upon the description given by the seller – then there could be no sale by description.

Implied Terms about Quality or Fitness

Section 14 of the Act contains what are known as the merchantable quality and fitness for purpose provisions. Section 14(2) states: "where the seller sells goods in the course of a business, there is an implied condition that the goods supplied under the contract are of merchantable quality, except that there is no such condition –

a. as regards defects specifically drawn to the buyer's attention before the contract is made; or
b. if the buyer examines the goods before the contract is made, as regards defects which that examination ought to reveal."

The phrase merchantable quality is defined in Section 14(6), This states that "goods of any kind are of merchantable quality if they are as fit for the purpose or purposes for which goods of that kind are commonly bought as it is reasonable to expect having regard to any description applied to them, the price (if relevant) and all the other relevant circumstances."

In *Bartlett v Sydney Marcus Ltd (1965)*, the court held that a minor repair to a second hand car some weeks after purchase would not indicate that the car had not been of merchantable quality. Note – the Act makes no distinction between "new" and "second hand" goods; but this merchantable quality provision would not apply if the buyer had examined the goods and had not spotted the defects. Likewise the provision would not apply if the seller had made it clear that he was selling "seconds".

The "fitness for purpose" condition is contained in Section 14(3). This section states that "Where the seller sells goods in the course of a business and the buyer, expressly or by implication, makes known:

a. to the seller, or
b. where the purchase price or part of it is payable by instalments and the goods were previously sold by a credit broker to the seller, to that credit broker,

any particular purpose for which the goods are being bought, there is an implied condition that the goods supplied under the contract are reasonably fit for that purpose, whether or not that is a purpose for which such goods are commonly supplied, except where the circumstances show that the buyer does not rely, or that it is unreasonable for him to rely, on the skill or judgement of the seller or credit broker".

Note that in each case of these implied conditions as to

quality or fitness then the seller must have been selling the goods in the course of a business. In other words the conditions are not implied in the case of a private sale. Also there may be an overlap between the merchantability and fitness for purpose sections, sometimes there will be no overlap. An article may be of merchantable quality yet still not be fit for the purpose stated by the buyer. Equally if the buyer states the purpose for which he wants the goods then notwithstanding that they are of merchantable quality, if they are still not fit for the purpose stated then again the seller will be in breach of the fitness for purpose condition.

In *Baldry v Marshall Ltd (1924)* B told M who were dealers in motor cars that he wanted a car which "was comfortable and suitable for the ordinary purpose of a touring car". M sold B a Bugatti car for £1,050. B found the car unsatisfactory for touring, and as he had relied on the seller's skill and judgement M was in breach of the condition that the goods should be reasonably fit for the purpose specified.

In *Crowther v Shannon Motor Co Ltd (1975)* the plaintiff paid £390 for a 1964 Jaguar car in 1972, with 82,000 miles on the clock. He drove 2,000 miles within three weeks of buying it and the engine seized up. *Held*: that when the car was sold the engine must have been near the point of failure and so the seller was in breach of the condition that the car should be reasonably fit for the purpose of being driven on the road.

Sale by Sample

The final condition implied into every contract for the sale of goods is that if the sale is by sample then there is an implied condition –

a. that the bulk will correspond with the sample in quality.
b. that the buyer will have a reasonable opportunity of comparing the bulk with the sample.
c. that the goods will be free from any defect, rendering them unmerchantable, which would not be apparent on reasonable examination of the sample.

Chapter Eleven
Transfer of Property in the Goods

In this section we shall deal with the transfer of property and in the following section with the transfer of title. There is a confusion sometimes between these two phrases. Property signifies total control over an object – "the sum of all the ways in which a movable or immovable thing can be lawfully used and enjoyed, together with the right to the possession of the same." Property is said to be a right, or a sum of rights. However preceeding such a right there is a title. And title is a fact which vests the right of property in the person who enjoys it. Thus property may be transferred from the seller to the buyer and that means that, at that moment in time, the buyer assumes the risk of loss or damage to the goods because property has been transferred to him. However a title may be valid or defective and it does not necessarily follow that because the property in the goods has passed from the seller to the buyer that the buyer will be able to keep the goods as his own. For example some third person may claim the goods from the buyer on the ground that he has a better title to them.

Some authors write of the transfer of property as a transfer of risk being transferred to the buyer. This is quite acceptable because once the property has been transferred to the buyer then he becomes responsible for any loss or damage to the goods.

Note that the transfer property is a matter of law and does not refer to the physical transfer of the goods. So it is important to remember that the property in goods may be transferred from the seller to the buyer notwithstanding the fact that the goods physically remain in the possession of the seller. Thus even though the goods remain in the possession of the seller, if property in those goods has passed to the buyer, then he, the buyer, will be liable for any loss or damage to them.

Time When the Property Passes

The question of the time when the property in the goods passes from the seller to the buyer may often be of considerable importance. If the goods are being transported some distance then it may be that the buyer, who may be the owner of them at that time will wish to insure against loss or damage to them. Also if the buyer were to be made bankrupt then only the goods he owns may be taken over by the Trustee in Bankruptcy for liquidation and distribution of the proceeds to creditors.

Thus the rules for determining the precise moment when the property in goods is transferred to the buyer are of considerable importance.

Specific Goods

Section 16 provides that no property in the goods may be transferred to the buyer unless and until the goods are ascertained. However some goods are called specific goods and this means that they are goods which both parties have agreed upon at the time of the sale. Thus if A is selling to B the Vauxhall Astra motor car, registration number A123 BCD, this is an example of specific goods, because the thing to be sold has been identified and agreed upon when a contract of sale was made.

When the goods are specific goods then the rules for the transfer of property are as follow.

Rule 1 – Where the goods are in a deliverable state the property passes to the buyer when the contract is made and it is immaterial whether the time of payment or the time of delivery or both be postponed.

This reinforces a point made earlier that property in goods may pass from the seller to the buyer even though the buyer has not paid for them and even though the goods themselves physically remain in the possession of the seller. The point is that when the property in the goods has passed to the buyer then he of course will from that moment be responsible for any loss or damage to them, irrespective of where they may be located.

Rule 2 – This provides that where there is a contract for the sale of specific goods and the seller is bound to do something to put them into a deliverable state then the property does not pass until the thing is done and the buyer has notice that it has been done.

This means that if the seller has agreed, for example, to put four new tyres on the car then he must put these new tyres on the car before the car is in a deliverable state, and must inform the buyer.

Rule 3 – This provides that if the seller is bound to weigh/measure or to do something to the goods for the purpose of ascertaining the price again the property does not pass to the buyer until what needs to be done has been done and again the buyer has been notified that it has been done.

In this case an example would be where a person goes to a fishmongers and on the counter is a whole salmon which is priced at £2.50 per pound. The buyer agrees to buy the salmon but of course the salmon then has to be weighed in order to find out what the total price is going to be.

Rule 4 – This concerns goods which are delivered to the buyer on approval or on sale or return. In such a case the property in the goods passes to the buyer either when he signifies his approval or acceptance to the seller or does any act adopting the transaction. If he does not signify his approval or acceptance to the seller but keeps the goods without giving notice of rejection then the property will pass when the time has been fixed for the return of the goods has passed or if no time has been fixed when a reasonable time has passed.

In *Kirkham v Attenborough* the jewellery was delivered "on sale or return" and the person to whom it was so delivered pledged it with a pawnbroker who took it in good faith. It was held that the original seller could not recover it from the pawnbroker because by pledging it the original purchaser had done an act "adopting the transaction" and the property in the goods had passed to him and so therefore he could give the property to the pawnbroker.

The original owner of the jewellery of course had his remedy in an action on the contract for the price.

These are four rules which indicate the moment in time when the property in specific goods will pass from the seller to the buyer. However it is important to keep in mind the fundamental principle, which is that the property in the goods will be transferred to the buyer at such time as the parties to the contract intend it to be transferred. The above rules will only apply unless a contrary intention appears.

Unascertained Goods

If the goods cannot be identified when the contract of sale is made then they are called unascertained goods. This situation will arise when the goods being sold form part of a bulk or of a large number of identical things and the precise things being sold are not immediately identifiable. If A is selling to B 10 tons of coal and A has 500 tons in his stock yard then the exact 10 tons of coal B is to receive will not have been identified when the contract of sale was made. They are then said to be unascertained.

Rule 5 of Section 18 concerns the moment when the property in unascertained goods passes from the seller to the buyer. This rule provides that the unascertained goods will become ascertained when the seller takes the goods out of bulk and is said to appropriate them to the contract. Property will pass at this moment because the goods have then, by being taken out of bulk, become specified goods.

The method of appropriation to the contract will usually be where the seller delivers the goods to the buyer or to a carrier and does not reserve the right of disposal.

In *Pignataro v Gilroy (1919)* G sold to P 140 bags of rice, the particular bags being unascertained. On 27 February P sent a cheque for the price and asked for a delivery order. G sent a delivery order for 125 bags from a wharf, and wrote saying that the remaining 15 bags were ready for delivery at his place of business. P did not send for the 15 bags until 25 March when it was found they had been stolen without any negligence on G's part. P sued to recover from G the price he had paid for the 15 bags. *Held*: he could not succeed, because G had appropriated the 15 bags to the contract, and P's assent to the appropriation was to be inferred from his conduct in not objecting. The property in the 15 bags therefore passed to P.

Reservation of Right of Disposal

Above, reference was made to reservation of right of disposal which means that the seller may on some occasions state that he does not intend the property in the goods to pass to the buyer until certain conditions have been fulfilled by the buyer. The effect of this is that notwithstanding the physical delivery of the goods to the buyer, the property in the goods will not pass to the buyer until the conditions imposed by the seller have been fulfilled.

The Romalpa Clause

A further development along these lines is provided by the Romalpa clause which may be inserted in a contract of sale. The case *Aluminium Industrie Vassen BV v Romalpa Aluminium Ltd (1976)* concerned the sale of aluminium foil by a Dutch company to an English company. The seller had inserted a clause to the effect that the ownership of the foil would only pass to the buyer when payment in full had been made. It was further made a term of the contract that if the foil was mixed with other foil then the seller would become the owner of the goods manufactured with the foil. When the English company became insolvent it was held that the seller's claim to the unsold foil and a claim to the money received by the English company had priority to any claim by other creditors.

Thus a Romalpa clause, as it is now called, is very advantageous to the seller of goods. Since the original case, there have been many cases in which the clause has been held to be ineffective. This has usually been because the clause has been interpreted as a charge placed on his goods by the buyer and he has not registered the charge (s.395 Companies Act 1985). Re. *Bond Worth Ltd (1908)*.

If the goods sold remain identifiable then it would appear that the retention of ownership clause (Romalpa clause) will be effective in relation to the unmixed goods, but would not be effective in relation to the mixed goods.

The clause will be effective, if drawn correctly, in the case of unmixed goods provided such a clause provides for separate accountability for the proceeds in the event of a re-sale by the original buyer. There are considerable difficulties in the case of mixed goods. *Clough Mill Ltd v Martin (1986)*.

Transfer of Title

The general rule is that only a person who is the owner of goods can pass the ownership of these goods on to the purchaser. This is expressed by the Latin phrase "Nemo dat quod non habet". Thus if a person has stolen goods and then sells these to an innocent purchaser, a purchaser who knows nothing about the fact that he is buying stolen goods, the fact remains that he cannot become the rightful owner of the goods. The reason of course is that the seller of the goods, the thief, had no title to them.

However there are exceptions to this rule and these are contained in the Act as follows:

1. *Market Overt*

    This is any legally constituted market. Anyone who buys goods in the hours of daylight with no knowledge that he is buying the goods from someone who is not the true owner will get a good title to them. A market overt is any legally constituted market or any shop in the City of London and this provision originally came into being when the local market was the only place available for a person to buy goods. Consequently, being able to rely on this rule meant, and still does mean, that goods may be purchased in market overt without the fear of having to give up the goods to the rightful owner if it should turn out that the seller did not have title to the goods.

In *Bishopsgate Motor Finance Corporation v Transport Brakes Ltd (1949)* the hirer of a car under a hire-purchase agreement took it to Maidstone market to be sold by auction. Having failed to sell it that way it was sold privately. *Held*: the market was a market overt and its rule permitted private sales and so the purchaser acquired a good title to the car.

2. *Sale by a seller under a voidable title*

When a person acquires goods and the right of ownership in those goods by deception, he is said to have a voidable title because he acquired ownership by means of a voidable contract. In this case whoever acquires the goods will get a good title to them provided he does so before the rightful (and deceived) owner has taken steps to escape liability under the contract.

In *Car and Universal Finance Co Ltd v Caldwell (1965)*, on 12 January 1960. C, the owner of a Jaguar car, was persuaded to sell and deliver the car to a rogue who gave C a car of much lower value and a cheque. On the next morning C ascertained that the cheque was worthless and at once asked the police and Automobile Association to recover his car. The rogue sold the car to a person who did not acquire it in good faith, and only on 15 January the car was acquired by a purchaser in good faith. It passed through several hands and eventually was acquired by the Car and Universal Finance Company Ltd which acted in good faith. *Held*: that while normally the rescission of a voidable contract must be communicated to the other contracting party, that was not necessary if – as in the present case – the other party, by deliberately absconding put it out of the power of the rescinding party to communicate. Consequently, C had rescinded the contract on 13 January when he notified the police and the Auto-mobile Association and the finance company had not acquired the title to the car.

In *Lewis v Averay* which was mentioned earlier the rogue deceived Lewis into letting him take his (Lewis's) car. The rogue then sold it to Averay. The rogue did not have a good title to the car, it was merely a voidable title which meant that Lewis could avoid the contract if he did so before a third party became involved. Unfortunately for Lewis, Averay acquired the car before Lewis had taken sufficient steps to avoid his contract with the rogue and so Averay got a good title to the car.

3. *Seller in possession of goods after sale*
When a person having sold goods continues to be in possession of the goods or of the documents of title to the goods and then resells the goods to another person who takes delivery of these goods, then the third person will get legal ownership or title to the goods. The moral of the story seems to be that once you have bought goods you should take possession of them as soon as you can. Of course the original buyer will have his remedies against the seller but that is not always a satisfactory solution.

4. *Sale by buyer in possession*
Section 25 provides "where a person having bought or agreed to buy goods obtains, with the consent of the seller, possession of the goods or the documents of title to the goods, the delivery or transfer by that person, or by a mercantile agent acting for him, of the goods or documents of title, under any sale, pledge or other disposition thereof, to any person receiving the same in good faith and without notice of any lien or other right of the original seller in respect of the goods, has the same effect as if the person making the delivery or transfer were a mercantile agent in possession of the goods or documents of title with the consent of the owner."

The importance of this Section 25 is that if a buyer obtained possession of the goods with the consent of the seller, then notwithstanding that he, the buyer, may not have become the owner of them, if he then sells to a third person, then the third person gets a good title to the goods. This provision is particularly important in recent years because of the widespread use of the Romalpa Clause which was mentioned earlier. Thus if a buyer obtains goods from a seller and in the contract of sale there was a

Romalpa Clause by which the seller retained ownership of the goods until such time as the buyer paid for them, then if the buyer now resells to a third person that person will get a good title to the goods.

This provision will only apply in a sale contract. A person who possesses goods subject to a hire purchase contract cannot pass a good title under Section 25. The same applies to a person who obtains possession under a conditional sale agreement.

The above examples of circumstances in which a person who is not the owner may nevertheless still sell the goods to a third party so that the third party can become the owner, are contained in the *Sale of Goods Act 1979*. There are a couple of additional examples.

5. *Sale by agent*

If an agent has the authority of his principal to sell the goods then obviously anyone buying from the agent will obtain ownership of the goods. Other points relating to agency will be dealt with separately.

6. *Sale of a motor vehicle under hire purchase agreement*

A general rule is that a person who is buying goods under a hire purchase agreement cannot sell those goods so as to pass a good title to any purchaser because the person who is buying the goods under the hire purchase agreement is merely hiring them and the ownership lies with the finance company. However the *Hire Purchase Act 1964* provided that in the case of the sale of a motor vehicle which is subject to a hire purchase agreement then any private purchaser can claim protection. In other words a private purchaser will get a good title to a motor vehicle; whereas a car dealer or a car finance house will be unable to do so. The reason for this is that Parliament decided that as a most important purchase of ordinary private persons is the buying of a motor vehicle then such people should be protected. Car dealers of course have access to a register of hire purchase agreements and so therefore they can, and will, before purchasing a vehicle check whether it is subject to an HP agreement.

Performance of the Contract

It is the duty of the seller to deliver the goods and of the buyer to accept and pay for them in accordance with the contract of sale.

Delivery means the voluntary transfer of possession from the seller to the buyer and Section 28 provides that delivery of the goods and payment of the price are concurrent conditions. In other words the seller must be ready and willing to give possession of the goods to the buyer and the buyer must be ready and willing to pay the price for the possession of the goods.

Rules of Delivery

1. Delivery will take place at the seller's place of business or his residence. However as in a number of other cases this provision of law may be varied by agreement between the parties. Obviously if a person is buying a large quantity of products from the seller then it probably will be in the agreement that the seller will undertake to transport the goods to the buyer's place of business.
2. Where the seller is bound to send the goods to the buyer and no time for sending them has been fixed, then he is bound to send them within a reasonable time.
3. Where the goods, at the time of sale, are in the possession of a third person, then there is no delivery by the seller to the buyer until the third person has acknowledged to the buyer that he holds the goods on his behalf.
4. Delivery in the sense of transporting the goods to the buyer must be made at a reasonable hour.
5. Finally unless otherwise agreed the expenses of putting the goods into a deliverable state must be borne by the seller.

Delivery of Wrong Quantity

Where the seller delivers to the buyer a quantity of goods less than he contracted to sell, the buyer may reject them. If the buyer accepts the goods as delivered he must pay for them at the contract rate.

Where the seller delivers to the buyer a quantity of goods larger than he contracted to sell, the buyer may accept the goods he has agreed to buy, and reject the rest or he may reject the whole.

Where the seller delivers a quantity of goods larger than he contracted to sell and the buyer accepts the whole of the goods so delivered then he must pay for them at the contract rate.

Where the seller delivers to the buyer the goods he contracted to sell mixed with other goods of different descriptions then the buyer may accept the goods which are in accordance with the agreement and reject the rest or he may reject the whole.

These particular provisions are as always subject to any usage of trade or any special agreement or course of dealing between the parties. These rules are illustrated in *Re Moore & Company and Landauer & Company (1921)*. This case has been mentioned earlier and illustrates that the seller must keep very strictly to the terms of the agreement.

In practice it will usually be the case that the parties will agree in their contract of sale that a certain variation from the strict contract quantity will be permitted.

Instalment Deliveries

Unless otherwise agreed the buyer of goods is not bound to accept delivery of them by instalments.

Where there is a contract for the sale of goods to be delivered by stated instalments which are to be separately paid for, and the seller makes a defective delivery in respect of one or more instalments; or the buyer neglects or refuses to take delivery or to pay for one or more instalments – then it is a question in each case depending on the terms of the contract whether the defect in respect of one instalment is a repudiation of the whole contract or whether it is a severable breach giving rise to a claim for compensation but not to a right to treat the whole contract as repudiated.

The tests to be applied are firstly, the ratio quantitatively which the breach bears to the contract and secondly the degree of probability or improbability that such a breach will be repeated. For example if the buyer fails to pay for one instalment under such circumstances as to suggest that he will not pay for future instalments; or the seller fails to deliver goods of the contract description under similar circumstances then the contract can be repudiated. In *Regent OHG Aisenstadt und Barig v Francesco of Jermyn Street Ltd (1981)* – a clothing manufacturer contracted to sell 62 suits to a retailer, delivery to be by instalments over an agreed period, the number of size of each delivery to be at the seller's descretion. The buyer informed the seller that the buyer wished to cancel the order. The seller insisted on making deliveries because the seller was already in production. Each of the attempted deliveries (five in all) was rejected by the buyer. In defence to the seller's claim for damages for non-acceptance, the buyer claimed that as the attempted deliveries had been 1 suit short of the total contract quantity of 62, the buyer was entitled to reject all the goods under Section 30(1). *Held*: giving judgement for the seller, Section 30(1) which provides that in the case of a short delivery the buyer can reject all the goods, does not apply in the case of a severable contract. Section 30(1) was inconsistent with and had to yield to Section 31. Applying Section 31 the short delivery was not sufficiently serious to amount to a repudiation of the whole contract.

Acceptance

The buyer for his part has a duty to accept the goods and Section 35 provides that acceptance is deemed to take place when the buyer

a. intimates to the buyer that he has accepted the goods or
b. does any act to the goods which is inconsistent with the ownership of the seller or
c. retains the goods, after the lapse of a reasonable time without intimating to the seller that he has rejected them.

Section 34 provides that a buyer has a right to examine the goods for the purpose of ascertaining whether they are in conformity with the contract. The seller on his part must give the buyer a reasonable opportunity to examine the goods for that purpose.

Once the buyer, as stated above, either tells the seller that he has accepted them or does any act inconsistent with the ownership of the seller such as reselling the goods or pledging them; or if he keeps the goods after a reasonable time has elapsed, then in all these cases he will be held to have accepted the goods.

It is often made a term of the contract that if fourteen days have elapsed after delivery of the goods to the buyer then the buyer will be deemed to have accepted the goods. The purpose of this is naturally to clear up any confusion which might arise as to whether or not the buyer has accepted the goods.

The importance of acceptance from the point of view of the buyer is that when he has accepted the goods then he is bound to pay for them at the contract price. Furthermore when the buyer has accepted the goods then he will be able then to reject the goods if in fact there is some defect. In *Bernstein v Pamsons Motors (Golders Green) (1986)* the buyer took delivery of a new car and having travelled 140 miles in three weeks the engine ceased up. The cause of the trouble was traced to drops of sealent which had got into the car's lubrication system during the assembly process. Repairs had been carried out but the buyer wished to reject the car and recover the price. The court held that the car was unmerchantable but the buyer had lost his right to reject by lapse of time. The judge observed that Section 35(1) allowed a reasonable time to inspect the goods and try them out generally, however, the fact that the defect was not discovered until after delivery was irrelevant in assessing what was a reasonable time. He commented that the length of time required would vary according to the nature of the goods; what was a reasonable time for a bicycle would scarcely be adequate for a nuclear submarine.

Remedies of Buyer and Seller

Buyer's Action against the Seller
Whether the property in the goods has passed or not, the buyer is entitled under the contract of sale to delivery in accordance with the rules. If the seller wrongfully neglects or refuses to deliver the goods to him, the buyer may bring an action for damages for non delivery. Section 51(2) provides that the measure of damages is the estimated loss directly or naturally resulting, in the ordinary course of events, from the seller's breach of contract.

That provision is merely a restatement, in statutory form, of the general rule with regard to damages for breach of contract. However the Act gives a particular application of it where it provides in Section 51(3) that "where there is an available market for the goods in question a measure of damages is prima facie to be ascertained by the difference between the contract price and the market or current price of the goods at the time or times when they ought to have been delivered, or (if no time was fixed) at the time of the refusal to deliver."

However a buyer will often be buying goods in order to resell these goods to a third party and the seller's failure to deliver may render the buyer unable to fulfill his obligations under the subcontract. The question then arises whether the buyer can claim as damages the profit which he would have made on the subcontract, had he been able to fulfill it, and also any liability incurred to the other party to the sub-contract by reason of its non fulfillment. Normally such damages cannot be recovered as they cannot be said to be "a loss directly and naturally resulting, in the ordinary course of events from the seller's breach of contract." However Section 54 of the Act expressly provides that nothing in the Act will affect the right of the buyer or the seller to recover special damages in any case where by law special damages are recoverable. It is well settled that a party suing for breach of contract may recover as special damages loss which, although it does not arise naturally from the breach, may be recoverable provided it should have been in contemplation of both parties at the time they made the contract.

Finally, the buyer may sue the seller for damages where there has been a breach of warranty by the seller or where the buyer chooses to treat any breach of condition by the seller as a breach of warranty. Remember that the breach of condition entitles the buyer to reject the contract completely; whereas a breach of warranty will only entitle him to sue for damages.

Specific Performance
The buyer's remedies are not confined to an action for damages but he may in special cases obtain from the court an order for a specific performance of the contract.

The *Sale of Goods Act* provides in Section 52 that "in any action for breach of contract to deliver specific or ascertained goods a court may, if it thinks fit, on the application of the plaintiff direct that the contract shall be performed specifically". This Section merely gives a statutory statement to an equitable jurisdiction which the court would already possess apart from the *Sale of Goods Act*.

Specific performance is an extraordinary remedy which will only be granted in extraordinary cases. It will only be ordered where the court can effectively superintend and enforce the carrying out of its order. It would seem to follow that specific performance would not be decreed of a contract for the delivery of goods by instalments, for it might require the constant supervision of the court to see that each instalment was delivered. In the same way the Section confines the remedy to cases where the goods in question are specific or ascertained. If the court were to order specific performance of a contract for the sale of unascertained goods, the court itself might have to ascertain the goods which were to be delivered.

However even if the goods are ascertained the court may still not grant specific performance. It will never do so for example, in a case where damages would afford adequate compensation to the injured party, and this rule precludes specific performance of most contracts for the sale of goods. "If a contract is for the purchase of a certain quantity of coals this court will not decree a specific performance because a person can go in to the market and buy similar articles and get damages for the difference in the price of the articles in a court of law" – *Falcke v Gray (1859)*.

Thus it is only in exceptional cases such as where the article in question is unique such as an heirloom or where it possesses some peculiar value to the buyer over and above the ordinary market value of similar goods where the order of specific performance will be made. The normal remedy of the buyer is an action for damages for non delivery.

It should always be remembered that over and above an action for damages for non delivery and an action for specific performance a buyer always has a right to reject the goods and to end the contract when the term broken by the seller is a condition (not a mere warranty). Most of the terms implied by Sections 12–15 are conditions. Also the courts have held that late delivery by a seller is a breach of condition which entitles a buyer to reject the goods and to end the contract. Section 11(4) provides that where the contract of sale is non severable, the rights to reject the goods and treat the contract as repudiated are lost as soon as the buyer has accepted the goods, or part thereof. A buyer is deemed to have accepted the goods when he does any act outlined in Section 35.

Seller's Action Against the Buyer
The seller has corresponding rights of action against the buyer if he, the buyer, neglects or refuses to perform his side of the contract. Section 49(1) provides that "where under a contract of sale the property in the goods has passed to the buyer, and the buyer wrongfully neglects or refuses to pay for the goods according to the terms of the contract, the seller may maintain an action against him for the price of the goods." Usually delivery of the goods and payment of the price are concurrent conditions; but the contract may provide for payment irrespective of delivery. Section 49 provides that "where under a contract of sale price is payable on a day certain irrespective of delivery, and the buyer wrongfully neglects or refuses to pay such price, the seller may maintain an action for the price, although the property in the goods has not passed and the goods have not been appropriated to the contract".

156 Transfer of Property in the Goods

In addition if the buyer breaks a contract by not accepting the goods then the seller may maintain an action against him for damages for non acceptance. Again the measure of damages, as in the case where the seller is at fault, is the estimated loss naturally resulting from the buyer's breach of contract. The measure of damages is to be ascertained by reference to the contract price and the market price.

Note that in the references to an action by the seller for the price of the goods and an action by the seller for damages, a distinction must be made between each of these. Remember that if the seller has a right to recover the price that is quite straight forward. If he can merely sue for damages then the amount he will be awarded will depend on the amount of compensation he deserves, which in some cases may amount to little or nothing.

W. L. Thompson Ltd v Robinson (Gunmakers) Ltd (1955). The defendants brought a Standard "Vanguard" motor car from the plaintiffs and then refused to accept it. The seller's profit would have been £61. As the supply of this particular vehicle exceeded the demand the sellers could not re-sell it and so lost their profit. They succeeded in recovering the whole loss of profit.

Charter v Sullivan (1957). The defendant bought a Hill-man Minx motor car from the plaintiff. The latter's profit would have been £97.15s. When sued for non-acceptance the defendant was only ordered to pay nominal damages because it was proved that the seller could sell as many Hillman Minx cars as he could obtain. Therefore he had not incurred any appreciable loss.

Also because the rights of seller against the buyer will usually only be enforced because the buyer has not paid for the goods then it may be of no help to the seller to allow him to bring an action against the buyer because the buyer will not be able to pay damages. It will be much preferable if the seller can exercise rights against the goods themselves.

Rights of the Unpaid Seller Against the Goods
In addition to the remedies by way of action, the Act gives to

the seller, in certain circumstances, rights against the goods themselves. To be able to claim these rights he must be an unpaid seller i.e. one to whom the whole of the price has not been paid or tendered, or who has received as conditional payment, a bill of exchange or other negotiable instrument which has been subsequently dishonoured. *(S.38.)* To such an unpaid seller the Act gives, in certain circumstances three rights against the goods themselves. Namely:

1. *A lien*

    A lien is a right to retain the goods of another. In this case it is the right of a creditor who is in possession of the goods belonging to his debtor to retain possession of them until payment is made. A lien is a right over the property of another. For a seller to exercise his lien merely because he has not been paid is not sufficient. One at least of the following conditions must be satisfied:

    a. The goods must have been sold without any stipulation as to credit.
    b. Where the goods have been sold on credit the term of credit has expired.
    c. The buyer must have become insolvent. The meaning of insolvent is to be found in Section 61(4). This provides that a person is deemed to be insolvent if he has either ceased to pay his debts or he cannot pay his debts as they become due.

    Lien is founded on possession, and so it follows that once possession is lost the lien, as a rule, is lost also.

    The unpaid seller of goods will lose his lien or right of retention:

    a. when he delivers the goods to a carrier for the purpose of transmission to the buyer without reserving the right of disposal of the goods.
    b. when the buyer or his agent lawfully obtains possession of the goods.
    c. by waiver of the lien or right of retention.

Merely because an unpaid seller has made part delivery of the goods does not of itself deprive him of his right of lien on the remainder, unless the circumstances under which the part delivery was made show an agreement to waive the lien. In other words a lien is only lost in such cases if it appears that both parties intended the part delivery to be regarded as constructive delivery of the whole.

2. *Stoppage in transit*

When the unpaid seller has delivered the goods to a carrier it may be that he has lost his lien. Therefore this second remedy of the unpaid seller is that in certain circumstances he can stop the goods in transit. This means that he can order the carrier to re-deliver the goods to him. *Section 44* provides that when the buyer of the goods becomes insolvent the unpaid seller who has parted with the possession of the goods has the right of stopping them in transit. In other words he may resume possession of the goods as long as they are in the course of transit and may retain them until payment or tender of the price. It is therefore important to determine whether or not the goods are in the course of transit. They are deemed to be in the course of transit from the time when they are delivered to a carrier for the purpose of transmission to the buyer until the buyer or his agent takes delivery of them. If the buyer or his agent obtains delivery before their arrival at the appointed destination the transit is at an end. The essence of stoppage in transit, it has been said, is that the goods should be "in the possession of a middle man". It is not necessary that the goods should actually be in motion for if the goods are deposited with a person who holds them merely as an agent to forward them, then they are as much in transit as if they were actually moving. Sometimes it is agreed that the goods shall be sent to some intermediate place, and the question then arises whether the delivery of them at that place terminates transit or transit continues until the goods reach their ultimate destination. Thus A in India may order goods from B in Manchester to be sent to London whence they are to be forwarded to India. Does transit terminate when the goods reach London or not until they reach India? The answer to that question depends on whether the intermediate place is merely a place of rest in the course of one journey or whether, having reached the intermediate place, the goods cannot again be set in motion without fresh orders from the purchaser. In the latter case transit ends at the intermediate place, but in the former transit continues until the goods arrive at their ultimate destination.

If goods are delivered to a ship chartered by the buyer then a difficulty may arise. The Act provides Section 45(5) that it is a question depending on the circumstances of the particular case whether the goods are in the possession of the master as a carrier or as an agent for the buyer. Of course if the ship is owned by the buyer, transit is usually at an end as soon as the goods are put on board.

In order to stop the goods in transit it is not necessary for the seller to recover actual physical possession of them. He may exercise his right of stoppage in transit either by taking actual possession of the goods or by giving notice of his claim to the carrier in whose possession the goods are. Such notice may be given either to the person in actual possession of the goods or to his principal. In the latter case the notice must be given at such time and under such circumstances that the principal may communicate it to his servant or agent in time to prevent delivery to the buyer. *Section 46(3)*.

Where the carrier in possession of the goods receives notice of stoppage in transit from the seller, it is his duty to re-deliver the goods to the seller and seller must bear the expense of such re-delivery. *Section 46(4)*.

The third remedy of the unpaid seller is:

Right of resale
Merely because the seller has retained possession of the goods or has had them stopped in transit and now

possesses them does not give him automatically a right of resale. However *Section 48* of the Act gives the unpaid seller a right to resell the goods in following circumstances:

1. Where a right of resale is expressly reserved by the terms of the contract.
2. Where the goods are of a perishable nature or
3. Where the unpaid seller gives notice to the buyer of his intention to resell and the buyer does not within a reasonable time pay or tender the price.

Where the resale is at a profit, so that the seller gets more than the original contract price, the seller can keep the profit. If an unpaid seller resells wrongfully e.g. without giving reasonable notice, the new buyer gets a goods title but in this event the seller must account to the old buyer for any profit as compared with the original contract price.

In the above cases the unpaid seller may resell and he also has, against the buyer, a claim for damages for breach of contract.

Chapter Twelve
Consumer Protection/ Product Liability

If a person is injured by a defective product then he will wish to sue for damages. The question is whom may he sue and what is his right of action. The situation is well illustrated in the famous case of *Donoghue v Stevenson (1932)*. In that case Mrs Donoghue's friend purchased for her a bottle of ginger beer which contained the decomposed remains of a snail. The friend gave the ginger beer to Mrs Donoghue who, having drunk some of the poisonous liquid and seen the remains of the snail slither out on to her ice cream, suffered injury. The question was, whom could she sue? As Mrs Donoghue had not herself purchased the ginger beer she was not in contractual relationship with the seller of the ginger beer therefore there was no question of suing that person under the *Sale of Goods Act*. The only possible person who might be liable was the manufacturer of the ginger beer and the importance of *Donoghue v Stevenson* is that it established that a manufacturer, in certain circumstances, may be liable for a defective product if he should have had reasonable foresight of harm occurring to persons whom he should have foreseen were likely to be harmed by his negligence. In the end Mrs Donoghue succeeded in her action against the manufacturer but of course the action was framed in tort because there was no contract between Mrs Donoghue and the manufacturer.

Thus the situation is that the purchaser of defective goods can sue the seller of these goods and in that case the seller will be strictly liable to the purchaser. This means that the purchaser who has been injured is not required to show any fault on the part of the seller. The seller will be automatically liable merely because he has sold defective goods. On the other hand if, as in the case of Mrs Donoghue, the injured party wishes to sue someone other than the seller then she had to prove that the manufacturer was at fault in not taking reasonable care in relation to the ginger beer. This is an action in the tort of negligence.

This then was the situation before 1 March 1988. On that date the *Consumer Protection Act, 1987* came into force. This Act was passed by the United Kingdom Parliament in response to a European Community Product Liability Directive which called upon member States to pass legislation making the producer of defective products liable without any proof of fault.

The second recital of the Directive states "whereas liability without fault on the part of the producer is the sole means of adequately solving the problem, peculiar to our age of increasing technicality, of a fair apportionment of the risks inherent in modern technological production."

Part 1 of the Consumer Protection Act now stands along side the *Sale of Goods Act* and an action in negligence.

A person injured by a defective product may wish to rely on the *Sale of Goods Act* and this he can do if he was the purchaser. If he was not the purchaser, then he may have to prove negligence but it may be that he will be able to make use of the *Consumer Protection Act* in which case negligence need not be proved.

Who May Sue?

Under the *Consumer Protection Act* any person may sue who has been injured by a defect in the product. The plaintiff will only succeed if he can prove that his injury was caused by a defect in the product. Section 3 of the Act states that a product will be regarded as defective when "the safety of the product is not such as persons generally are entitled to expect". The section goes on to give some guidance as to determining whether or not a product is defective "in determining what persons generally are entitled to expect in relation to a product all the circumstances shall be taken into account, including –

a. the manner in which, and purposes for which, the product has been marketed, its get-up, the use of any mark in relation to the product and any instructions for, or

warnings with respect to, doing or refraining from doing anything with or in relation to the product;
b. what might reasonably be expected to be done with or in relation to the product; and
c. the time when the product was supplied by its producer to another person;

and nothing in this Section shall require a defect to be inferred from the fact alone that the safety of a product which is supplied after that time is greater than the safety of the product in question."

Thus it has made it imperative for producers to be careful as regards the packaging of their products and they must not suggest by the packaging that the product can be used in any manner which is unsafe.

Who is Liable?

Liability will fall upon the following

1. The producer.
   Section 1(2) defines the producer as

   a. the person who manufactured it
   b. in the case of a substance which has not been manufactured but has been won or abstracted, the person who won or abstracted it. "This covers mining and quarrying"
   c. in any other case a person who has applied an industrial or any other process affecting the essential characteristics of the product.

2. Any person who puts his own name on the product or uses a trademark of other distinguishing mark in relation to the product – in other words has held himself out as being the producer of the product. This is increasingly occurring in supermarkets who put their own brand on products made by other persons.

3. Any person who imported the goods into a member State of the European Community from a place outside the

Community for the purpose of supplying it in the course of a business.
4. Any person to whom Section 2(3) applies i.e. any supplier who cannot identify the person who produced the product or who supplied it to him. This provision is inserted because on occasions it may be difficult for the injured party to identify the producer or the person who imported the product into the European Community. In this case then the supplier can be made liable provided he supplied the product to someone else and provided
   a. he is requested by a person suffering damage to identify any producer, own brander or importer into the European Community.
   b. the request is made within a reasonable time after the damage occurs.
   c. at the time of the request it is not reasonably practicable for the injured party to identify all of the potential defendants.
   d. he fails, within a reasonable time, to comply with the request or to identify the person who supplied the product to him.

It can be seen that a number of persons then may be made liable for the damage to the plaintiff and in that case the person who is sued may be entitled to a contribution from any other person who may be liable under the *Civil Liability (Contribution) Act 1978*.

As has been stated the basis of liability under the *Consumer Protection Act* is strict. This means that where the injured person can show that there is a causal relationship between the defect and the damage then one or other of the above defendants will be strictly liable.

Types of Loss

Section 5 provides that damages are recoverable for death or for personal injury. However there is no liability for loss of or damage to

a. the product itself.
b. any property in respect of which the amount of the claim would be below £275.
c. any commercial property i.e. property of a type which is not ordinarily intended for private use, occupational consumption and which is not actually intended by the plaintiff for his own private use, occupation on consumption.

If the plaintiff wishes to claim for these excluded losses then he may pursue his claim in contract or negligence.

The *Consumer Protection Act* prohibits absolutely any limitation or exclusion of liability arising under the Act. It will be remembered that exclusion or limitation of liability may be possible in contract or in negligence and subject to the *Unfair Contract Terms Act, 1987*.

What Defences are Available to the Defendant?

Apart from the obvious defences of showing that there was no causal relationship between the defect and the damage or that the product was not in fact defective, the following specific defences are stated in Section 4 of the *Consumer Protection Act*:

1. That the defect was attributable to the defendant's compliance with a legal requirement.
2. That the defendant did not supply the goods to anyone.

In this connection the term "supply" has been widely defined in Section 46 and in a hire purchase case involving dealer – hire purchaser – finance company, the Section provides that the dealer and not the finance company is to be treated as supplying the product to the hire purchaser. Also, where a finished product incorporates component products or raw materials, the supplier of the finished product will not be treated as the supplier of the component products or raw materials merely because he has supplied the finished product.

3. Section 4 enables the defendant to escape liability if he can show that he had not supplied the goods in the course of

his business and that he had not own-branded, imported into the EC or produced the goods with a view to profit. The effect of this is that homemade goods which cause injury will probably not make the supplier liable.
4. That the defect did not exist in the product at the relevant time. The relevant time means the time when the producer supplied it to another person.
5. Section 4 provides what is called "the development risks defence". This means that the state of scientific and technical knowledge at the relevent time was not such that a producer of products of the same description as the product in question might be expected to have discovered the defect if it had existed in his products while they were under his control.

It has been argued that this "development risks" defence reduces the effectiveness of the Act. It means that, in effect, any manufacturer will now escape liability provided he can show that he took all reasonable precautions in the light of scientific knowledge at that time. Thus if there were a repetition of the Thalidomide tragedy then the victims of that drug would be in no better position now to pursue their claim, than they were at the time of the tragedy.

6. Where the defendant is the producer of a component part of a product, he will have a defence under Section 4 if he can show that the defect in the finished product is wholly attributable to its design or to compliance with instructions given by the producer of the finished product.

Time Limit for Claims

The basic limitation period as far as the injured party is concerned is three years from;

1. the date on which the right to take action arises or
2. the date on which the plaintiff is aware
   a. that he has suffered significant damage
   b. that the damage is attributable to a defect in the product,

    c.   of the identity of the defendant.

The limitation period is the same whether there is personal injury or property damage.

As for the supplier there is a 10 year cut off period for each supplier. This is known as a "period of repose" in the United States, and relates to the particular product and not to the product line.

Chapter Thirteen

Insurance

The owner of a house or of goods on a ship can never be certain that any of these things is not going to be damaged or lost. It is of the greatest importance therefore that the owner of any of these things should take out insurance cover.

The nature of an insurance contract is that it is a contract by which a person called the insurer agrees, in return for a premium, to pay a sum of money to another person (the insured) on the happening of some future event.

The future event may be certain to happen or it may merely be a possibility. Thus the two categories of insurance are:

1. Indemnity Insurance. This provides an indemnity against loss as in a fire policy on a house, or a marine policy for on a ship.
2. Contingency Insurance. This provides not an indemnity but payment on some contingent event. This is to be found in a life policy or a personal injury policy.
    The sum to be paid is not measured by the loss but is stated in the policy. The contracted sum is paid if the life ends or an injury is sustained, irrespective of the value of the life or injury.

Like any other contract a contract of insurance is an agreement whereby the parties make promises to each other. In this particular contract, one party approaches the insurance company and pays, or promises to pay a sum of money called a premium; in return the insurer promises to pay out a sum of money if a certain thing occurs in the future.

On the face of it, it appears that a contract of insurance is like a wager – which is also a contract in which one party agrees to pay a sum of money to the other party dependent upon the happening of some uncertain future event. A contract of insurance is enforceable where as a wager is not. *Gaming Acts 1835–1968.*

Insurable Interest
The difference between a wager and a contract of insurance lies in the fact that in the latter there must be "an insurable interest". *Life Assurance Act 1774.*

An insurable interest has not been defined by Parliament but in *Halford v Kymer (1830)* it was stated that a person who will suffer pecuniary loss as a consequence of the happening of the risk insured against, as opposed to a chance of winning money, as in the case of a wager, can be said to have an insurable interest.

It is up to the courts to decide whether an insurable interest exists as they have so decided in the following cases:

1. A creditor may insure the life of his debtor. *Anderson v Edie (1795)*. Thus according to Paget "a bank may insure the life of its debtor but in practice never does so, preferring to take as security, a policy on the life of another person."
2. A guarantor may insure the life of a principle debtor.
3. An employer may insure the life of his employee *Hebdon v West (1863)*. In this connection an employer will frequently insure his employees lives and agree that any benefits be paid to their next of kin.
4. A litigant may insure the life of his judge. This has been done in a long complicated will case where it was apparent that if the judge were to die a re-trial would necessitate heavy expense.
5. A husband or wife can insure the life of the other spouse.
6. A father does not have insurable interest in the life of his child unless he can show some E.g. the daughter is looking after him. He can of course take out a policy on his child, for his child's benefit.
7. An assignee such as a bank does not need to have an insurable interest – *Ashley v Ashley (1829)*.

The *Life Assurance Act 1774* does not apply to insurance on goods. Section 4 of that Act provides "nothing here in contained shall extend or be construed to extend to insurance bona fide made by any person or persons on ships, goods or merchandise." Thus the requirement for an insurable interest in goods is not so stringent as in the case of a life. Even if the insurer has no interest at all the contract may still not be a wager as everything will depend on the intention of the parties as expressed in the policy.

The three factors which give an insurable interest under a contract for the sale of goods are property, possession and risk. If the goods are still at the seller's risk or if the property has not yet passed or if the seller has possession as in the case of an unpaid seller then he, the seller, can insure the goods without the contract being invalidated as a wager. In the same way the buyer can insure if he has acquired property, possession or risk. Even if the buyer has not acquired property, possession or risk he can insure against loss of profit on re-sale as soon as he has agreed to buy the goods. In marine insurance an insurable interest is also required. A person has an insurable interest if he is interested in a marine adventure in consequence of which he may benefit by the safe arrival of insurable property or be prejudiced by its loss, damage or detention.

Uberrimae Fidei

Insurance is a contract *uberrimae fidei*. All forms of insurance require that there should be the fullest disclosure of all material facts. If a material fact has been omitted to be disclosed then it may render the contract voidable. A circumstance is material if it would influence the judgment of a prudent insurer in fixing the premium or determining whether to take the risk. In *Mutual Life Insurance Company of New York v Ontario Metal Products Company (1925)* a proposal form asked the name of any physician whom the proposer had consulted in the last five years. The proposer said "none", though in fact, he had consulted a doctor and received tonics, but he had never been away from his work. The insurers' doctor said that if he had known of this he would still have recommended the acceptance of the risk at the ordinary premium. *Held*: there was no material concealment and the policy was not avoided.

In *London Assurance v Mansel (1879)* M in reply to questions asking whether previous proposals on his life had been made to any other office, and if so, whether they had been accepted at the ordinary rate, said that he was then insured at two offices at the ordinary rates. He omitted to disclose that his life had been declined by several other offices. *Held*: this was a material failure to disclose and the policy could be set aside.

Indemnity

As has been stated insurance may be either an indemnity insurance or a contingency insurance. Contingency insurance covers life policies and personal injury policies. Indemnity insurance provides indemnity against the loss as in a fire policy on a house or a marine policy on a vessel. In an indemnity contract the fundamental rule is that the insured cannot recover or retain for his own benefit more than his actual loss. An exception of this principle occurs if the parties have agreed at the time of the contract on the value of the subject matter of the insurance. This is known as a valued policy. In this case where a total loss occurs, a sum representing the agreed value is recoverable by the insured, even though it exceeds his actual loss. The most common type of valued policy to be found in non marine insurance is a policy insuring against loss of profits.

In the event of a total loss the insurers under an unvalued policy are liable to pay the market value of the property at the time and place of the loss or the sum insured that is agreed between the parties whichever is less. This is why a car owner should reduce the cover on his car each time he pays his annual premium because almost certainly the value of the car will decrease year by year. If the car is written off then the insured will only receive the current market value and not the market value at the time when he originally entered into the contract of insurance.

The indemnity is based on the market value of the property and not the cost of its purchase or production or reinstatement unless there has been an agreement to this effect.

If the property has no market value then the insurers are liable to pay the cost of reinstatement or the sum insured whichever is less. Finally where the goods are merely damaged then the insurers liability is based on cost of repairs or the sum insured whichever is the less.

Average Clause
If the insured insures for less than the full value of the property, the insurers are nevertheless liable to indemnify the insured up to the total amount insured. If there is total loss there is no difficulty and the insured will receive the sum insured. However if there is only partial loss then the insurers are liable to indemnify the insured up to the full amount insured even though they have only received a small premium. To guard against under insurance it is very common to insert "an average clause" in a policy. The words "subject to average" in a Lloyd's policy involve the following standard clause:

"Where ever a sum insured is declared to be subject to average, if the property shall at the breaking out of any fire be collectively of greater value than such sum insured, then the insured shall be considered as being his own insurer for the difference and shall bear a rateable share of the loss accordingly". Thus if goods worth £50,000 are insured for £25,000 under a policy containing an "average clause" and damage is caused totalling £25,000 then the insurers will only be liable to pay half of the damage i.e. £12,500. This is the proportion which the sum insured bears to the total value of the property i.e. 50%.

Chapter Fourteen
Intellectual Property

Patents, Copyright and Trademarks

All these matters are included in the term intellectual property or sometimes it is called industrial property. Also included under this term would be plant breeders rights, registered designs and the new unregistered design right.

Intellectual property is generally taken to describe all those things which emanate from the exercise of the human brain, such as ideas, inventions, poems, designs etc. When we look at intellectual property we will consider the rights and the protection of these rights that exist over such things as patents, copyright and trademarks. We will see that these rights in the main give to the owner of the rights a monopoly right to enjoy the benefits of the invention or the trademark or the writing for a particular period of time. The law gives rights to the owner of the intellectual property so that he may get the benefit from the time and money that he has expended in producing the item.

It should be remembered that usually there will be an overlap of these intellectual property rights – for example a person may have invented a particular machine and so therefore he will obtain a patent in respect of that invention; there will probably be drawings of the machine and so he will then own the copyright in those drawings. And finally very often there will be a trademark which will link the machine with his business so that members of the public, when they purchase the machine, can identify the product.

Patents

Patent is the name given to a bundle of monopoly rights which give the patentee the exclusive right to exploit an invention for a stated period of time and to prevent anyone else from exploiting that invention.

Because a patent may well have an international application then there has been a certain amount of international co-operation concerning the filing of an application for a patent.

In 1970 the *Patent Co-operation Treaty (PCT)* was entered into and this came into operation in 1978. By this Treaty about 40 States have agreed that their respective national patent offices will accept and accord a priority date to "international applications" which have been filed at an international receiving office within the previous 20 months. The applicant still has to satisfy local requirements in order to obtain his grant. The scheme is operated under the World Intellectual Property Organisation in Geneva.

The *European Patent Convention 1973 (EPC)* which came into operation in 1978 creates a common system of law for the grant of patents. The steps leading to a grant, as well as the grant itself, are undertaken by the European Patent Office (EPO) in Munich. The application is searched and examined at the European Patent Office and if the invention satisfies the requirements of the Convention then a separate national patent will be granted for each of the specified countries. Thus a single application may result in what has been termed "a bundle of national patents".

At the moment there is no single patent for the whole of the European Community but the *Community Patent Convention 1975 (CPC)* is designed to provide a patent which will take effect throughout the European Community.

The three requirements which determine whether or not an invention is capable of being patented are:

1. Novelty.
2. An inventive step.
3. Industrial application.

Novelty
The *Patents Act 1977* contains the law on patents for the United Kingdom and Section 2 of that Act states that "an invention

shall be taken to be new if it does not form part of the state of the art". "The state of the art comprises all matters (whether a product, a process, information about either, or anything else) which has any time before the priority date of that invention been made available to the public (whether in the United Kingdom or elsewhere) by written or oral description, by use or in any other way."

Therefore an applicant for a patent must ensure that his invention is new. However there are three cases of prior disclosure which cannot be used for purposes of objecting to the application. These are;

1. disclosures occurring not earlier than six months before the filing date and made in breach of confidence or resulting from such breach or any unlawful acquisition of information.
2. information disclosed at an international exhibition which does not include a trade exhibition.
3. where the applicant claims a novel use of a known substance "for use in a method of treatment of the human or animal body by surgery or therapy or of diagnosis – provided that the former use was not a medical one."

An Inventive Step

It is a matter of some difficulty to decide on occasions whether in fact an invention does involve an inventive step. The test is directed to a man skilled in the art. He has been described as "a skilled technician who is well acquainted with workshop techniques and who has carefully read all the relevant literature." *Technograph Printed Circuits Ltd v Mills & Rockley (Electronics) Ltd (1972)*. Therefore if the invention is not obvious to such a person who is skilled in the art then it probably means that an inventive step has been taken by the inventor.

Capable of Industrial Application

The third requirement is that the invention should be capable of industrial application. In other words any method of treatment of the human or animal body by surgery or therapy or diagnosis is excluded. Subject to that, the requirement of "capable of industrial application" will be satisfied by any invention if it can be made or used in any kind of industry, including agriculture.

Ownership of the Patent
Any person may apply for a patent but if the applicant is not the inventor then he must file a statement identifying that person and showing why he is applying for the patent.

A difficulty may sometimes arise where the inventor is an employee. The question may be whether the employee or the employer is the owner of the invention. It is not enough for the employer to show that the invention was made in the course of his employee's duties. *Section 39* of the Patents Act 1977 must go further and show that the duties were the normal duties of the employee or specifically assigned to him or performed by an employee having a special obligation to further the employer's undertaking. Not only that but there is a further requirement that an invention might reasonably have been expected to result from the employees carrying out those duties. All other employee inventions belong to the employee.

Where an employer obtains a patent in respect of an employee's invention and it is shown that the patent is of great benefit to the employer then the employee inventor may apply under *Section 40* to the court or to the Controller of Patents for an award of compensation.

If the owner of the patent does not wish to develop the invention himself then he may licence another person to do so. A licence may be granted orally and may be non-exclusive or exclusive. In the case of an exclusive licence then the licensee can bring infringement proceedings in his own name.

Infringement
There will be direct infringement of a patent if a person:

1. makes a patented product.
2. disposes or offers to dispose of or import or keeps for disposal a patented product.

3. uses a patented process.
4. offers a patented process for use in the United Kingdom when the infringer knows, or it would be obvious to a reasonable person, that its use in the United Kingdom would be an infringement without the consent of the owner of the patent.

There will also be infringement if a person supplies or offers to supply "means essential for putting an invention into effect" to a person not entitled to work the invention.

Defences

A person who is accused of infringing a patent has the following defences in addition of course to the main one which is that he holds a licence to use the patent.

1. acts done privately for non-commercial purposes.
2. acts done for experimental purposes relating to the subject matter of the invention.
3. extemporaneous preparation by pharmacies of individual prescriptions.
4. certain uses in respect of foreign ships and aircraft temporarily in United Kingdom jurisdiction.
5. a right to continue to use the invention which had been commenced before the priority date of the patent.

Revocation of a Patent

Obviously a person will only be guilty of infringing a patent if in fact the patent has been validly granted in the first place. It follows therefore that if the defendant can show that the patent should never have been granted then that will be an adequate defence. A patent may be revoked because:

1. the invention is not a patentable invention – the ground most frequently invoked in practice.
2. the patent was granted to a person not entitled to the grant.
3. the specification lacks the clarity and completeness required for the invention to be performed by a person skilled in the art.

4. the matter disclosed in the specification of a patent extends beyond that disclosed in the applications filed.
5. protection has been extended by an amendment which should not have been allowed.

These issues may be related by way of defence or counter-claim to an action for infringement:

1. by applying to the comptroller or court for an order revoking the patent or by applying to the comptroller or court for a declaration that an act or proposed act does not infringe, the applicant having failed to obtain an acknowledgement to like effect from the patentee.
2. by instituting proceedings for groundless threats.
3. at the instance of the Crown in proceedings relating to use for Crown services.

Remedies for Infringement
Before the trial it may be possible to use an action for discovery as explained in *Norwich Pharmacal v Customs and Excise (1974)*. There is also an Anton Piller Order which compels the defendant to permit entry and search and to deliver into the custody of the plaintiff documents and articles specified in the order. Finally, before action, an interlocutory injunction may be obtained. The principles on which this may be awarded are contained in *American Cyanamid v Ethicon (1975)*. They are that the plaintiff should satisfy the court:

1. that should he succeed at the trial damages would not compensate him for the continuance of the activity complained of until final judgment.
2. that should he lose at the trial (having been granted such relief) the defendant will be adequately compensated by damages payable pursuant to the normal undertaking required of the plaintiff.

As for final Orders which the court may grant, these are:

1. *Damages* – the award of damages is subject to some limitations and will not be made if the defendant can

prove that he was not aware and had no reasonable grounds for supposing that the patent existed.
2. *Account of profits* – this is an equitable remedy and may be awarded as an alternative to damages. It may be applied for where the provable loss is less that the ill-gotten gains.
3. *Order for delivery up or destruction of infringing goods* – this is another equitable remedy designed to reinforce an injunction. It is usual for the defendant to be given a choice between the destruction of the goods or delivering them up.

Final injunction
In the case of a continuing infringement or where there is a possibility that the infringement may be repeated then an injunction may be asked for.

Copyright

The Law relating to Copyright may be found in the *Copyright Act 1956* and more recently in the *Copyright Designs and Patents Act 1988*.

Copyright is intended to protect the skill, labour and effort which have been expended in producing the work. The author of the work is the only one with a right to copy it in the sense of using it again or publishing it. It follows therefore that no-one else has this right. Copyright arises merely by bringing a work into existence. Unlike a patent there is no need for any registration.

The owner of a copyright, in the same way as the owner of a patent owns a monopoly. However in the case of copyright the monopoly of its owner is only of a limited variety. The owner of a patent has complete control over the marketability of the invention patented. In the case of copyright the owner can prevent other people from copying his work; but similar works may continue to be produced by competitors.

Subject Matter of the Copyright
Section 1 of the 1988 Act states that copyright is a property

right which subsists in an original literary, dramatic, musical or artistic works.

Sound recordings, films, broadcast or cable programmes.

Typographical arrangements of published editions.

The definition of these terms is quite wide – for example, literary works would include any table or compilation or a computer program. Also artistic works would include a graphic work, a photograph or a sculpture irrespective of any artistic quality. Thus in this way the football association own the copyright in the fixtures list to be played by the football clubs of this country.

Ownership of Copyright

The first owner of copyright is the author of the work and this means the person who created the work.

In the case of employer and employee then if the employee produces any literary, dramatic, musical or artistic work in the course of this employment then the employer will own the copyright. In any other case then the author will own the copyright himself.

Under the 1956 Act there were commissioning conditions which meant that when a person commissioned for payment the taking of a photograph or painting or drawing of a portrait then the copyright belongs to the person who commissioned the work. There is no similar provision in the 1988 Act and so the first ownership of the copyright will belong to the author of the work. However, an exception exists in the case of a design right when the design is created following a commission by a person. In that case the commissioner owns the design right. Naturally, this position can be reversed by the making of a contract in writing between the commissioner and the author of the work by which the copyright in the finished work will in fact become the property of the commissioner.

A copyright may be assigned and this must be in writing signed by or on behalf of the assignor. In addition copyright may be transmitted by testamentary disposition or by operation of law as in the case of personal property. An example of his occurred by Agatha Christie leaving the copyright in her play

"The Mousetrap" by Will to her nephew who will of course continue to receive royalties in respect of the production of the play.

Period of Protection
A period of protection for published works is the life of the author plus 50 years and for works which are not published it continues until the end of 50 years from the date on which it was published. These are the provisions in the 1956 Act. The 1988 Act merely provides that protection will be given for the author plus 50 years after the end of the year in which the author died and there is no distinction made between published and unpublished works.

Moral Rights
Sections 77–89 of the 1988 Act create new moral rights for English law. These have been introduced to enable the United Kingdom to comply with the Berne Convention.

These so-called "moral rights" may be conferred upon the author of a copyright work and these are:

1. the paternity right i.e. a right to be identified as the author of a copyright work.
2. the integrity right i.e. a right not to suffer derogatory treatment of the work.

The paternity right must be specifically asserted by the author and this is increasingly being done in new editions of books. The right not to suffer derogatory treatment is defined in the Act as "a distortion or mutilation of the work or treatment prejudicial to the honour or reputation of the author".

Copyright Infringement
Under both the 1956 and the 1988 Acts the copyright owner may ask the court for an injunction to prevent the continuation of the infringement. He may also claim damages for the loss he has suffered or an account of profits gained as a result of the infringement. Exceptions to infringement include dealing for the purposes of research and private study or for the purposes of

criticism or review. Reproduction for the purposes of judicial proceeding or for certain educational purposes.

Unregistered Design Right

Prior to the 1988 Act protection of an industrial design could be made by a registration under the *Registered Designs Act 1949* but this would only apply if the design had an aesthetic value. Protection still existed under the *Copyright Act 1956* but this was usually not used to any extent.

However the protection under the *Copyright Act* has now, by Section 51 of the 1988 Act, been withdrawn to the extent that the article is not itself an artistic work. In its place a new design right has been created by Sections 213–264 of the 1988 Act. In the same way as copyright, protection of an unregistered design right will arise automatically and no registration is required.

However there must exist documentary proof of the industrial design.

Section 213(2) states that a design is "any aspect of the shape or configuration (whether internal or external) of the whole or part of an article".

Section 213(3) states what an industrial design is not i.e. (a) a method of principle of construction (b) features of shape or configuration which enable an article to be connected to, or placed in, around or against, another article so that either article may perform its function (the "must fit" exception) (c) features of shape or configuration dependent upon the appearance of another article of which the article is intended by the designer to form an integral part ("the must match" exception) (d) surface decoration.

The owner of a design right has the right to reproduce the design for commercial purposes.

Infringement
The owner of a design right may sue for damages, ask for an injunction or an account of profits. The defendant may have a defence as regards damages if he can show that he infringed the design right, "innocently".

Ownership of the design right
The designer of the original design is the first owner of the design subject to two exceptions:

1. if the design is created in the course of employment, then the ownership belongs to the employer
2. designs created under a commission belong to the person who commissioned them.

The period of protection for a design right expires 10 years after the first marketing of articles made from the design, subject to an overall limit of 15 years from creation of the design if there has been a delay in marketing the article. In the last 5 years licences of right will be available. The terms of these licences will be settled by the Comptroller of Patents in the absence of agreement.

Trademarks

A trademark is any word or symbol or combination of both which is used to indicate a connection in the course of trade between the goods in relation to which the mark is used and the owner of the mark. Such trademarks are protected by the common law of "passing off" and under the *Trademarks Act 1938*.

Passing Off
This is a common law tort and has been described by the House of Lords as "the principle of law may be very plainly stated, that nobody has the right to represent his goods as the goods of somebody else."

The most recent case which contains the judgment of Lord Diplock is *Warninck v Townend (1980)*. In that case Lord Diplock stated "there are five characteristics which must be present in order to create a valid cause of action for passing off:

1. a misrepresentation.
2. made by the trader in the course of trade.
3. to prospective customers of his or ultimate customers of goods or services supplied by him.

4. which is calculated to injure the business or goodwill of another trader (in the sense that this is a reasonably foreseeable consequence).
5. which causes actual damage to the business or goodwill of the trader by whom the action is brought or will probably do so."

It is the case that the plaintiff in a passing off action may need to show the defendant is engaged in competing business activities. If in fact the defendant is in a totally different line of business then the plaintiff will be in difficulties in convincing the court that there has in fact been confusion in the public mind.

As regards remedies a plaintiff who is successful will be entitled to an injunction and to damages or an account of profits. He may also obtain an order for obliteration or modification of the mark, name or wording complained of.

Registered Trademarks
The *Trademarks Act 1938* establishes a procedure for registration of certain marks and gives the owner of the trademark exclusive use. Only marks used in connection with goods can be registered.

Registrability
The trademarks register is divided into part A and part B. To be registrable in part A a mark must consist of or contain at least one of the following:

1. the name of a company, individual or firm represented in a special or particular manner
2. a signature of the applicant
3. an invented word or words
4. a word or words having no direct reference to the character or quality of the goods and not being a geographical name or a surname
5. any other distinctive mark.

In order for a mark to be accepted for registration then it must be shown to be distinctive. This means that the mark must be adapted to distinguish the goods of the owner from those of other traders.

If it is impossible to have a mark registered in Part A then it may be possible to have the mark registered in Part B. The test in this case is less stringent than for Part A and the Registrar of Trademarks must be satisfied that the mark is capable of becoming distinctive where as in Part A it must be shown that it is already distinctive.

Infringement
The owner of a trademark registered in Part A has the exclusive right to use that trademark in relation to the goods for which it is registered. Any other person using that mark in the course of trade and without permission is guilty of infringement. The test for infringement of a mark registered in Part B is the same as for Part A except that it is a defence for the person who is alleged to have infringed the mark to show that his use of the mark was not likely to deceive or cause confusion.

Defences to Infringement
The defences available are:

1. that the mark is invalid e.g. it has not been used for a period of five years or that its registration contravenes provisions of the Act. Once registered for seven years a Part A mark can only be attacked for contravention of Section 11, i.e. non-use or if its registration was fraudulent.
2. that there is no infringement
3. that the defendant used his mark prior to the first use by the proprietor of the mark sued upon or prior to its registration whichever is the earlier
4. that the defendant is bona fide using his own name or that of his place of business
5. that the defendant is using a bona fide description of the character or quality of his goods
6. that the defendant is himself the registered proprietor of the mark complained of

7. that the plaintiff has no title
8. general defences such as acquiescence, estoppel or that the plaintiff's use of the mark is fraudulent or deceptive.

Remedies

A successful plaintiff will be able to obtain an injunction and also an award of damages or an account of profits for an infringement. Also he may be granted an order for destruction or modification of the offending material.

Licensing

Any person who is the owner of a mark used or intended to be used by him may apply for registration. Once a mark has been registered then it may be assigned either in connection with the goodwill of the business in which it is used, or as a separate assignment.

If the assignment is made without transferring the goodwill of the business then it will not take effect unless the assignee applies to the Registrar of Trademarks within six months from the date of the assignment for directions with respect to advertising the assignment in a suitable trade journal. The assignment agreement must give the owner of the trademark some sort of continuing control over the way the mark is to be used. The Registrar has recognised as adequate three types of control:

1. that of a holding company over its subsidiaries
2. that given by a contract entitling the owner of a mark to control the quality etc. of the goods
3. that of a patentee over licencees of his patent.

Whether or not in fact control may be exercised effectively is questionable.

Intellectual Property and the European Community

It is of course a fundamental principle of the European Community that competition for goods or services is the best way of keeping prices down and ensuring that industrial output keeps pace with existing consumer demand.

Articles 30–36 of the Treaty of Rome intend to prohibit any unjustifiable restriction upon the goods that can be imported into or exported from one member State to another.

Article 85 prohibits the operation of cartels and agreements with the effect of distorting or preventing competition.

Article 86 prohibits the abuse of a position of dominance within the Community by any commercial undertaking.

Thus it is apparent that when one considers that the purpose of Intellectual Property is to grant to the owners of such property exclusive rights then this is in conflict with the European Community's principle.

The European Court of Justice has attempted to resolve the conflict between the pro and anti-competitive laws by stating that there is a distinction between the *existence* of Intellectual Property Rights and the *exercise* of these rights.

The existence of these Intellectual Property Rights is a matter for each member State. The exercise of them is a matter for Community Law.

Thus Intellectual Property Rights may continue to be used provided that by making use of such rights then prohibitions or restrictions are not merely a means of arbitrary discrimination nor are they a disguised restriction on trade.

In *Deutsche Grammophon v Metro-SB Grossmarkte (1971)* it was held that Article 36 permitted a departure from the provisions of Articles 30 and 34 of the Treaty of Rome but only to the "extent to which they are justified for the purpose of safeguarding rights which constitute the specific subject matter of such property".

In the case of a patent the specific subject matter is the right to exploit an invention by manufacturing and selling a product coupled with the right to prevent an infringement by a third party. This was established in *Centrafarm B.V. v Stirling Drug Inc. (1974)*.

Centrafarm v Winthrop B.V. (1974) established that the specific subject matter of a trademark was the grant to the holder of the exclusive right to use the mark and to be the first to market the product under that mark. This principle was extended in *Centrafarm v American Home Products (1979)* and now includes the right of the proprietor to prohibit the repackaging of a product to which the trademark has been affixed by a person without authority.

Article 36 provides "the provisions of Articles 30–34 shall not preclude prohibitions or restrictions on imports, exports or goods in transit justified on grounds of public morality, public policy or public security; the protection of health and life of humans, animals or plants; the protection of national treasures possessing artistic, historic or archaeological value; or the protection of industrial and commercial property. Such prohibitions or restrictions shall not, however, constitute a means of arbitrary discrimination or disguised restriction on trade between member States."

Merck & Co. Inc. v Stephar B.V. (1981) the European Court held that a patentee may not exercise his rights so as to exclude from one market goods which he has marketed in another member State.

Also in *Van Zuylen Frères v Hag A.G. (1974)* the European Court held where trademarks share a common origin, the user of a mark in one member State may not use his rights to exclude the goods of the user in another member State. "Common origin" means that the trademark was originally owned by the same undertaking even though ownership had subsequently become split. This might have occurred because of a takeover or a merger.

Apart from Articles 30 and 34 which are concerned with the free movement of goods Articles 85 and 86 may also be affected by intellectual property rights. Article 85 is most likely to apply to an agreement for the exploitation of an intellectual property right. This probably would be a licence granted by the owner of the right to another to manufacture and sell the product which may be restrictive in its terms. Such an agreement would probably come within the terms of the block exemption on patent licensing.

In the same way Article 86 may be considered in connection with intellectual property rights because it is true to say that the owner of any such right has a dominant position in respect of the subject matter of that particular right. However in both these cases the Commission will only be concerned if it can be shown that fair trading has been affected.

As regards the future it is fairly certain that intellectual property law will be harmonised within the European Community. The greatest amount of progress has been made towards a common trademark law. The Trademarks Approximation directive 1988 lays down principles which should be common to the Community's national or regional trademark systems.

The directive must be implemented by each member State by the end of 1992. However it does not follow that harmonisation will result in the creation of a single trade mark throughout the E.C. The political problems still remain as to the location of the Community Trade Mark office and the language to be used.

As regards patents the majority of the member States of the European Community have basically identical laws regarding patentability. A Community Patent Convention which would provide one single patent is quite likely to come into force in the near future.

The least amount of progress has been made in copyright as there appears to be the greatest amount of divergence in copyright law in the various member States of the Community. There is a proposed directive on software protection which was published in 1988 and so it may be that any advance in harmonisation in copyright law will come through this channel.

Part 3
Financial

Money is the life blood of commerce and so we must consider such topics as are concerned with loans, financial advice, cheques and – if the money runs out – insolvency.

Chapter Fifteen
Consumer Credit Act 1974

Credit, in the sense of payment being deferred for goods or services, has become a feature of our modern life. For many years attempts have been made to control the credit industry and to protect the consumer. This has been done by regulating the supply of credit and by the advertisement of credit by the *Pawnbrokers Act 1872–1960*, the *Moneylenders Acts 1900–1927*, the *Hire Purchase Act 1965* and the *Advertisements (Hire Purchase) Act 1967*.

These Acts gradually became less and less effective and it was evident that some of the legislation was being bypassed. For example the Moneylenders Acts applied only to moneylenders, and to loans made by moneylenders. They did not apply to other forms of credit and certain types of business e.g. banking, in the course of which loans of money were made, were exempted from the operation of the Acts.

The *Consumer Credit Act 1974* now regulates many different forms of credit. It is comprehensive in its scope and it controls the business of giving credit by the issue of licenses. It restricts advertising and canvassing and gives wide supervisory powers to the Director General of Fair Trading. It also controls agreements made by individuals by stating the formalities required and it deals with the matters of termination, cancellation and default of agreements.

What sort of transaction is affected by the Act?

The two transactions regulated by the Act are:

1. a consumer credit agreement
2. a consumer hire agreement.

The titles given to these agreements bring up a number of concepts which must now be examined in some detail.

Sections 8–20 deal with the various types of credit and hire agreements and linked transactions.

Credit is defined as a cash loan and any form of financial accommodation.

All types of loan are covered and examples are given in Schedule 2 Part II of the Act e.g.

1. moneylenders loans
2. bank loans
3. overdrafts
4. pawnbrokers loans
5. advances on mortgage
6. the sale of goods on instalment credit terms (e.g. credit sales, conditional sales, budget accounts, option accounts, subscription accounts)
7. the supply of services on credit, check and voucher trading
8. credit cards
9. check cards

In all of these cases in return for goods *or* services payment is deferred whether the payment is to be made in one amount or by instalments.

A Consumer Credit Agreement

A consumer credit agreement is defined as a personal credit agreement by which the creditor provides the debtor with credit not exceeding (at present, 1992) £15,000.

A personal credit agreement is an agreement between an individual called "the debtor" and any other person called "the creditor" by which the creditor provides the debtor with credit. The term individual includes a partnership or other unincorporated body of persons not consisting entirely of bodies corporate. Therefore an agreement to provide credit for a company will not be a personal credit agreement and so will not be affected by the Act. An agreement with a partnership can be a personal credit agreement even though the partnership is in business and the loan is for business purposes. Whether or not the Act applies to the transaction will be determined by the status of the debtor and not by the purpose for which the loan has been made and by the amount advanced.

A Regulated Consumer Credit Agreement

This is a consumer credit agreement which is not an exempt agreement.

Exempt Agreements

These are specified in section 16 and include:

1. Consumer credit agreements secured by a mortgage over land where the creditor is a local authority or a building society.
2. Agreements secured by mortgage over land where the creditor is one of a number of Insurance Companies, Friendly Societies and Land Improvement Companies specified by the Secretary of State or is a Trade Union of employers or workers.
3. Fixed sum debtor-creditor-supplier agreements (other than hire purchase or conditional sale agreements) when the number of payments to be made by the debtor does not exceed four.
4. A running-account credit agreement where the debtor is required to repay the debt in one single payment. Examples of this type of agreement would be a credit card issued by American Express or Diners Club.
5. Low cost debtor-creditor agreements when the rate of interest does not exceed 13% or 1% above the base rate determined by the Bank of England.
6. Any agreement made in connection with trade in goods or services between the United Kingdom and an overseas country.

The above agreements are exempt agreements and so are not

affected by the provisions of the Act. However the fact that an agreement is exempt does not exclude the power of the Court to investigate a bargain which it considers to be extortionate in regard to the rates of interest required and other factors (Sections 137–140). Thus the Court has power to re-open any agreement regulated or not, whether it is below £15,000 or not.

If the debtor convinces the Court that the credit bargain is extortionate then the Court may make one of the orders listed in Section 139(2) of the Act, viz:

1. direct accounts to be taken to between any persons
2. set aside the whole or part of any obligation imposed on the debtor or a surety by the credit bargain or any related agreement
3. require the creditor to repay the whole or part of any sum paid under the credit bargain or any related agreement by the debtor or a surety whether paid to the creditor or any other person
4. direct the return to the surety of any property provided for the purposes of the security or
5. alter the terms of the credit agreement or any security instrument.

Any application to have a credit agreement set aside must be made by the debtor or any surety to the High Court or County Court. In England and Wales application in respect of a regulated agreement or any other agreement, not being a regulated agreement under which the creditors provides the debtor with a fixed sum credit or running-account credit, must be made in the County Court.

Fixed-Sum and Running-Account Credit

Section 10 describes the two types of credit. A *fixed sum credit* is a once and for all credit. The amount of the credit is fixed and agreed between the parties. It may be paid by the creditor to the debtor as a lump sum or by instalments. Examples would be moneylenders and bank loans, pawn-brokers loans, hire purchase, a credit sale and conditional sale agreements and check and voucher trading.

In determining whether the amount of credit comes within the £15,000 limit a distinction must be made between credit and the total charge for credit. Thus the important figure is the amount of the loan or the capital sum not including the interest.

A *running-account credit* is sometimes named as a revolving credit. In this case the debtor does not have to apply for further credit but by his agreement with the creditor he has a right to further credit – usually subject to a credit limit. In order to decide whether or not a running-account credit falls within the definition of a consumer credit agreement the credit limit must not exceed £15,000. However this limit may be exceeded merely temporarily (Section 10(2)). Furthermore there are three situations where the agreement will still be subject to the Act even though there is no credit limit or that it exceeds the specified amount (£15,000 at present).

1. If the debtor is not allowed to draw at any time an amount that exceeds £15,000 as credit but excluding any charge for credit. This situation could arise if a bank has allowed a customer overdraft facilities of say £60,000 (or even without limit) but stipulates that he can only draw say £10,000 in any one month.
2. The agreement provides that if the debt exceeds a sum not exceeding £15,000 then the rate of interest will increase.
3. If at the time the agreement was entered into, it is probable that the debit balance will not rise above the specified amount (£15,000).

In each of these cases the agreement would be within the financial limit (£15,000). These exceptions have been made so as to avoid the situation where a creditor might agree to provide credit in excess of the specified amount, knowing that the debtor will not require more than the specified amount (e.g. £15,000) but so as to take the agreement outside the provisions of the Act.

Consumer Hire Agreements

So far we have considered consumer credit agreements. A consumer hire agreement is an agreement made by a person called the owner with an individual (not a company) called the hirer. The agreement must be capable of lasting more than three months and must not require the hirer to pay more than £15,000. Also Section 15 makes it clear that a consumer hire agreement is not a hire purchase agreement.

All consumer hire agreements will be regulated agreements if they are not exempt agreements. Such exempt agreements are those exempted by order of the Secretary of State where the owner is a company authorised to supply electricity, gas or water or where the subject of the agreement is a meter or metering equipment owned by the Post Office.

A hire purchase agreement differs from a consumer hire agreement in that in the former case the hirer who has possession of the goods will become the owner of them if the agreement is complied with and he opts to purchase the goods. In a consumer hire agreement there is no question of the hirer becoming the owner of the goods.

Small Agreements

These are regulated consumer credit agreements for credit not exceeding £50 other than a hire purchase or a conditional sale agreement or a regulated consumer hire agreement which does not require the hirer to make payments exceeding £50 provided that in either case the agreement is an agreement which is either unsecured or secured by a guarantee or indemnity only.

In the case of a running-account credit the credit limit must not exceed £50.

The provision relating to small agreements is included in the Act so that such small agreements may be excluded by other sections in the Act from certain technical requirements of those sections. Therefore Section 17 makes provision to prevent the splitting up of agreements into two or more agreements below the £50 limit, so as to circumvent the provisions of the Act.

Non-Commercial Agreements

Such an agreement is a consumer credit agreement or a consumer hire agreement not made by the creditor or owner in the course of a business carried on by him. Such private agreements are excluded from some of the provisions of the Act.

Multiple Agreements

Section 18 provides that an agreement that falls within more than one type of agreement, such as a running-account credit and a fixed-sum credit, shall be called a multiple agreement. Where there is a multiple agreement each part is to be treated as a separate agreement (Section 18(2)).

A credit card agreement will be multiple if the card can be used to obtain goods or services (a debtor-creditor-supplier agreement) or cash (a debtor-creditor agreement).

It should be noted that Section 18(5) provides that in the case of a running-account credit, a term of the agreement that allows the credit limit to be exceeded only temporarily, shall not be treated as a separate agreement or as a separate agreement providing fixed-sum credit in respect of the excess. This will permit a bank to honour cheques drawn on it in the case of a temporary excess of an agreed overdraft.

Linked Transactions

When a person enters into an agreement to obtain goods on credit or to hire goods it is quite usual for an additional agreement to be entered into such as one for installation, insurance or maintenance. Such agreements will be linked to the regulated agreement if:

1. It is entered into in compliance with a term of the principal agreement.
2. The principal agreement finances the linked transaction. This may occur if the debtor obtains a loan from a finance company to finance his purchase from a dealer. This is known as a debtor-creditor-supplier agreement. The

contract between the debtor and the dealer is a linked transaction.

It will also arise where a debtor uses a credit card or check or voucher in order to obtain goods from a supplier. The contract for the goods or services is a linked transaction.

3. If the creditor, owner, negotiator or credit broker suggests to the debtor or hirer that he should enter into an agreement so as to induce him to enter into a principal agreement. Such as when it is suggested by dealer or broker arranging a loan that an insurance policy be entered into with a particular company. That transaction would be linked with the principal agreement.

Control of Credit Agreements

The foregoing is concerned with the various types of credit agreements and the nomenclature used in the *Consumer Credit Act 1974*. The important point to be borne in mind is that certain agreements are regulated by the Act and whether or not an agreement is regulated must be established.

The Director General of Fair Trading has been given powers to issue licences to bodies involved with various activities of the credit industry. Basically a person requires a licence if he carries on a business in the course of which regulated agreements are made with customers (debtors or hirers) (Section 21).

A licence is not required if the business:

1. provides credit only in excess of £15,000 or which rents goods where the hirer must pay more than £15,000.
2. provides credit or hire only to companies.
3. provides credit or hire only under exempt agreements.

Unlicensed Trading

Section 39 provides that a person who trades when unlicensed has committed an offence and will be liable to criminal sanctions. Furthermore Section 40 provides that the agreement itself may not be enforced against the debtor or hirer unless the Director General of Fair Trading authorises it. In deciding whether or not to allow the agreement to be enforced the Director must consider to what extent other debtors or hirers have been prejudiced, whether or not he would have been likely to grant a licence and the creditor's degree of culpability in failing to obtain a licence.

Seeking Business

This may be done by advertising, by canvassing or by giving quotations.

Advertising
The provisions related to advertising and quotations apply not only to persons who are carrying on a consumer credit business or a consumer hire business but also to those who carry on a business in the course of which they provide credit to individuals secured on land and that the advertisement or quotation need not relate to a regulated agreement.

The provisions extend to any form of advertising – by television, radio, distribution of samples, catalogues, exhibition of models or in any other way.

The Secretary of State is empowered to make regulations concerning the form and content of advertisements. The charge for credit must be expressed as an annual percentage rate (A.P.R.).

Quotation
A quotation is a document in which prospective customers are given information about the terms on which the person who carries out a consumer credit or hire business is prepared to do business. These are all subject to controls.

Canvassing
This occurs where the canvasser solicits the entry of a consumer into a regulated agreement by making oral representations

during a visit not previously arranged. The canvassing is said to be "off trade premises" if it takes place somewhere other than the place of business of the creditor or owner, the supplier, the canvasser or the consumer. Such off trade premises canvassing is an offence unless it is in response to a written invitation from the person making the invitation.

It is also an offence to send a document to a minor inviting him to borrow money, obtain services, goods or hire on credit.

Finally it is an offence to give a person a credit-token if he has not asked for it in writing. Such a credit-token may be given, without request, if it is given under a credit-token agreement already made or in renewal or replacement of a credit-token previously accepted by the debtor.

Making a Regulated Agreement

The agreement between the creditor and the debtor or the owner and the hirer will be made when it has been signed or executed by both parties. Section 61(1)(a).

The document must contain all the terms of the agreement and these shall be legible.

The form and content of the agreement are laid down by the Secretary of State. In any case the debtor or hirer must be made aware of

1. his rights and duties
2. the amount and rate for the total charge for credit
3. the protections available to him.

If the agreement is

1. a non-commercial agreement
2. a debtor-creditor agreement enabling the debtor to overdraw on a current account or
3. a debtor-creditor agreement to finance the making of payments, arising on or connected with the death of a person, then, the above provisions will not apply (Section 74)

Mortgage of Land

If the security for the loan or hire is land then Section 58 will apply. This provides that the creditor/owner must give to the debtor/hirer a copy or the unexecuted agreement not less than seven days before the unexecuted agreement is sent for signature. This is called the consideration period and during it no approach must be made by the creditor/owner to the debtor/hirer. This provision will not apply if:

1. the loan is a restricted-use loan to finance the purchase of mortgaged land. This would apply if a person borrows money from a bank or building society to buy the land which is to be used as security for the loan.
2. the agreement is for a bridging loan in connection with the purchase of the mortgaged land or other land.

Restricted-use Credit

Under a credit agreement the credit may be restricted-use or unrestricted-use credit. If the credit is granted by a regulated consumer credit agreement and can only be used in a particular way, e.g.

1. to finance a transaction between the debtor and the creditor
2. to finance a transaction between the debtor and a person (the supplier) other than the creditor or
3. to refinance any existing indebtedness of the debtor whether to a creditor or to another person.

then in these cases the credit is said to be "restricted-use credit".

If it is possible for the credit to be used in any way the debtor chooses even though that might be contrary to an agreement between the creditor and debtor, the credit will be said to be "unrestricted-use credit".

Copies of the Agreement

Not Signed by Creditor/Owner
If, when the unexecuted agreement is presented personally to the debtor/hirer for his signature but it has not become an executed agreement (because the creditor has not signed) then the debtor/hirer must be given a copy of it. If the unexecuted agreement is sent to the debtor/hirer for his signature then a copy of it must also be sent together with any supporting documents. Later when the creditor/owner signs, a second copy of the agreement must be sent within seven days of the creditor/owner signing unless it is a credit-token agreement.

Signed by creditor/owner
If the unexecuted agreement is presented personally to the debtor/hirer for signature and when he signs it becomes an executed agreement, then a copy of the executed agreement and any supporting documents must be then and there delivered to him, but no further copy is required.

If the unexecuted agreement is sent to the debtor-hirer for him to sign a copy must be sent at the same time. No further copy is required if the debtor/hirer signs because the creditor/owner has already signed it before sending it.

Cancellation

The normal rule for making a contract requires that a valid offer is made which is accepted unconditionally. So long as the parties really are in agreement i.e. there is no mistake or deception, then an agreement has been entered into which cannot be set aside easily. However as regards regulated agreements it may be possible for an individual to change his mind after entering into an agreement provided certain rules are complied with.

Section 67 of the Act provides that a regulated agreement may be cancelled by debtor or hirer if the antecedent negotiations included oral representations made in the presence of the debtor or hirer unless the agreement is signed by the debtor or hirer on trade premises. Also the agreement may not be cancelled if, although signed off trade premises, the debtor has not been subject to face to face persuasion.

This provision is intended to protect individuals who are subject to persuasion by door to door salesmen and sign the agreement on the doorstep. This would also apply if the negotiations are conducted at a dealer's place of business and if the debtor takes home the agreement to sign. On the other hand if there has been no face to face persuasion, such as in a Mail Order transaction, contracts made in this way cannot be cancelled. Neither can the following agreements be cancelled:

1. a non-commercial agreement
2. an agreement enabling the debtor to overdraw on a current account if the Director General of Fair Trading so determines.
3. a debtor-creditor agreement to finance the making of payments arising on the death of a person provided the Director General so determines.
4. a small debtor-creditor-supplier agreement for restricted use.

A Cooling-off Period
The period in which the debtor/hirer is permitted to serve notice of cancellation (the cool-off period) is a period ending on the fifth day following the day on which he received the second copy of the agreement or if no second copy is required the notice informing the debtor of his cancellation rights.

Effect of Notice of Cancellation
The notice of cancellation is effective at the time of posting whether or not it is actually received.

The notice of cancellation must be served on the creditor/owner, the credit-broker or supplier who took part in the antecedent negotiations or any agent of the debtor/hirer or creditor/owner.

The notice of cancellation will cancel the agreement and any linked transaction. Any payments made are recoverable. If however the creditor has advanced a sum of money during the cooling-off period this does not become immediately repayable (Section 71).

Connected Lender Liability

A credit card transaction may be two-party or three-party. If the supplier of the goods issues his own credit card this will be a two-party credit agreement.

A three-party transaction is where the issuer of the credit card is not the supplier of the goods. Section 75 of the *Consumer Credit Act 1974* is of importance in this case because that section makes liable the issuer of the credit card jointly and severally with the supplier in respect of any claim of the debtor for misrepresentation or breach of contract in relation to the transaction financed by the agreement.

In the case of a two-party transaction then the supplier and the issuer of the card are one person and of course the supplier will be liable directly to the debtor. This provision whereby the creditor may be made liable together with the supplier is intended to ensure that creditors will take care to associate only with reputable suppliers. Of course Section 75 is of particular value if the supplier himself should become insolvent and then the debtor will still be able to enforce his rights against the creditor. This has occurred quite frequently when Tour Operators have gone into liquidation and their customers have been able to recover against the credit card company.

Section 75, at present, only applies to a transaction where the cash price exceeds £100 and does not exceed £30,000.

Also remember that Section 75 does not apply to exempt agreements and so does not apply to American Express or Diners Club credit card agreements.

Extortionate Credit Bargains

An important provision of the *Consumer Credit Act 1974* is contained in sections 137 to 140. These are concerned with extortionate credit bargains and Section 137 gives the Court power to re-open a credit agreement. This power may be exercised by the High Court, the County Court or the Sheriff's Court in Scotland, if the Court considers that an agreement is extortionate. All credit agreements are subject to this power not only regulated ones and exempt, small and non-commercial agreements are affected.

Section 138 states the factors to be taken into account in deciding whether or not an agreement is extortionate. In deciding whether a bargain is extortionate the following matters shall be considered:

1. interest rates prevailing at the time the agreement was made
2. the debtor's age, experience, business capacity and state of health
3. the degree to which the debtor was under financial pressure when he made the bargain
4. the degree of risk accepted by the creditor
5. the creditor's relationship with the debtor
6. whether or not the cash price was quoted for any goods or services
7. in relation to a linked transaction factors applicable include how far the transaction was required for the protection of the debtor or the creditor or was in the interest of the creditor
8. any other relevant consideration.

If the Court decides that a credit bargain is extortionate then it may relieve the debtor from any sum in excess of what is fair and reasonable or it may alter the terms of the agreement or even require the creditor to repay any sums already paid.

Matters Arising During the Currency of an Agreement

The creditor has a duty to supply unrequested periodic statements of account in the case of an overdraft or credit card agreement (a running-account credit agreement).

In the case of a fixed-sum credit agreement the creditor, if so requested by the debtor, must give him a copy of the agreement and inform him of the total sum paid, the sum which has become payable and the dates when payment must be made.

If a debtor is liable to make payments to the same creditor in respect of two or more regulated agreements then he has a choice as to which debt a payment he makes may be linked or appropriated. This is the normal rule relating to appropriation.

In the case of credit-tokens which include credit cards the general rule is that the debtor is not liable to the creditor for any loss arising from the use of the credit card by another person who is not the agent of the debtor. In any case Section 66 provides that a debtor shall not be liable under a credit-token agreement unless he has accepted it

1. by signing it
2. by giving a receipt for it
3. by using it.

If, after accepting the credit card the debtor permits its use by another person then he will be liable to the creditor.

Termination of the Consumer Credit Agreement

Section 94 provides that a debtor may repay his debt at any time by notice to the creditor and payment of the debt to him. The debtor may then be entitled to a rebate for early settlement (Section 95). He is also entitled to a statement from the creditor of the amount he owes and if the creditor fails to provide this information the agreement cannot be enforced and if the information is not given within one month an offence will have been committed.

Chapter Sixteen
The Financial Services Act 1986

The FSA received the Royal Assent on 7 November 1986 and came fully into force on 29 April 1988.

The act came about as a result of the appreciation that it was necessary to have the means of regulating investment business and that investors required protection.

Prior to the Act there were some methods of protection contained in the *Prevention of Fraud (Investments) Act 1939* which was re-enacted by the *Prevention of Fraud (Investments) Act 1958*.

Professor L. C. B. Gower was appointed in 1981 to head a committee charged with the review of the protection required by investors and the need for some control of dealers in securities, investment consultants and managers.

The Financial Services Act itself has effected a complete overhaul of the legal framework for the regulation of investment business. The Act is divided into 10 parts:

Part 1. This creates a framework for the regulation of investment business.
Part 2. Extends the investment control to Life Assurance when it is used as a form of investment.
Part 3. Establishes a framework for the regulation of Friendly Societies.
Part 4. Introduces a new regime for the official listing of securities on the Stock Exchange.
Part 5. Deals with offers of unlisted securities.
Part 6. Provides new rules relating to the take-over offers.
Part 7. Makes a number of changes to the law on Insider dealing contained in the *Company Securities (Insider Dealings) Act 1985*.
Part 8–10. Deal with disclosure of information, reciprocity

of access for financial business in foreign markets and miscellaneous matters.

It will be apparent that Part 1 is the most important part as far as bankers are concerned and we must now consider that section in some detail.

Definition of Investments

An investment is defined very widely and includes any right, asset or interest which falls within the following categories.

1. Shares and stock in the share capital of a company.
2. Debentures, including debenture stock, loan stock, bonds, certificates of deposit and any other instrument creating or acknowledging indebtedness. A cheque or other bill of exchange, a bankers' draft and letter of credit; bank notes; current, deposit or savings accounts are excluded.
3. Government, local authority or other public authority securities.
4. Warrants or other instruments entitling the holder to subscribe for investments in the above categories.
5. Certificates or other instruments conferring rights to acquire, dispose of, underwrite or convert any investments falling within the above categories.
6. Units in collective investment schemes. This includes units in unit trusts.
7. Options to acquire or dispose of investments as defined.
8. Futures for investment purposes.

A definition of investments excludes by implication, land and physical commodities such as works of art, antiques and old coins. Similarly gold and silver will not be regarded as investments unless they are expressed in the form of options.

Investment business

This is defined as dealing in investments: buying, selling,

subscribing for or underwriting investments or offering or agreeing to offer investments, either as principal or as agent.

Arranging deals in investments: making, offering, or agreeing to make arrangements with a view to another person buying, selling, subscribing for or underwriting the particular investment.

Managing investments: managing, offering or agreeing to manage assets belonging to another person if these assets consist of or include investments.

Advising on investments: giving or offering or agreeing to give advice to investors on the merits of the purchase, sale, subscription for or underwriting of investments or on the exercise of rights conferred by investments to acquire, dispose of, underwrite or convert an investment.

Certain activities which might be considered to constitute investment business are specifically excluded. These include dealing as a principal as where a person buys securities on his own account. Such a person will not be regarded as carrying an investment business unless he is making a market or is soliciting the public to buy or sell investments. Also it will not be regarded as investment business where a financial package is linked with the sale of goods or supply of services; where a company operates a "share shop" for its employees; a trustee manages investments for his beneficiary or advice is given in the course of a profession, provided the investment dealing is not predominant. Also many daily newspapers contain financial columns which contain investment advice. Even so newspaper proprietors and financial journalists are not required to seek authorisation provided that their primary purpose is not to lead persons to invest in any particular investment.

The Framework for Regulation

The Security of State for Trade and Industry is authorised under the Act to regulate the investment industry so as to protect investors. He may delegate his tasks to a designated agency which is, in the first instance, the Securities and Investments Board (SIB).

The Securities and Investments Board

This is a private company limited by guarantee and financed by a levy on certain organisations. It may exercise its powers flexibly and quickly but is subject to the control of the Secretary of State. He may remove Board members, he may withdraw in whole or in part the powers given to the SIB or he may direct the SIB to alter its rules or practices. In addition the SIB must also submit an annual report to parliament which will be debated. The SIB will delegate its powers to other bodies, the main categories being Self Regulating Organisations (SRO) and recognised professional bodies (RPB). In addition the SIB may recognise a recognised investment exchange (RIE) and a recognised clearing house (RCH).

So the structure will be as follows:

Secretary of State for Trade and Industry
|
Securities and Investments Board

| Self Regulating Organisations (SRO) | Recognised Professional Bodies (RPB) | Recognised Investment Exchanges (RIE) | Recognised Clearing Houses (RCH) |

Self Regulating Organisations

The SIB has recognised the following as SROs.

The Securities Association (TSA) – these are firms dealing and broking in securities, international money market instruments, forward agreements and related futures and options. They also are concerned with investment management and advice incidental to this business.

Association of Futures Brokers and Dealers (AFBD) – these firms deal in broking in futures and options also they are concerned with investment management and advice incidental to their business.

Financial Intermediaries, Managers and Brokers Regulatory Association (FIMBRA) – these are firms dealing and broking in securities and giving professional advice and management.

Investment Management Regulatory Organisation (IMRO) –these are investment managers and advisors including managers and trustees of collective investment schemes and in-house pension fund managers.

Life Assurance and Unit trust Regulatory Organisation (LAUTRO) – these are life companies and unit trust managers and trustees for the management and selling of insurance linked investments or units in a collective investment scheme by themselves and their sales forces.

Recognised Professional Bodies

In their practice professionals such as accountants, solicitors etc provide an important source of investment advice and other investment services such as insurance broking. These professional bodies will only be involved in investment business to an insignificant degree within the main body of their professional activities. However they may be authorised by the SIB provided:

1. the professional body regulates the practice of a profession which is not, wholly or mainly, the carrying on of an investment business.
2. it regulates the practice of a profession recognised for a statutory purpose or in the exercise of statutory powers.

The SIB has identified twelve professional bodies that are possible candidates for recognition. These are:

1. The Law Society of England and Wales
2. The Law Society of Scotland
3. The Law Society of Northern Ireland
4. The Institute of Chartered Accountants of England and Wales

5. The Institute of Chartered Accountants of Scotland
6. The Institute of Chartered Accountants in Ireland
7. The Chartered Association of Certified Accountants
8. The Institute of Cost and Management Accountants
9. The Institute of Consulting Actuaries
10. The Faculty of Actuaries
11. The Royal Institute of Chartered Surveyors
12. The Institute of Chartered Secretaries and Administrators

Whether or not any of the above bodies will apply for recognition by the SIB will probably depend upon the amount to which the membership of the profession is involved in public practice. When deciding to recognise a professional body the SIB must be satisfied that the rules of the profession will provide equivalent investor protection to that provided by its own rules. Also the professional body must have adequate arrangements and resources for the effective monitoring and enforcement of compliance to its rules. The enforcement arrangements must provide for the withdrawal or suspension of certification. Also the arrangements must provide a proper balance between the interests of persons certified by the body and the interests of the public. Furthermore arrangements must be made for the investigation of complaints against its members or its regulation of investment business.

Recognised Investment Exchanges and Clearing Houses

Persons running a market or exchange will normally be carrying on investment business and will therefore need to be authorised, unless that market or exchange obtains exemption by becoming recognised by the SIB.

Any body corporate or unincorporated association may apply for recognition as an RIE. The procedure is the same as for recognition as an SRO. The criteria for recognition include the following:

1. The exchange must have sufficient, financial resources to enable it to perform its functions in a proper manner.

2. Its rules and practices must ensure the orderly conduct of business and afford proper protection to investors.
3. It must limit dealings to investments to which there is a proper market.
4. It must impose information requirements on issues of investments so that people dealing in these can ascertain their current value.
5. It must have arrangements for ensuring the performance of transactions effected on it.
6. It must provide satisfactory arrangements for recording transactions effected on the exchange.
7. It must have adequate arrangements for monitoring and enforcing compliance with its rules.
8. It must have effective arrangements for the investigation of complaints.

The SIB will consider a number of candidates for recognition and these include:

1. The International Stock Exchange
2. London Commodities Exchange
3. London International Financial Futures Exchange (LIFFE)
4. London Metal Exchange
5. An Exchange for Unlisted Securities
6. An Association of International Bond Dealers
7. Certain Overseas Exchanges.

Authorisation

Anyone who carries on an investment business in the United Kingdom must be authorised subject to certain exemptions.

Exempt Persons

1. Bank of England
2. Lloyds
3. Listed Money Market Institutions
4. President of the Family Division of the High Court

5. Accountant General of the Supreme Court
6. The Public Trustee
7. The Central Board of Finance of the Church of England etc.

In this connection it should be noted that many financial conglomerates will be supervised under other regulatory systems –for example, by the Bank of England in the case of banks and by the Department of Trade and Industry in the case of Insurance Companies.

1. Members of Self Regulatory Organisation (SRO's) are entitled to operate an investment business, i.e.:

    a. to deal in investments
    b. to arrange investment deals for others
    c. to manage investments
    d. to advise on investments
    e. to operate a collective investment scheme such as a unit trust.

    The SRO's will have satisfied the requirements of the Securities and Investments Board (SIB).

2. Certain professional bodies will be recognised by the SIB and will be able to authorise persons applying to it to engage in investment business. Authorisation will be granted by means of the issue of an Investment Business Certificate. This may only be granted to persons whose main business is the practice of a profession rather than an investment business.
3. Direct authorisation by the SIB will be granted if the applicant is a fit and proper person to carry on the investment business.
4. Overseas persons will require authorisation if they conduct investment business in the United Kingdom, whether or not they have a place of business in this country.

    Nationals of other EEC Member States will automatically be authorised provided they have no permanent place of business in the United Kingdom and are authorised to conduct investment business in their own State.

Conduct of Investment Business

The Financial Services Act contains powers to enforce compliance with the statutory rules and other regulations. These powers may be exercised by:

1. Criminal prosecution brought by the Secretary of State or the Director of Public Prosecutions.
2. Civil action by any person who has suffered loss as a result of a transaction. Such a person may bring an action for damages against any person who has broken the rules and regulations (other than the financial resources rules) of the SIB, an SRO or a recognised professional body, as the case may be.
3. Other procedures. In this connection the Act provides for the establishment of a Financial Services Tribunal to serve as a forum to hear appeals against certain decisions made by the Secretary of State or the SIB. The tribunal will consist of three persons nominated from a panel of ten. They must be legally qualified and at least one member must have had recent business experience.

The persons who may refer a matter to the Tribunal will be those who have received from the SIB:

1. Notice that the SIB intends to refuse a grant authorisation or to withdraw or suspend authorisation.
2. Notice that the SIB intends to terminate or suspend authorisation by virtue of authorisation in another EEC member state.
3. Notice of intention to disqualify a person from employment in an investment business.
4. Notice of a proposed public statement relating to an authorised person's misconduct.
5. Notice of the imposition, rescission or variation of a prohibition or of a refusal to impose, rescind or vary one.

Any person affected has twenty eight days from the date on which the notice was served to require the SIB to refer the matter to the Tribunal.

From the above it will be apparent that the power to bring a criminal prosecution is the most effective sanction.

Misleading Statements and Practices

The Act (Section 47) creates two offences, the first of which is contained in Section 47(1). This section provides that a person who:

1. makes a statement, promise or forecast which he knows to be misleading, false or deceptive
2. conceals any material facts or
3. recklessly makes a statement, promise or forecast which is misleading, false or deceptive shall be guilty of an offence.

The second offence is contained in Section 47(2). This provides that any person who intentionally does any act or engages in any course of conduct which creates a false or misleading impression as to the market in or price of value of any investments shall be guilty of an offence.

For each offence the punishment for a person convicted on indictment is imprisonment for a term not exceeding seven years or to a fine or to both. If convicted before the magistrates the punishment is imprisonment not exceeding six months or a fine or both.

Rules for the Conduct of Business

Section 48 empowers the SIB to make rules relating to the conduct of business. The principles are set out in Schedule 8 of the Act.

1. Investment business should be carried on honestly and fairly.
2. Operators should carry out their responsibilities, capably, carefully and to the best of their abilities.

3. They should be fair to their customers, which implies avoiding conflicts of interest.

There are also certain general requirements such as:

1. *Know your customer*. This means that the authorised person must take steps to find out about his customers' personal and financial situation so that he may be given the "best advice".
2. *Cold calling*. Unsolicited calls are forbidden by Section 56 except in relation to life assurance and unit trusts. When a sale results from an unsolicited call in relation to these two matters the investor must be informed that he has a fourteen day cooling off period in which he can change his mind and cancel the agreement.
3. *Customer agreements*. The rules relating to customer agreements will apply to all firms except registered life offices and trustees of regulated collective investment schemes.

Two types of investor need not be asked to sign a full customer agreement i.e.

1. Occasional customers who may be offered "occasional customer agreements" and
2. Business, experienced or professional customers who may be offered a "terms of business letter".

Apart from these all customer agreements must include the following information:

1. Basic details about the investment business.
2. The type of services offered.
3. If the services include recommending purchases of single premium life policies or units in regulated collective schemes, a warning that the purchases cannot be cancelled, other than by mutual agreement.
4. A statement of whether the customer agrees to the firm making uninvited calls on the customer and if so the circumstances in which such calls may be made.
5. Where non business and non professional investors agree to unsolicited calls a warning that the investor will

forfeit his right under the cancellation rules to treat any agreement entered into in consequence of such a call as unenforcable.
6. The basic method and frequency of remuneration payable by the customer to the firm and a statement of whether the firm will earn any commissions other than from the customer and whether these will be passed on to the customer.
7. The customers' investment objectives e.g. Capital growth, income etc.
8. Restrictions or guidelines on what the business should put the investor in to.
9. Statement of particular exchanges or markets which the customer doesn't want to get involved with.
10. If the types of investment in which the investors funds are to be sunk are not easily realisable, a warning of the risks involved.
11. Arrangements by which a customer can terminate his contract without incurring any penalty charges.
12. Arrangements for receiving instructions and reporting any advice to the customer.
13. The accounting arrangements for the customer and arrangements for holding money or investments for the customer.
14. In the case of a managed portfolio, its initial composition and the periods of account for which statements are to be provided.

Where the customer agreement concerns futures, options and contracts for differences, the agreement, in addition to the matters noted above, must also include:

1. a warning of the risky nature of the investment
2. a statement of the circumstances in which an investor will have to apply a deposit or a margin in support of a transaction or supplement that payment
3. a statement of the circumstances in which the firm may close out existing contracts without reference to the customer.

The Financial Services Act 1986

A relationship with a customer for which a full agreement is required can be commenced only after the agreement has been received by the customer and he has signed and returned it.

An occasional customer agreement must outline the advice which the firm has given to the customer and any instructions that the customer has given to the firm. The agreement must be received and agreed by the customer before any transactions are conducted under it.

A "Terms of Business" letter must identify the investments and services for which the customer is to be treated as a business, professional or experienced investor.

Chapter Seventeen
The Data Protection Act 1984

Nowadays computers are common-place pieces of equipment which are capable of storing, processing and distributing information. It is a possibility that such facilities, in the wrong hands, might pose a threat to individuals and so should be controlled. Furthermore it was decided by the Government that the Council of Europe convention for the protection of individuals with regard to automatic processing of personal data must be ratified. If it had not been ratified, countries who had ratified it might place restrictions on the transfer of personal data to countries which had not ratified it.

The Data Protection Act was passed in 1984. It applies only to automatically processed information and does not cover information which is held and processed manually, for example in ordinary paper files. The Act does not cover all computerised information but only that which relates to living individuals. For example it does not cover information which relates only to a company or organisation and not to an individual. If a person wishes to record and use personal data he will be known as a Data User. It does not matter that the Data User does not have his own computer but uses a bureau or that the computer he has is only a desk top machine and not a mainframe. In each case he is still a Data User and has his responsibilities under the Act. The Act requires that every Data User who keeps personal data on a computer must register with the Data Protection Registrar. However there are exceptions. These exceptions apply where the Data User makes a limited use of information for one purpose, for example:

1. Personal data held by an individual in connection with personal, family or household affairs or for recreational purposes.

2. Personal data used only for calculating and paying wages and pensions, keeping accounts or keeping records of purchases and sales in order to ensure that the appropriate payments are made.
3. Personal data used for distributing articles or information to the data subjects.
4. Personal data held by an unincorporated members' Club e.g. a sports or recreational club which is not a registered company.
5. Personal data which the Law requires the user to make public such as personal data in the Electoral Register kept by an Electoral Registration Officer.
6. Personal data which is required to be exempt in order to safeguard National Security.

Also information which is processed only for preparing the text of documents is also outside the scope of the Act. This rule is sometimes referred to as the "Word Processor Exemption". Its effect is that the Act does not apply to information entered on to a computer with the sole purpose of editing the text and printing out a document.

In all the above examples where an exemption exists the effect is that the Registrar cannot take enforcement action and neither can an individual exercise his rights of access under the Act.

The Register

The Act creates a register of Data Users and every Data User who holds personal data must be registered unless the data are exempt. The Data User's register entry is compiled by the Registrar from the information give in the application. It contains the Data User's name and address together with broad descriptions of the type of data which the Data User holds, the purposes for which the data are used, the sources from which the Data User intends to obtain the information, the people to whom the Data User may wish to disclose the information and any oversea countries to which the Data User may wish to transfer the personal data. The register is open to public inspection at the Registrar's office in Wilmslow in Cheshire and an index to the register may be inspected in major public libraries throughout the country.

Data Protection Principles

The Act provides that in addition to registering with the Data Protection Registrar a Data User must abide by the eight Data Protection Principles. These state that personal data shall:

1. be obtained and processed fairly and lawfully
2. be held only for the lawful purposes described in the register entry
3. be used only for those purposes and only be disclosed to those people described in the register entry
4. be adequate, relevant and not excessive in relation to the purpose for which they are held
5. be accurate and where necessary kept up to date
6. be held no longer than is necessary for the registered purpose
7. an individual shall be entitled to have access to data held about himself and if appropriate to have such data corrected or deleted
8. the data must be surrounded by proper security.

In order to enforce compliance with the principles the Registrar can serve three types of notice. They are:

   a. An *Enforcement Notice* requiring the Data User to take specified action to comply with a particular principle. Failure to comply with the notice would be a criminal offence.
   b. A *Deregistration Notice* cancelling the whole or part of the Data User's register entry.
   c. A *Transfer Prohibition Notice*, preventing the Data User from transferring personal data overseas if the Registrar is satisfied that the transfer is likely to lead to a principle being broken. Again failure to comply with such a notice is a criminal offence.

A person on whom a notice is served is entitled to appeal against the Registrar's decision to the Data Protection Tribunal.

Rights of the individual whose personal data are held on file

Such a person is called a Data Subject and he is entitled to seek compensation through the courts if he has suffered damage caused by the loss, unauthorised destruction or unauthorised disclosure of his personal data. He may also seek compensation through the courts for damage caused by inaccurate data. If personal data are inaccurate then the Data Subject may complain to the Registrar or apply to the courts for correction or deletion of the data.

Every Data Subject is entitled on written request to be supplied by any Data User with a copy of any personal data held about him or her. This right is called "Subject Access Right".

If the Data Subject considers there has been a breach of one of the principles of data protection then he is entitled to complain to the Data Protection Registrar. If the complaint is justified and cannot be resolved informally then the Registrar may use his powers to prosecute or to serve one of the notices already mentioned.

Disclosure of personal data
The Act does not prevent a Data User from disclosing information about an individual and such disclosure may be made if either:

a. the person to whom the disclosure is made is described in the disclosure section of the Data User's register entry or
b. the disclosure is covered by one of the "non disclosure exemptions". These would include, for example, disclosures required by law or made with the Data Subject's consent.

The Data Protection Registrar

The Data Protection Registrar is an independent officer who reports directly to Parliament. His duties include establishing the register of Data Users, spreading information on the Act, promoting compliance with the Data Protection Principles, encouraging the development of Codes of Practice to help Data Users comply with the principles and finally to consider complaints about breaches of the principles of the Act and where appropriate to prosecute offenders or serve notices on registered Data Users who are breaking the principles.

If the Registrar is satisfied that a Data User has breached a principle he can serve an Enforcement Notice directing that person to take specific steps to comply with the principle within a specified time. If the Registrar considers that compliance with the principle cannot be secured by the service of an Enforcement Notice he can issue a Deregistration Notice. This cancels from the register the whole or part of any register entry.

Finally the Registrar can also issue a Transfer Prohibition Notice to prevent the transfer of personal data overseas. A Data User who receives one of these special notices can appeal to the independent Data Protection Tribunal. The tribunal has the power to substitute its own decision in place of the Registrar's.

Breach of an Enforcement or Transfer Prohibition Notice is a criminal offence. The Registrar employs teams of regional investigators who check whether Data Users are properly registered and investigate complaints of breaches of principle.

Chapter Eighteen
Negotiable Instruments – Generally

Property comprises anything that a person may own and remember that the word "own" means "has a right to". As always law is concerned with the rights of persons. Now what a person may own is either land or anything which is not land called personal property.

The law relating to land is a complex subject on its own so we can ignore that for our present purposes.

Let us consider personal property. This is a wide division of property and in itself it may be sub-divided into tangible things and intangible things.

Tangible things are designated by the old Norman French words of "choses in possession". Such things can be seen, touched and counted.

Intangible things are called "choses in action". This is because, as they cannot be seen and touched, then ownership of them can only be evidenced by a piece of paper (an instrument). So oranges can be seen and counted – they are choses in possession. The same applies to coins in my pocket. Instead of the oranges it may be that a cargo of oranges is being transported to this country and before they arrive they may be sold. The buyer can be given a document called a bill of lading which is evidence of his rights to the oranges when they arrive. Instead of the coins in my pocket, I can have a postal order or a cheque entitling me to the amount of the coins. The bill of lading, the postal order and the cheque all entitle the owner of these instruments to something – either the oranges or the money, but of course they are worthless themselves. It is only because of the form of the documents and what they contain that they entitle the owner to something of value. Admittedly, to say that a chose in action is a piece of paper is not entirely accurate because the goodwill of a business or the copyright of an author are choses in action but they are not evidenced by pieces of paper. One other principle of law must be observed here – that is that ownership is a right to something. When one buys goods one is hoping to acquire a right of ownership in the goods. It follows that if A has stolen something from B and then sells it to C, C will not become the owner, because A did not have the right of ownership and so is not in the position of being able to pass a right of ownership on to C. This principle applies to the transfer of choses in possession, and also to the transfer of choses in action generally.

The transfer of a chose in action
A piece of land may only be transferred by means of a document called "a conveyance" or one should write more correctly even though pedantically the legal ownership of a piece of land is transferred by a conveyance.

A chose in possession is transferred by delivery. Indeed, ownership is usually presumed to reside in the person who has possession of the chose in possession. This is sometimes described by the phrase "possession is nine tenths of the law".

A chose in action however must usually be transferred in a particular manner laid down by law. Thus to transfer a share certificate it is necessary to use a share transfer form and complete it with the details of the transferee. Also the company whose shares they are must be notified of the transfer. Finally, the principle regarding the right of ownership also applies; and so if a person transfers a chose in action to which he does not have the right of ownership then the transferee will likewise not get a good title.

Now some choses in action entitle the holder to goods but a number of them entitle the holder to a sum of money. As money is so vitally important in commercial transactions it gradually became desirable to have some rather less formal system of transferring a right to a sum of money. Thus it was that certain choses in action began to be treated differently from others – the need for a formal method of transfer was abolished, it was no longer necessary to notify the person who ultimately would be called upon to make payment, of the transfer. Most importantly of all, the transferee of these special choses in action would get a good title to it, in certain cases, even though the transferor did not have a good title. This last point was of particular importance and in fact is the basis of negotiability. These choses in action which received this special treatment became known as negotiable instruments. They include:

Bills of Exchange including cheques
Promissory notes
Divided Warrants
Bearer Bonds
Bearer Scrip
Debentures payable to bearer
Share warrants
Treasury bills

The attributes common to these documents are

1. They are transferable merely by delivery if payable to bearer or by indorsement if payable to order.
2. The party who will be called upon to pay on the document need not be notified of the transfer.
3. The transferee who takes in good faith and for value will get a good title notwithstanding any defect in the title of the transferor.

This last point requires some clarification. The transferee is known as the holder of the negotiable instrument. In order to get a good title to it he must have given value for it and the document itself must have been in order. If the document contains a forged indorsement for example, the person to whom it was transferred will not become the owner of it.

Example 1 A draws a cheque payable to bearer and gives it to B. X steals the cheque and gives it to C, to whom he owes money for goods he has purchased. C is the owner of the cheque, provided he took it in good faith.

Example 2 A draws an order cheque payable to B. X steals the cheque and gives it to C to whom he owes money for goods he has purchased. X will of course have to forge B's indorsement

230 *Negotiable Instruments – Generally*

and so even though C took the cheque in good faith he will not be the owner of it because of the forgery.

This then is the essence of negotiability. Of the instruments which are negotiable we shall only be concerned with bills of exchange, including cheques. Finally it should be remembered that in this context negotiable does not mean transferable. It refers to the fact that in certain cases a person may become the legal owner of an instrument even though he received it from someone who was not the owner.

Example 3 A cheque marked "not negotiable" may still be transferred. However the person who receives it will get no better title than that of the person from whom he received it.

Bill of Exchange

Let us now consider the operation of a bill of exchange. Say a manufacturer sold goods to a wholesaler for £1,000 and he in turn sold them to the retailer for £1,000. For the sake of simplicity let us ignore any profit margin. So W owes £1,000 to M and R owes £1,000 to W.

Assuming M and W had no more money and also, as is quite likely, W has given R the retailer 3 months credit. The situation is that W cannot pay M until he is paid by R and R does not have to pay for three months. Thus all the parties are at a standstill for 3 months.

```
            £1,000              £1,000
   R――――――――――――W――――――――――――M
```

However a bill of exchange could be used to break the impasse. W could draw a bill on R for £1,000 payable in 3 months time. He could do this because R owes him the money. Also as W owes M £1,000 it would be convenient if R were ordered to pay M. So the bill is drawn by W (the drawer) on R (the drawee) by which R is ordered to pay M (the payee) £1,000 in 3 months time. The bill is then given to M; so how much better off is he with the bill than without it? He can do any of three things.

1. He can do nothing and wait for payment from the drawee

for 3 months. Even here he is better off with the bill than without it because if he has difficulty in getting payment at least he has a signed acknowledgement by W (who has signed the bill as drawer) that he owes M £1,000.
2. M can sell the bill or discount it as it is called. If he does this he will receive £1,000 less the interest on that sum for 3 months plus handling charges.
3. M can use the bill as cash and transfer it to some person to whom he owes £1,000. In this way the bill may be passed from hand to hand until the time when the 3 months have expired (the bill is said to have matured) when the person who is the holder at that time can obtain his money from the drawee.

Points to note from the definition of a Bill in the *Bills of Exchange Act, 1882,* are:

1. It must be an unconditional order in writing. Usually the word "Pay" is used. It must not be a mere request.

    However an order may still be unconditional if it is coupled with

    a. an indication of the particular fund out of which the drawer is to reimburse himself or a particular account to be debited with the amount.
    b. a statement of the transaction which gives rise to the bill.

    Where a cheque bears a receipt form on the back the test to determine whether it is a valid bill is whether the direction is addressed to the drawee or the payee. If it is addressed to the drawee the bill is invalid.
2. The order must be for a sum certain in money. However the money can be paid with interest at a stated rate, by instalments or in foreign currency according to a rate of exchange.
3. These must be a certain or determinable time of payment. Thus the bill may be payable:

    a. on demand or at sight or on presentation
    b. at a fixed period after date or sight

c. on or at a fixed period after a person's death.
4. The bill must be payable to a payee who can be identified or to the order of that person or to bearer.

At this point one must remember that law is concerned with the rights of people and relating this to bills of exchange it is concerned with the rights of persons to the bill. If a person is the lawful owner of a bill then he can enforce his rights on it against anyone who has signed it. Initially only the drawer's signature will appear on the bill, it is then given to the payee. It is only natural that if it is a time bill (one payable at some future date) then it would be advisable to ask the person who eventually will be called upon to pay up to promise that he will make payment on that future date. This person is the drawee and so usually a bill will be presented to him for acceptance.

Acceptance When the drawee signifies that he has accepted the bill he must write "accepted" on the bill and sign it. His acceptance may be general or qualified. If it is qualified in any way then the payee may treat the bill as dishonoured by non acceptance.

General Acceptance
In this case the drawee agrees to fulfil all the terms of the order of the drawer without qualification.

Qualified Acceptance
This expressly varies the effect of the bill as drawn. In other words, the drawee states by his acceptance that he does not propose to honour all the terms of the order in the bill. It must be emphasised that a qualified acceptance does not make the order of the bill conditional. It is still unconditional and so the bill remains valid. This is because the drawee is not giving any order.

There are five types of qualified acceptance:

1. *Conditional*: This makes the payment by the acceptor dependent on the fulfilment of a condition stated in the acceptance. E.g. "Accepted, payable on giving up a bill of lading for seventy-six bags of seed."

2. *Partial*: An acceptance to pay part only of the amount for which the bill is drawn. E.g. bill drawn for £500 and accepted as to £300.
3. *Local*: Acceptance to pay only at a particular place. E.g. "Accepted payable at Barclays Bank, only." If the word "only" is omitted, the acceptance is general.
4. *Qualified as to time*: E.g. a bill drawn payable thirty days after date, accepted payable forty days after date.
5. *Acceptance by one or more of the drawees but not all*: E.g. where a bill is drawn on X, Y, Z is accepted by X and Y but not Z.

   Effect of a qualified acceptance:
   1. A holder may refuse to take a qualified acceptance and if he does not obtain an unqualified acceptance he may treat the bill as dishonoured (S.41(1)).
   2. If a qualified acceptance is taken and the drawer or indorser has not expressly or impliedly authorised the holder to take a qualified acceptance, or does not subsequently assent to it, such drawer or indorser is discharged from his liability on the bill.
   3. In the case of a partial acceptance, the holder may take it and subsequently notify the drawer and indorsers without discharging them from liability.
   4. A foreign bill which has been partially accepted must be protested as to the balance (S.44(2)).

Presentment for acceptance: Presentation for acceptance is essential only in three cases: (section 39)

1. Where a bill is payable after sight then presentment for acceptance is necessary in order to fix maturity date of the bill.
2. Where a bill is drawn payable elsewhere than at the residence or place of business of the drawee.
3. Where the bill expressly stipulates that it shall be presented for acceptance.
   a. Apart from section 39, bills should be presented for the following two reasons:

        i. Once the drawee accepts, he becomes liable on it.
        ii. If he refuses to accept, the holder has an immediate right to sue all prior parties without having to wait until the date of maturity.

  b. Where a drawee accepts a bill payable elsewhere than at this residence or place of business, the bill is said to be "domiciled" at the place of payment. Unless a banker has expressly or impliedly agreed to pay bills domiciled with him, he is under no legal obligation to do so even though the customer has a balance sufficient to cover the bills. If the banker pays, the relationship between him and the customer then is not debtor and creditor, but principal and agent.

Presentment for payment

By section 52(1) a general acceptance by the drawee to pay at maturity makes him liable and presentment to him for payment is not necessary. Presentment for payment is necessary where the acceptance is qualified.

The rules concerning presentment for payment are similar to those for acceptance but in this case emphasis is placed upon presentment at the proper place. This is defined in section 45(4) as the place of payment specified in the bill; if no place is specified then at the address of the drawee or acceptor given in the bill or his last known place of business or ordinary residence.

The time for presentment for payment is the last day of the time for payment or if that is not a business day then the succeeding business day. If the bill is payable after a period of time after date, after sight or after the happening of a specified event, the time for payment is determined by excluding the day from which the time is to begin to run and by including the day of payment.

Dishonour

A bill may be dishonoured by non acceptance or by non payment. If a bill is drawn payable on demand then the drawee must pay when it is presented to him, if he does not, then the payee may treat the bill as dishonoured by non payment. If the bill is payable at some future time then it may have been accepted but when the holder comes to present the bill for payment it may again be dishonoured by non payment. If a bill is dishonoured for whatever reason, the holder may enforce his rights against anyone who has signed the bill. In order to do this he must notify the drawer and each indorsee of the fact that the bill has been dishonoured. In practice the holder notifies his previous indorser, who notifies his previous indorser and so on. Thus in this way everyone who is liable on the bill is informed of his liability.

By section 52(3), notice of dishonour is not necessary to render the acceptor/drawee liable.

By section 48(1) if a bill is dishonoured for non-acceptance and notice of dishonour is not given, the rights of a subsequent holder in due course are not affected by the failure to give notice, e.g., A draws on B in favour of C (payee) who indorses it to D. D presents the bill to B who refuses to accept. The bill is dishonoured by non-acceptance (S.43(1)). D, the holder, must give notice of dishonour to A (drawer) and C (indorser) before he can enforce his rights against them. If he fails to do so A and C will be discharged. However, if he subsequently negotiates it to a holder in due course (say E), E can sue A and C and is not prejudiced by D's failure to give notice.

1. To be a holder in due course, E must take the bill without notice that it had been previously dishonoured.
2. If the bill had been dishonoured by non-payment there cannot be a subsequent holder in due course because the bill is then overdue. (See S.29).

The rules as to the giving of notice of dishonour are set out in section 49.

These require that the holder of the bill must give notice of dishonour, verbally or in writing or by the return of the bill, to anyone whom he intends to make liable on the bill. In practice he will merely notify his previous transferor. The notice of dishonour may be given as soon as the bill is dishonoured and must be given within a reasonable time. That means:

a. where the person giving and the person to receive notice reside in the same place the notice must be given or sent off in time to reach the latter on the day after dishonour of the bill.
b. where the person giving and the person to receive notice reside in different places, the notice must be sent off on the day after the dishonour of the bill, and if there be no such post on that day then by the next post thereafter.

Notice is deemed to have been given if it was duly addressed and posted, even if it was lost in the post.

The rules as to delay and excuses in giving notice of dishonour are contained in section 50.

Noting and Protesting

When a bill is dishonoured a distinction is made between an inland bill which is one which is drawn and payable in the British Isles, or which is drawn in the British Isles on a British resident; in any other case the bill is a foreign bill. When a foreign bill is dishonoured then it must be "noted and protested".

1. *NOTING*: Where a bill has been dishonoured the holder takes it to a notary public who then represents the bill. If it is again dishonoured, he notes on it:

    a. the date;
    b. a reference to his register;
    c. the noting changes; and.
    d. his initials.

    He will also attach a ticket stating the answer given when the presentment was made.
2. *PROTEST*: This consists of the obtaining of a certificate from a notary public attesting the dishonour of the bill.

The certificate is a formal declaration signed by the notary public. It must contain a copy of the bill. The details of a protest are given in section 51(7).

Where a bill requires to be protested and a notary public is not available, any householder or substantial resident of the place may in the presence of two witnesses, give a certificate, signed by them attesting the dishonour of the bill. A specimen form of "house-holder's protest" is given in the First Schedule to the Act.

A protest must be made by the day following the day of dishonour. In order to extend this period of time the dishonour of the bill may be noted and then a protest may be made at any time after the noting.

Noting and protesting are essential in the case of a foreign bill because the procedure provides evidence of the dishonour which will be acceptable to foreign courts. In addition an inland bill must be protested if payment from a referee in case of need is requested. A referee in case of need is a person whose name is inserted on the bill by the drawer to whom the holder may turn for acceptance or payment should the drawee refuse to accept it or pay upon it. In the same way a person may intervene if a bill is dishonoured, and accept the bill or pay it for the honour of a person who is liable. Legal proof of payment for honour should always be obtained, this is "a notarial act of honour".

Transfer of a Bill
When a bill has been issued it may then be transferred from one person to another and of course what is actually being transferred is the right to the sum of money that the bill will entitle the holder to receive.

If the bill is made payable to bearer then it may be transferred by simple delivery and the holder of such a bill will be the person who has possession of it.

If the bill is made payable to a named payee or order, then it is an order bill. It may be transferred by the payee indorsing the bill, designating the indorsee and giving delivery to him. The indorsee will then become the holder.

Holder in due course

As was mentioned earlier, a feature of bills of exchange is that a person can be the legal owner of a bill even though he received it from a person who was not the legal owner of it. Thus a thief may steal a bearer bill and pass it to X and X will become the legal owner of it, provided of course that X did not know he was receiving the bill from a thief and also provided X had given something of value for the bill.

However if the thief has stolen an order bill and because an order bill requires indorsing before it can be transferred, the thief had forged the indorsement of the person from whom he had stolen the bill and then passed it to X. X will now not become the legal owner of the bill because of the forged indorsement. Now this is rather hard on X who may have given something of value for the bill and may have received it not knowing he was taking it from a thief. The forged indorsement makes all the difference.

To summarise the position – the holder in due course, as he is called, is a holder who has a right to enforce payment on the bill against all parties who are liable on it. Also he will get a good title (become the legal owner) to the bill notwithstanding the fact that he takes it from a person who had no title to it. However in order to establish himself as a holder in due course he must have taken the bill in good faith not knowing of the lack of title of the person from whom he received it, and he must have given value for it – the bill itself must be complete and regular and especially must not contain a forged indorsement if it is an order bill. S.29(1).

Discharge of a bill
Finally, a bill is said to have been discharged, which means all rights of action on it are extinguished, in the following ways:

1. Payment by the drawee/acceptor to the holder. Payment to any other person such as one claiming under a forged indorsement will not discharge the drawee's liabilities.
2. By express waiver.

3. By cancellation.
4. By material alteration.

Chapter Nineteen
Cheques – in Particular

A cheque is defined as a bill of exchange drawn on a bank and payable on demand.

Thus the drawee of a cheque is always a banker. A cheque does not need to be accepted and the drawer is never discharged by the holder's failure to present the cheque for payment within a reasonable time.

The relationship between the drawer and the drawee, in the case of a cheque, is important because it is the relationship between a bank and its customer. This relationship is a contractual one that creates a debtor-creditor relationship and has been examined in Chapter 1.

By reason of the contract between bank and customer there are duties placed on each party. The main duty of the bank is to pay its customer's cheque up to the amount of the credit balance of their accounts provided the following conditions are complied with:

1. The cheque must be in writing, it must demand payment and be signed by the drawer (or customer).
2. The cheque must be drawn on the branch which holds a credit balance and the request for payment must be made during banking hours.
3. The cheque must be in unambiguous form. This means that as a cheque is a mandate from the customer to the banker then "the banker has a right to insist on having his mandate in a form which does not leave room for misgiving as to what he is called upon to do." Lord Haldane in *London Joint Stock Bank Ltd v Macmillan and Arthur (1918)*.
4. If any modifications to the contract between bank and

customer are to be made then they must be communicated expressly to the customer and it probably would not be sufficient for the banker to place a notice in the cheque book especially if there had been a course of dealing between the customer and the banker before the charges were made. *Burnett v Westminster Bank Ltd (1965)*.
5. There must be sufficient funds in the account on which the cheque is drawn. In this connection one should remember that a banker may be able to consolidate two accounts of a customer even if these accounts are at different branches – *Garnett v McKewan (1872)*. This facility applies to a bank but not to a customer. He has no right to insist on payment of a cheque at one branch where he has no funds merely because he has funds at another branch. Also, in England, a cheque is not an assignment of funds and so the holder of the cheque has no claim against the banker if he refuses, for whatever reason, to pay on the cheque. In Scotland, a cheque operates as an assignment to the payee of the amount for which it was drawn out of the credit balance of the customer's account. If therefore in Scotland a customer draws a cheque for an amount in excess of the credit balance on his account the practice is for the banker to transfer the balance to a separate account to be held for the holder of the cheque. In England a banker is not bound to pay part of a cheque if he has insufficient funds to pay the whole amount.
6. *Cheques out of date.* Sometimes called stale cheques, it is the custom of bankers not to pay cheques if six months or sometimes twelve months have elapsed after their issue.
7. *Postdated cheques.* Such cheques are not invalid but should not be paid by a banker because the customer may countermand payment before the due date of the cheque. Also if a banker pays a postdated cheque he may have to dishonour other cheques which he would otherwise have been able to pay.

Crossings

A particular feature of cheques is the crossing. This consists of two parallel transverse lines drawn across the face of the cheque. The effect of this is to ensure that the cheque cannot be cashed across the counter of the paying (drawer's) bank but must instead be paid into another bank and that bank will collect the proceeds for its customer. The purpose of crossing a cheque is obviously to make it more difficult for the wrong person to get his hands on the proceeds.

In addition to the general crossing just referred to there are also the following crossings:

A special crossing – where the name of a banker is written across the face of the cheque and the cheque is only payable to that named bank.

Account Payee

This is an instruction to the collecting banker to collect the proceeds for the account of the person named on the face of the cheque as payee. However, before June 16th 1992, the words "account payee" did not prevent the cheque being transferred, and so if a cheque bearing these words was indorsed in blank and then stolen, a holder in due course would get a good title.

This situation began to cause some anxiety in financial circles. The advice then given was to always add on the words "not negotiable" after the "account payee" crossing. Another aspect was that a banker who credited the account of a person other than the payee would forfeit his right to protection under *Section 80* of the *Bills of Exchange Act 1882* and also under *Section 4* of the *Cheques Act 1957*, on the grounds that he was negligent in crediting someone other than the payee.

However on June 16th 1992, the *Cheques Act 1992* came into force and it states that a cheque crossed and bearing across its face the words "account payee" or "a/c payee" either with or without the word "only", shall not be transferable, but shall only be valid as between the parties thereto.

Furthermore if a banker credits an account other than that of the payee he shall not be treated for the purpose of section 80 nor section 4 as having been negligent by reason only of his failure to concern himself with any purported indorsement of a cheque which is not transferable. The purpose of this change in the law is to ensure that the drawer of a cheque, by crossing it "account payee" can be certain that only the payee named will have a right to the proceeds of it.

The change caused a problem for the banks as to whether or not to print the crossing "account payee" on their cheques. The effect of this is to destroy one feature of a cheque by withdrawing its transferability. This is inconvenient to a person without a bank account who receives an "account payee" cheque. However in this day and age larger numbers of people than ever before have bank accounts and in any case the place of cheques is being taken over, to some extent, by credit and debit cards.

To summarise the situation – if a person steals an "account payee" cheque no person to whom he fraudulently indorses it can ever become the owner of it. Also if a bank does credit the wrong person with the proceeds then the bank will not be liable.

Not negotiable – these words may be added to a general or a special crossing and they have the effect of destroying the cheque's negotiability. This means that although it may still be transferred, the person who receives it will get no better title than that of the person from whom he received it. *Universal Guarantee Property Ltd v National Bank of Australasia (1965)*.

In the case of a bill of exchange other than a cheque the words "not negotiable" prevent the bill being transferred. *Hibernian Bank v Gysin and Hanson (1939)*.

Revocation of a banker's authority

Section 75 of the *Bills of Exchange Act 1882* provides that "The duty and authority of a banker to pay a cheque drawn to him by his customer are determined by (1) countermand of payment, (2) notice of the customer's death".

1. A banker will require the written and signed authority of his customer, accompanied by the date, number, amount and name of the payee of the cheque. If a verbal request to

stop payment is received the bank may merely suspend payment pending the receipt of written confirmation. If the account is joint and the bank's mandate does not require all parties to draw a cheque then a countermand of a cheque drawn by one party may be lodged by another party. *Gaunt v Taylor (1843)*.

The conditions for a countermand to be effective are:

a. The countermand must actually come to the notice of the banker. In *Curtice v London City and Midland Bank Ltd (1908)* a customer sent a telegram to his bank countermanding payment of a cheque but the telegram was left in the bank's letter box until 2 November. On 1 November a cheque had been paid and so the customer claimed against the bank. The Court of Appeal held that the claim must fail as the cheque had not been effectively countermanded.

b. The stop notice must be sent to the branch of the bank where the account is held. *London Provincial and South-Western Bank Ltd v Buszard (1918)*.

c. If the customer fails to adequately identify the cheque he wishes to be stopped he cannot blame the bank if it pays on that cheque *Westminster Bank Ltd v Hilton (1926)*.

d. The countermand must be given to the bank before payment of the cheque and the question may arise as to what moment of time payment takes place.

The customer must not have agreed not to countermand payment, which would be the case if a cheque card were used. Also it is only the drawer who can stop a cheque, not the payee. If the payee notifies the bank that he has lost the cheque then the bank should get in touch with the customer.

2. *Notice of customer's death or insanity*
Note that it is the notice of death or insanity and not the event itself that terminates a banker's authority to pay cheques. In general any credit balance of a customer must be held by a banker and only paid to an executor,

administrator or Committee in Lunacy after the appropriate legal formalities have been complied with.

Other events that determine a bankers authority

1. Insolvency of the customer.
2. Garnishee proceedings. This is an order of the Court which a judgment creditor may obtain to restrain a bank from paying funds it owes to a judgment debtor, the service of a garnishee order on a bank will suspend its duty to honour its customer's cheques. So if A has obtained judgment against B for a sum of money but B has omitted to pay up, A can get a garnishee order from the court directed at any person who owes money to B, such as his bank. This person is called the garnishee.
3. An injunction restraining a bank from paying out money from a customer's account (e.g. a Mareva injunction).
4. Outbreak of war between the country where the bank is situated and the country of which the customer is a national.

Breach of contract
If a bank fails to pay its customer's cheque when there are adequate funds in his account then the bank would be in *breach of contract* and would be liable to the customer. If the customer is a trader he may claim substantial damages without proof of actual loss. If he is not a trader he can only claim nominal damages unless he can establish actual loss.

Defamation
In addition the banker runs the risk of a libel action on the grounds that by not honouring his customer's cheques (incorrectly) he has given the payee and others the impression that the customer is the sort of person who issues "dud" cheques.

A bank therefore should make every effort to avoid a libel action if possible, by taking care as to the comments it makes on the cheque. Answers such as "Requires confirmation", "Words and figures differ", or "Indorsement irregular" would not be libellous. If such phrases cannot be used then "Refer to drawer" would be in order.

In *Evans v London and Provincial Bank (1917)* the wife of a naval officer, who sued for the dishonour of a cheque, received only one shilling in damages.

In *Cox v Cox and Co (1921)* when a cheque had been returned marked "N.S. Present again in a few days" the plaintiff sued for dishonour of the cheque and for libel. The bank paid £50 into court in respect of the breach of contract which the plaintiff accepted and continued the action for alleged libel. The jury found in favour of the defendants and Darling J stated that he considered the plaintiff would not have recovered the amount of £50 if it had not been paid in.

The customer for his part owes the bank a duty to take care in drawing his cheques and a duty to disclose to the bank any forgeries of which he is aware.

Bearer cheques and other cheques

In order for an instrument to be a valid cheque it must be made payable to a specified person or his order or to bearer.

Bearer Cheques

These do not require indorsement and so a person who receives a bearer cheque from a thief who has stolen it from the rightful owner will nevertheless become the rightful owner of it provided he took it without the knowledge that he was receiving it from a thief. An order cheque will be teated as a bearer cheque in the following circumstances

1. if it is indorsed in blank. In other words if the rightful owner of the cheque indorses it merely by signing his name without naming the indorsee. In that case the order cheque will require no further indorsement.
2. Section 7(3) of the Bills of Exchange Act 1882 provides

> "Where the payee is a fictitious or non existing person the bill may be treated as payable to bearer."

If therefore a clerk issues a cheque of his employer payable to a fictitious person and then the clerk indorses the cheque to an innocent person for value, the innocent person will get a good title to the proceeds of the cheque because of S.7. The person who receives the cheque will be able to enforce it against the drawer and the fact that it is not a genuine indorsement will be irrelevant because the cheque/bill has become a bearer cheque/bill by virtue of section S.7(3).

The question that remains is what is a fictitious person? The courts have decided that depends on whether the drawer intended the payee to receive the money. This is a good reason for making the bill not negotiable.

Bank of England v Vagliano Brothers (1891)
Glyka, an employee of Vagliano Brothers, forged a signature of a person named Vucina as drawer of a bill in favour of Petridi and Co, with whom Vagliano did business. Vagliano accepted the bill which had been drawn on him, and Glyka then forged Petridi's indorsement before presenting it to Vagliano's bank for payment. The bank, having paid Glyka, then debited Vagliano's account but Vagliano, on learning of the fraud, claimed that his account should not have been charged by the bank.

Held: Although Petridi was an actual person, the drawer of the bill (i.e. Glyka) never intended that he should receive payment under the bill. Petridi, as payee, was therefore in effect a fictitious person so far as the bill was concerned; consequently the bill was payable to bearer. As the bank had paid the bearer of the bill (namely, Glyka), Vagliano's claim failed, and the bank was in order in charging his account with the amount of the bill.

Vinden v Hughes (1905)
X, an employee of Vinden, persuaded V to draw cheques in favour of certain persons who were actual customers of

V, by telling V untruthfully that the amounts of the cheques were owing to the persons concerned. X then forged the indorsements of the payees and obtained payment of the cheques by purporting to negotiate them to Hughes.

Held: As the payees were existing person, and the drawer of the cheques (Vinden) intended payment to be made to those payees, the forgeries by X prevented Hughes from obtaining a good title. Vinden was therefore able to recover from Hughes the amount paid to Hughes by Vinden's banker.

In *North and South Wales Bank v Macbeth (1908)* Macbeth was induced by the fraud of White to draw a cheque in favour of Kerr who was an existing person. Macbeth intended him to receive the money.

White obtained the cheque, forged Kerr's indorsement and paid the proceeds into his account with the appellant bank.

Macbeth sued the bank, claiming it had converted his money. The bank replied that the cheque was drawn in favour of a fictitious person and so it became a bearer cheque.

The House of Lords decided the section did not apply as the drawer intended the payer to receive the money. The bank was therefore liable.

Order cheques

Cheques are usually payable to the payee or to his order. Thus the payee may receive the proceeds of the cheque or he may indorse the cheque in favour of an indorsee so that person may receive payment. Sometimes a cheque is made payable to "wages or order" or to "cash". Such an instrument is not a cheque but is a mandate to pay money. The collecting banker has the same statutory protection as he has in relation to cheques.

Orbit Mining and Trading Co Ltd v Westminster Bank Ltd (1962)
Mr Epstein had an account at the Westminster Bank. Some years after opening it he became a director of the plaintiff company, Orbit. Cheques in Orbit's account required the signatures of two directors. Before leaving for a business trip abroad, one director, Mr Woolf, signed a number of crossed blank cheque forms and left them with Epstein who took one, made it out to "Cash or order", added his own signature and the words "For and on behalf of Orbit Mining and Trading Co Ltd", and paid it into his private account. He did this on two other occasions. Epstein was authorised to sign cheques only for company business and so these three documents were fraudulent. The company claimed the money bank and the bank claimed its statutory protection as collecting for a customer under S.4(2). The Court of Appeal found for the bank. "It cannot be the duty of the bank to keep itself up to date as to the identity of a customer's employer" (Harman, LJ). Epstein's signature as drawer of the cheques was illegible and the bank could not be expected to recognise the name signed as being the same as that of the holder of the account into which the mandate for payment (it was technically not a cheque as it was payable "To cash") was being paid.

Liability of Paying Bank to Drawer and to Rightful Owner of the Cheque

The main duty of a bank, as was stated above, is to pay its customers cheques quickly. In doing so it runs the risk of paying one to the wrong person. How may this occur? Say, A draws a cheque payable to B. X, a thief, steals the cheque and now wants to get the money. If it is an uncrossed cheque then X can go to A's bank and if the cheque is for a reasonable amount, he will probably be paid over the counter.

If it is a crossed cheque then the proceeds of the cheque can only be paid into a bank account. So X, the thief, must either forge B's indorsement and then pay the cheque into his own or another person's account; or X may open an account in the name of B and pay the cheque into that. The second method is obviously more difficult because it requires X to obtain references who will state that he (X) is in fact B.

These then are the two methods by which a thief may obtain the proceeds of a stolen cheque. Note that in either of these two situations A's bank (the paying banker) will pay the proceeds of the cheque to the wrong person. On the face of it that bank will then be liable to A (for paying A's money to someone other than A had designated) also to B the rightful owner of the money (for wrongfully interfering with B's goods).

The bank on which the customer has drawn his cheque is called the paying bank because that bank will be paying the money to the bank into which the cheque has been paid for collection called the collecting bank.

The paying bank then will be liable to its customer and to the rightful owner of the money and the collecting bank will be liable only to the rightful owner of the money.

If this state of affairs had been allowed to continue then banks would have found it very difficult to operate. Consequently Parliament stepped in and provided the following protection for banks.

Banker's Protection

Paying Banker

A banker is under a duty to pay his customers cheques quickly and in doing so it may be that he pays the wrong person.

1. *Section 59 of the Bills of Exchange Act 1882* provides protection for a bank which pays the holder of a bearer bill and that holder was not entitled to the money.

    The section reads

    > A bill is discharged by payment in due course by or on behalf of the drawee or acceptor. "Payment in due course" means payment made at or after maturity of the bill to the holder thereof in good faith and without notice that his title to the bill is defective.

It will be noticed that reference is made to a bill and not merely a cheque, so this section covers all bills of exchange; also payment must be to the "holder". Now the only person who can be a holder of a cheque to which he is not entitled is the bearer of a bearer cheque. If it is an order cheque then the indorsement must have been forged by the thief and so consequently the person to whom he negotiates the cheque cannot be "a holder" because of the forged indorsement.

Therefore Section 59 is not of great importance to bankers because it only applies to bearer cheques which are not particularly common.

2. *Section 60* of the *Bills of Exchange Act 1882* provides protection if the bank pays out on a cheque bearing a forged indorsement. The section reads

> "Where a bill payable to order on demand is drawn on a banker, and the banker on whom it is drawn pays the bill in good faith and in the ordinary course of business, it is not incumbent on the banker to show that the indorsement of the payee or any subsequent indorsement was made by, or under the authority of the person whose indorsement it purports to be, and the banker is deemed to have paid the bill in due course, although such indorsement has been forged or made without authority".

It will be seen that Section 60 covers the situation where there is a forged indorsement, also the protection only applies to cheques. In addition, in order to get the protection, the banker must have acted in good faith and in the ordinary course of business.

Probably the good faith of a banker would not be doubted but the requirement that payment must be made "in the ordinary course of business" was examined in *Baines v National Provincial Bank (1927)*.

In that case the bank cashed a cheque payable to Mr Wood at five minutes past three o'clock, which was five minutes outside normal banking hours. In the ordinary course of business the bank ceased trading for that day at 3 p.m. The next day Mr Baines cancelled payment on the cheque but the cheque had already been paid the day previously. Mr Baines then claimed the bank had not acted in the ordinary course of business.

The court held that normally paying a cheque outside banking hours would not be in the ordinary course of business but five minutes leeway was permitted so far as people already on the bank's premises were concerned. The meaning of payment in due course was further considered in

Auchteroni and Co v Midland Bank Ltd (1928)
In this case a fraudulent person presented a bill to the paying bank and was paid cash over the counter. The court held this was unusual but did not deprive the bank of its protection under S.59.

Examples of payments *not* in the ordinary course of business would be

a. Payment to a tramp, postman or office boy.
b. Payment after hours – but a few minutes could make no difference particularly if the payees were in the building.

3. *Section 80* of the *Bills of Exchange Act 1882* provides

> *Protection to banker and drawer where cheque is crossed.* Where the banker, on whom a crossed cheque (including a cheque which under section 81A below or otherwise is not transferable.) is drawn, in good faith and without negligence pays it, if crossed generally, to a banker, and if crossed specially, to the banker to whom it is crossed, or his agent for collection being a banker, the banker paying the cheque, and, if the cheque has come into the hands of the payee, the drawer, shall respectively be entitled to the same rights and be placed in the same position

as if payment of the cheque had been made to the true owner thereof.

In other words if a banker pays out on a cheque according to the crossing and if he does so in good faith and without negligence then he is protected if he pays to the wrong person.

The above are the main sections which protect the paying banker. Section 59 applies to bills of exchange, generally where payment is to a holder of the bill. Section 60 covers the case of a forged indorsement on a cheque and section 80 deals with crossed cheques.

Analogous instruments
The above protection is extended to instruments other than bills of exchange and cheques by the following provisions:

Section 1 of the Cheques Act 1957

Protection of bankers paying unindorsed or irregularly indorsed cheques

1. Where a banker in good faith and in the ordinary course of business pays a cheque drawn on him which is not indorsed or is irregularly indorsed, he does not, in doing so, incur any liability by reason only of the absence of, or irregularity in, indorsement, and he is deemed to have paid it in due course.
2. Where a banker in good faith and in the ordinary course of business pays any such instrument as the following, namely:
    a. a document issued by a customer of which, though not a bill of exchange, is intended to enable a person to obtain payment from him of the sum mentioned in the document;
    b. a draft payable on demand drawn by him upon himself, whether payable at the head office or some other office of the bank; he does not, in

doing so, incur any liability by reason only of the absence of, or irregularity in, indorsement, and the payment discharges the instrument.

Section 1 of the *Cheques Act 1957* gives to a paying banker the same protection that he will get in the case of unindorsed or irregularly indorsed cheques to banker's drafts and conditional orders – crossed or uncrossed. Section 1 extends the protection given to a paying banker if he pays to the wrong person

1. a banker's draft
2. a mandate for payment. This is not a cheque but is intended to enable a person to obtain payment from the banker.

The bank must of course be acting in good faith and in the ordinary course of business.

A banker's draft is drawn by a banker upon himself and it is not "addressed by one person to another". A conditional order lacks an essential requirement of a cheque which is that it must be an unconditional order.

Section 1 of the *Cheques Act 1957* does away with need for an indorsement on cheques except for the purpose of negotiation.

However on 23 September 1957 the *Committee of London Clearing Banks* issued a memorandum to their members.

This requires a paying bank to obtain indorsement of a cheque if it is either (a) a cheque marked "R" (by this the drawer signifies that he requires a receipt for payment of the cheque) or (b) an open cheque presented at the counter for payment in cash.

In addition promissory notes, travellers cheques and ordinary bills of exchange will also require indorsements.

Section 5

Application of certain provisions of Bills of Exchange Act 1882, to instruments not being bills of exchange
The provisions of the Bills of Exchange Act 1882, relating to crossed cheques shall, so far as applicable, have effect in relation to instruments (other than cheques) to which the

last foregoing section applies as they have effect in relation to cheques.

Section 5 of the *Cheques Act 1957* gives to a paying banker the same protection he will get under *Section 80* of the *Bills of Exchange Act*.

Section 5 applies to instruments other than cheques (i.e. instruments that do the work of cheques but do not comply with the definition of a cheque) e.g.

Banker's drafts
Conditional Orders
Drafts drawn upon the Paymaster-General or the Queen's and Lord Treasurer's Remembrancer.

Therefore Section 80 gives similar protection to a paying banker in respect of these instruments if they are crossed, as he gets for crossed cheques.

Section 19 of the *Stamp Act* covers crossed or uncrossed bankers drafts.

Collecting Banker

If a banker collects the proceeds of a cheque for his customer he will incur liability in conversion if the cheque did not belong to his customer. The rogue may have opened an account in the name of the payee named on the cheque or he may have forged the payee's indorsement and paid the cheque into his own account. In either case the banker who collected the proceeds of the cheque will have done so (albeit innocently) for the wrong person. He will therefore, prima facie, be liable to the rightful owner of the money. The collecting banker may be protected as follows:

By *Section 4(1)* of the *Cheques Act 1957*,

Where a banker, in good faith and without negligence;
1. receives payment for a customer of a cheque or other instrument specified in Section 4(2). The instruments referred to in Section 4(2) are:

a. cheques (including cheques which under section 81A (i) of the Bills of Exchange Act 1882 or otherwise are not transferable.)
b. any document issued by a customer of a banker which, though not a bill of exchange, is intended to enable a person to obtain payment from that banker of the sum mentioned in the document
c. any document issued by a public officer which is intended to enable a person to obtain payment from the Paymaster General or the Queen's and Lord Treasurer's Remembrancer of the sum mentioned in the document but is not a bill of exchange.
d. any draft payable on demand drawn by a banker upon himself, whether payable at the head office or some other office of the bank; or

2. having credited a customer's account with the amount of the cheque, etc, receives payment thereof for himself, and the customer had no title (e.g., because the indorsement was forged), or a defective title (e.g., he obtained the cheque by fraud).
3. The banker does not incur liability to the true owner of the instrument by reason only of having received payment thereof.

Before the banker can claim the benefit of the protection, however, he must satisfy the following conditions;
1. *Good faith*: He must have acted in good faith. This means that what he does when collecting the cheque must be done honestly.
2. *Customer*: Section 4(1) confers protection only where the person for whom payment is collected is a customer.

   A customer is a person who has a banking account with a banker even if the cheque with which he opened the account is the subject-matter of the action in respect of which the banker claims the protection of section 4(1):

Ladbroke & Co v Todd (1914). On one occasion thieves intercepted letters which Ladbrokes the bookmakers, had sent to clients containing their winnings cheques. The thieves took out the cheques and substituted forgeries. One such cheque was for £75 11s 3d payable to a Mr Jobson and crossed "A/c payee only".

One of the thieves took this cheque to the John Bull Bank, which was owned by Mr Todd, and opened an account in Jobson's name using the stolen cheque as an initial deposit and asked for that cheque to be specially presented. This was done and the cheque was paid. The next day "Mr Jobson" withdrew the money from his account and disappeared. Mr Todd said that he had not made any enquiries at all about "Mr Jobson" because he was obviously a University man and told a plausible story about not wishing his usual banker to see a cheque drawn by a bookmaker. The court held that "Mr Jobson" was a customer of the bank from the moment his account was opened but that the banker had been negligent in not making enquiries, for example, at the college he claimed to attend, which would have revealed him as an imposter.

The account may be a deposit or a current account: *Great Western Railway Co v London and County Banking Co Ltd (1901)*.

Section 4(1) applies to all cheques, whether crossed or uncrossed. It also applies to bankers' drafts, conditional orders and Paymaster-General's warrants (see Section 4(2) of the *Cheques Act 1957*).

3. *Without Negligence*: The banker must have collected without negligence. The meaning of negligence must be ascertained from the cases, but Section 4(3) of the Act provides that he is not to be treated as having been negligent by reason only of his failure to concern himself with the absence of, or irregularity in, indorsement of an instrument.

Whether the banker has been negligent or not will be decided by reference to the practice of reasonable men carrying on the business of banking and endeavouring to do so in a manner calculated to protect themselves and others against fraud.

Through the cases it has been established that a bank may be negligent in the following areas:

1. *Opening an account*
   Failure of the bank to obtain or follow up references when an account is being opened for a prospective customer may be negligence. If the banker acts on the reply from only one referee, he is not necessarily negligent, though where the prospective customer is a foreigner, it may be desirable for the bank to confirm the reply by an examination of the customer's passport: *Marfani & Co v Midland Bank Ltd (1967)* Marfani & Co's office manager, calling himself Mr Eliaszade (with whom the company did business) cultivated the acquaintance of a restaurant proprietor called Akkadas Ali. Shortly before Mr Marfani left to visit Pakistan, the office manager opened an account in the name of Eliaszade at the Midland Bank giving Ali's name as a reference. Ali was well known as a substantial customer of the bank, and he had previously introduced good new customers. The office manager then got Mr Marfani to sign a cheque for £3,000 payable to Eliaszade, pretending that money was owed to him in the normal course of business. He paid this cheque into his account, withdrew the money and disappeared. The bank claimed statutory protection as collecting for a customer but Marfani & Co claimed the bank had been negligent. The court found for the bank but said, "If the defendant bank here exercised sufficient care, it was in my view only just sufficient." The bank had not enquired about the employment of "Eliaszade" and had presented the cheque before receiving Ali's reference.

   Lumsden & Co v London Trustee Savings Bank (1971)
   In this case a collecting banker was found guilty of conversion without the protection of Section 4, *Cheques Act 1957* in that he failed to obtain a satisfactory introductory

reference relating to a new customer. The latter was a stranger who offered the name of "Dr Blake" as a referee who replied favourably to the bank but did not supply the name of his own bankers. The bank was informed that Dr Blake had recently arrived in the UK from Australia. Cheques drawn by Lumsden & Co were misappropriated and passed through the defendant bank, the proceeds being quickly withdrawn. The whole story of the thief turned out to be a lie which would have been revealed, said the court, if the defendant bank had been more diligent, demanding at least the sight of the "Dr Blake" with his passport.

The case is notable, however, for the fact that the damages awarded to the plaintiffs, were reduced by 10% because they had been contributorily negligent in not drawing the cheques correctly.

2. *In collecting for a customer who is an employee a cheque drawn by or in favour of the employer*

When opening an account, the banker is under a duty to inquire as to the name of his new customer's employer if the banker knows that the customer occupies a position which involves the handling and opportunity of stealing his employer's cheques.

If the customer is a married woman, the banker must inquire as to the name of her husband's employer. *Savory & Co v Lloyds Bank (1932)*. E B Savory & Co were London stockbrokers and two of their clerks, Perkins and Smith, from time to time misappropriated bearer cheques drawn by their employers payable to stock jobbers and paid them into London branches of Lloyds Bank for the credit of, in the case of Perkins, his account at the Wallington branch of that bank and in Smith's case for his wife's account at the Redhill, and later, the Weybridge branches of that bank. The branches of Lloyds Bank that conducted these accounts had not, on opening the accounts

a. in the case of Perkins, ascertained the name of his employers and

b. in the case of Mrs Smith, ascertained the name of her husband's employers.

The bank failed to obtain statutory protection from its common law liability for conversion since it was considered to be guilty of negligence in two respects, viz.,

a. the branches which maintained the accounts were not possessed of information to enable the bank to keep watch on what was paid into the account so to detect any misappropriation of the employers' cheques.
b. the London branches failed to pass on to the "home" branch details of the cheques paid in by Perkins and Smith and cleared by the London branches on behalf of the "home" branches.

However in 1968 – the Marfani case – Diplock LJ said of Savory's case that it depended on its own facts and there were matters to arouse suspicions in the social conditions of the 1920's. The case is merely an illustration of the principle that a banker must exercise reasonable care in all the circumstances of the case. Savory was decided in the light of banking practice as it was at that time.

3. *In not enquiring further into circumstances which should have set the alarm bells ringing*

Where there is evidence on the face of the cheque of possible misappropriation the banker who fails to inquire further may be negligent. In the following cases further inquiry will be needed before a banker:

a. Collects payment for a private account a cheque payable to a public official. *Ross v London County, Westminster and Parr's Bank Ltd (1919)*
b. Collects for an employee's private account or his wife's account cheques drawn by or in favour of his employer. *Savory (E B) & Co v Lloyd's Bank Ltd (1932)*
c. Collects for a customer's private account cheques payable to the customer as "agent for the Marquis of Bute". *Bute v Barclays Bank Ltd (1954)*

McGaw had been the Manager of three sheep farms owned by the Marquis of Bute. After the termination of his employment he received three warrants totally £546, being subsidies, payable to McGaw "for the Marquis of Bute". They were collected and credited to McGaw's private account without enquiry by Barclays Bank, Barnsley.

In defence, Barclays Bank stated that:

(i) As the warrants were payable to McGaw he was the true owner notwithstanding that he was accountable for the proceeds to the Marquis.

(ii) The Marquis was estopped against the bank since he knew that the warrants would be issued payable to McGaw.

(iii) The bank was entitled to statutory protection if its defence in (i) had failed.

The court held that although the warrants were payable to McGaw, the intention of the drawer was that the Marquis should receive the money and not McGaw – the latter was merely accountable to the Marquis. Consequently conversion of the warrants had taken place and the bank was guilty of conversion. The statutory protection it claimed was lost because the court declared that it was clear that McGaw was to receive the money only as an agent and so such documents should not have been credited to the agent's private account without enquiry.

d. Collects for a director's private account a cheque payable to his company. The bank was unaware the company had an account at another bank. *A L Underwood Ltd v Bank of Liverpool and Martins Ltd (1924)*.

e. Collects a cheque marked "account payee" or "account payee only" for some other account. *Ladbroke v Todd (1914)*

f. Collects an amount inconsistent with the status of the customer: *Nu-Stilo Footwear Ltd v Lloyds Bank Ltd (1956)*.

Nu-Stilo Footwear Ltd v Lloyds Bank Ltd (1956)
Nu-Stilo Footwear employed M as its Secretary. M opened an account at Lloyds Bank in the false name of B saying he, B, was a freelance agent just commencing business. For references he gave his real name and address and later, when Lloyds Bank followed up the reference he, not surprisingly, said that "B" was a suitable person to be given banking facilities. Subsequently 9 cheques drawn by Nu-Stilo, most of them payable to B were collected by Lloyds Bank for "B's" account. Since the total of these cheques was £4,855 the court ruled that the amount was inconsistent with B's commencing business as a freelance agent. Consequently negligence was attributed to the bank which therefore failed to get the statutory protection it claimed.

Banker acting both as collecting and paying banker

Where a banker acts in the dual capacities of collecting and paying banker, he must, to escape liability to the true owner of the cheques he has dealt with (in an action for conversion), bring himself within the scope of the statutory protection afforded to both the paying and collecting banker. In other words, he cannot, for example, say "I concede I was negligent when I was acting as collecting banker but in my separate capacity as the paying banker, I am entitled to the protection of Section 1 of the *Cheques Act 1957*."

In *Carpenters' Co v British Mutual Banking Co (1937)* a clerk of the Carpenters' company procured cheques from the company dishonestly and paid them into his private account at the defendant bank, which also acted as the company's bankers. The bankers claimed to be protected either by Section 60 or Section 82 (now Section 4 of the *Cheques Act 1957*). It was held that, although the bankers were protected by Section 60, they had been negligent in the collection of the cheque and were therefore liable to the company.

Collecting banker as holder for value

It should be remembered that a banker may collect the proceeds of a cheque in one of two capacities.

1. He may collect as agent of his customer and then *Section 4* of the *Cheques Act 1957* may protect him.
2. He may collect the proceeds of the cheque for himself. In order for that situation to arise he must have given value for the cheque. In that case he will come within the definition of a holder for value or in due course and so will be able to sue the drawer of the cheque. The fact that the cheque, paid in by the customer, will probably not be indorsed will not affect the situation. *Section 2* of the *Cheques Act 1957* provides that a banker who gives value for, or has a lien on, a cheque payable to order which the holder delivers to him for collection without indorsing it has such (if any) rights as he would have had if upon delivery, the holder had indorsed it in blank. In other words the unindorsed cheque will be treated as a bearer cheque.

A banker will be deemed to have given value for a cheque if

   a. He lends further sums to the holder on the strength of the cheque.
   b. If he pays over the amount of the cheque or part of it in cash or on account before it is cleared.
   c. If he agrees either then or earlier, or as a course of business, that the customer may draw against the cheque immediately, before it is cleared.
   d. If the cheque is paid in specifically to reduce an existing overdraft.
   e. If he gives cash over the counter for the cheque at the time it is paid in for collection.
   f. If he has a lien on the cheque.

Section 2 of the *Cheques Act 1957* covers only cheques and it will not apply if the cheque bears a forged indorsement.

Westminster Bank v Zang (1965)
The application of Section 2 of the Cheques Act is illustrated by the above case, the facts of which are:

Zang lost money gambling. He asked Tilley who was then watching if he could let him have £1,000 in return for a cheque. Tilley gave Zang the money in return for the cheque. Tilley had taken the £1,000 from a company, Tilley Autos Ltd. He was the company's managing director and controlling shareholder. Consequently he paid it in for the company's account but as the cheque had been made payable to himself he should have indorsed it before paying it in. This he did not do and this omission was not noticed by the collecting branch cashier. On presentation the cheque was dishonoured and Tilley borrowed it to sue Zang on it but abandoned his action. The bank later sued Zang themselves because Tilley Autos' account was overdrawn. To do so successfully they had to establish that they were holders for value.

The bank lost the action because even though *Section 2* of the *Cheques Act* could be satisfied, the bank was held not to have given value for the cheque. The bank's argument, that by crediting the cheque to the account of Tilley Autos Ltd, and reducing the company's overdraft by £1,000 they had given value, was dismissed on the ground that the bank's paying-in slip had a note to the effect that the bank reserved the right to refuse to pay against uncleared effects. This prevented an implied agreement from arising in the circumstances. The bank lost its lien when it lent the cheque to Tilley.

It was further held that the words "for collection", which appear in *Section 2* of the *Cheques Act 1957*, are not to be confined to cases where the bank is to collect for a customer's account. It applies if the cheque is being collected for any account.

Electronic Transfer of Funds

The physical movement of paper used in the transfer of funds is a very expensive process. Consequently in recent years a number of electronic systems have been developed using computers and designed to reduce the amount of paper used.

B.A.C.S. (Bankers' Automated Clearing Service)

B.A.C.S. Ltd is the company which operates the service. It deals with standing orders, direct debits, salary credits and other credits, such as traders settling amounts due. The B.A.C.S. system is used by the banks and by customers. The user prepares details of the transactions i.e. sort code number, account number, account name, amount and reference number. The details are sent to the B.A.C.S. computer centre at Edgware, Middlesex. They are contained on a tape or disc and are then read by computer at the centre. The entries are then sorted electronically, placed on magnetic tapes which are then passed to the appropriate bank. The advantages are – reduced clerical costs, lower bank charges cash flow benefits, interest saved and increased security.

C.H.A.P.S. (Clearing House Automated payments system)

This is a high value clearing system which is operated electronically. At present the system is available for payments of £5,000 or more. The settlement bank transmits the payment to the computer systems of the other settlement banks. When a payment has been fed into the system it cannot be stopped and so the funds are guaranteed as having been cleared. The C.H.A.P.S. system has taken over from the Town clearing which only applies to the City of London. This new system operates throughout the U.K. and is used when a guaranteed and speedy method of payment is required. Apart from that, the payee's bank account is credited immediately the payer orders his settlement bank to make the transfer.

E.F.T.P.O.S. (Electronic funds transfer at point of sale)

This is the technical name for the system which makes use of plastic cards – either debit cards issued by banks or building societies, or by credit cards. This method of transfer of funds sometimes goes under the names of – "Connect" "Switch", "P.D.Q." or "Accept".

When the customer presents his card the retailer "swipes" it through the electronic reader. Details of the transaction are transmitted to a central computer, the cost of the goods is checked against the cardholder's balance in his bank or building society. The customer's account is then debited and the retailer's account is credited.

If it is an "off-line" E.F.T.P.O.S. system then all the transactions for a day are collected together and then sent to the central computer by disc or tape or the bank's own computer system is used.

The advantages to the customer are: convenience, no need to write a cheque. To the retailer: it means greater efficiency, less cash to handle and a guaranteed payment once acceptance has been made.

A.T.M.S. (Automated Teller machines)
Most banks now have an A.T.M. outside their premises. The user operates the A.T.M. by inserting his card into the machine and keying in his P.I.N. (Personal identity number). The machine looks up the account in the bank's computer and then carries out the orders of the user. These may be:

cash withdrawal
statement request
cheque book request
some machines will also accept deposits and carry out payment of bills.

The advantages to a customer are that these machines allow him to pay bills and withdraw cash without drawing a cheque. Over the years the banks have co-operated and created shared A.T.M. networks e.g.

Midland, National Westminster, TSB and Clydesdale
Barclays, Lloyds, Royal Bank of Scotland and the Bank of Scotland.
Link Co-op bank, Girobank and some building societies.
Matrix a building society network.

1992
The transfer of funds is being currently studied in view of the advent of the single market which will be brought about by 31 December 1992.

The European Commission is critical of many of the existing transfer procedures as they are often slow, expensive and labour intensive. The European consumer organisation has calculated that simply exchanging £100 through each of the E.C. countries will lose £50 in charges. This risk has been reduced by the success of E.R.M. in bringing about greater exchange rate stability. Also in the final stages of EMU the risk would disappear but pending a single currency, one option would be for national bank notes to carry an indication of their ECU value printed on them. Banks would then exchange them at par value for notes of other Member States. These disadvantages are not faced by business in the USA. A New York based business man investing in Texas has no such problems because the value of the dollar is always the same anywhere in the USA. A similar arrangement was followed in the U.K. after the merger of Scotland and England. For 100 years after the union in 1707 bank notes in Scotland showed values both in pounds sterling and Scottish pounds. The Commission considers the ACHs (Automated Clearing houses) should be expanded and standard practices be adopted in order to provide efficient cross border services. This will require wider banking co-operation including central bank involvements. Priority is likely to focus on improvements in electronic payments via Eurocheques. However if machine readable code lines for electronic processing can be standardised in the E.C. ordinary cheque usage could increase.

Since 1987 progress has been made with the acceptance of payment cards at ATMs in all Member States. The U.K. leads with nearly 16,000 but surprisingly Germany had fewer than 6,000 in June 1989.

Chapter Twenty
Insolvency

Corporate Insolvency

Often the words insolvency, bankruptcy and winding-up or liquidation become intermixed in a person's mind. However one should be clear to what one is referring when using these words. Insolvency simply means inability to pay ones debts. Assuming B owes A £1,000 then A may have to establish his right to that sum of money by going to a court of law. If A wins then he can say he has obtained judgment against B and so B becomes a judgment debtor and A is the judgment creditor. But A still has not received his money.

If that is the case A must consider enforcing his judgment against B and will have to seek the help of the court. This may consist of the court ordering the bailiffs to distrain on B's goods, to sell them and from the proceeds to pay A. Other methods would be – if B is employed to get an attachment of earnings order by which B's employer is ordered to deduct a certain sum each week or month from B's wages and to pay the money deducted to A. However all these methods are only used in order to assist A to recover his money. If B owes money not only to A but also to C, D, E and F etc it might mean by concentrating on one creditor the other creditors could be unfairly teated and may not be able to recover any part of their debt. In that case it may be advisable from the point of view of all the creditors that a united front is maintained against B and that he is made bankrupt. The main purpose of bankruptcy proceedings is to ensure that each creditor is dealt with fairly. Also when one considers the assets of B a personal action against him would only succeed in gaining control of assets he owns at that time. Whereas a feature of bankruptcy is that it may be possible in certain cases to follow assets which formerly belonged to the debtor and to recover them so that they can be distributed amongst the creditors. In the case of companies the procedure for collecting in their assets and distributing them amongst the creditors is called winding-up or a liquidation. One point to be observed is that a human person is made bankrupt because he cannot pay his debts; a company may be wound up for reasons other than that it cannot pay its debts although the insolvency of a company is probably the main reason why it is wound up.

Thus insolvency means inability to pay debts and from that there may follow the formal procedures of winding-up or liquidation in the case of a company or bankruptcy in the case of an individual. However if these formal procedures are adopted it may result in there being less for distribution amongst the creditors because the expenses of these formal procedures will have to be paid before there is any distribution. Consequently it may be preferable for the creditors to come to some arrangement with the debtor company or the individual debtor. These voluntary arrangements are a feature of the new legislation contained in the *Insolvency Act 1986* and the Act facilitates the making of such arrangements.

The various methods of dealing with an insolvent company other than having it wound up are:

1. *Bank rescues*. Sometimes, instead of winding up a company it is advisable to lend it more money, in the hope that it will become profitable and eventually the creditors will recover the full amount of their debts. In such a case if a bank lends money then it will take a fixed debenture as security.
2. *Receivership*. An ordinary receiver is one appointed by the creditors under power contained in the debenture certificate. An administrative receiver is a receiver or manager of the whole of the company's property. He is appointed by the holders of any debentures secured by a floating charge.
3. *Administration Order*. The Insolvency Acts, have intro-

duced a new procedure whereby the court may make an "administration order" in regard to a company. The effect of this is to place the management of the company in the hands of an administrator and while the administration order is in force no resolution may be passed nor any order made for the winding up of the company, nor may an administrative receiver be appointed.

The appointment of an Administrator may be blocked by the holder of a floating charge but not by the holder of a fixed charge.

The administrator is given specific powers in particular to carry on the business of the company, to take possession of the company's property and to raise or borrow money and in that connection to grant security over the property.

Voluntary arrangements

These may be arrangements, assignments or compositions.

An *arrangement* may include a reorganisation of the company's share capital so the creditors can convert some debts into ordinary shares.

A *composition* is an agreement of creditors not to take action against the company in return for payment by the company of part of their debts.

An *assignment* involves a traansfer of the company's property to the creditors or to a nominee of them all *S.425 Companies Act 1985*.

In addition the *Insolvency Act 1986* has created a new scheme of voluntary arrangements. This requires supervision by a nominee, who must be an insolvency practitioner.

If these voluntary arrangements are unsuccessful it may be necessary to have the company wound up.

Winding up

The procedures for the winding up of a company are contained in the *Insolvency Act 1986* which consolidates parts of the *Companies Act 1985* and the *Insolvency Act 1985*. A company is usually wound up because it is unable to pay its debts but it may be wound up also on technical grounds such as the company did not commence business within a year after it was incorporated, or the number of its members has been reduced below two. Also a company may be wound up merely because the shareholders wish it to be wound up.

A company may be wound up compulsorily by the court or voluntarily by its members or creditors.

Winding up by the Court

The court may order the winding up of a company only if one or several of the following grounds for winding up are present. Applications to the court is made by petition, called a *winding-up petition* which if successful will result in the court making a winding-up order.

Grounds for petition: under section 122 of the *Insolvency Act 1986*, a company may be wound up by the court if:

1. the company has by special resolution resolved that the company be wound up by the court; or
2. the company does not commence its business within a year from its incorporation or suspends its business for a whole year.
3. the number of members is reduced below two.
4. the company is unable to pay its debts.
5. the court is of opinion that it is just and equitable that the company should be wound up.

Company unable to pay its debts

Section 123 of the *Insolvency Act 1986* provides that a company may be deemed unable to pay its debts in the following cases;

1. If a creditor to whom the company is indebted in a sum exceeding £750 has served on the company (at its registered office) a written demand for the payment of the debt and the company has for three weeks thereafter neglected to pay the sum or to make some other arrangement satisfactory to the creditor about its payment; or

2. If in England and Wales, execution or other process issued on a judgment of any court in favour of a creditor of the company is returned unsatisfied in whole or in part. Execution is where a judgment creditor is seeking to enforce his judgment against the debtor company.
3. If it is proved in any other way to the satisfaction of the court that the company is unable to pay its debts. In this case, the court has a discretion and the amount owed need not exceed £750. Usually, the fact that the petitioner has made repeated demands for payment, and that the company has neglected to pay affords *cogent evidence* that the company is unable to pay its debts. Unless the company bona fide disputes the claim, a winding-up order will be made.
4. Asset Test: if it is proved to the satisfaction of the court that the liabilities of the company exceed its assets. S.123.

Just and Equitable

The power of the court to wind up a company on "just and acquitable grounds" is discretionary. What is "just and equitable" will depend upon the allegations made by the petitioner. In the following situations the courts have made winding-up orders.

1. Where the main object of the company can no longer be realised.
2. If the company is a "bubble", i.e. if it never had any business or assets.
3. If the company was formed for purposes of fraud or to conduct illegal business.
4. That the articles of association provided for a winding-up in the event which has happened.
5. That in a small private company, the company was in substance a partnership and the facts would justify the dissolution of a partnership. This happens usually where the relationship between the persons owning its share capital is analogous to a partnership relationship: *Re Yenidje Tobacco Company Ltd (1916)*.

Who can petition for winding-up?

A petition may be presented by the following:

1. The company or its directors
2. A creditor.
3. A contributory
4. The Official Receiver
5. Department of Trade and Industry or Bank of England may petition in special cases.

A petition by the company would be very unusual because it only needs to pass an appropriate special resolution to be wound up.

Contributories also are not very common because they only exist in the case of shares which are not fully paid. The liquidator must prepare a list of persons who are liable to contribute to the assets of the company in the event of its being wound up. "A" list contains the names of present members of the company and "B" list the names of past members who ceased to be members within a year preceding the winding-up. In the event of a person on "A" list being unable to contribute the unpaid amount of his share, a person on "B" list may be asked to contribute – but only in respect of debts incurred before he ceased to be a member. The more likely petitioner will of course be a creditor.

The Official Receiver may petition if the company is in voluntary liquidation and he feels that the interests of creditors or contributories are in danger.

The Secretary of State for the Department of Trade and Industry may petition under *Section 440* of the *Companies Act 1985* if it appears that it is expedient in the public interest that the company should be wound up on the basis of information he has been given from his inspectors.

Consequences of a winding-up order
If a winding up petition is successful, the court will make an order for winding up.

The order relates back to the date of the commencement of

the winding-up. Under *Section 129 Insolvency Act 1986* the winding-up commences either:

1. at the time of the presentation of the winding-up petition, or
2. where, before a petition was presented, the company was in voluntary liquidation, on the passing of the resolution for voluntary winding up.

The effect of a winding-up order is:

1. To make void all dispositions of the company's property and any transfer of shares made after the commencement of the winding-up is void. S.127 unless sanctioned by the court.
2. Any attachment, sequestration, distress or execution against the estate of the company after the commencement of the winding-up is void. S.128.
3. After a winding-up order has been made or a provisional liquidator has been appointed, no action can be proceeded with or commenced against the company except by leave of the court. S.130(2).
4. The Official Receiver becomes provisional liquidator until he or another person is made a liquidator. S.136(2)(3).
5. The employment of employees and other agents of the company is terminated. Further the directors are dismissed and their powers to act on behalf of the company cease.
6. All invoices, orders for goods or business letters of the company must state that the company is in liquidation. S.188.

Proceedings after a winding-up order has been made
The court may require a statement of affairs to be produced by the official receiver. He must also carry out two investigations:

1. if the company has failed – into the reason for the failure.
2. in any case, into the promotion, formation, business dealings, and affairs of the company.

In order to assist him in his investigation, he may apply to the court for the public examination of:

1. any one who has been an officer of the company
2. has acted as liquidator, administrator, receiver or manager of its property or
3. anyone else who has been concerned in the promotion, formation or management of the company.

The official receiver must apply for a public examination if so requested by one half of the creditors or three quarters of the contributories. S.133(2).

Appointment of liquidator
The official receiver becomes the first liquidator until another person is appointed. Within 12 weeks of the winding up order the official receiver must decide whether or not to summon separate meetings of the company's creditors and contributories in order to choose a liquidator. If he decides not to call a meeting he must notify the creditors and then he may be obliged to call a meeting if requested by one quarter in value of the creditors.

The official receiver may apply to the Secretary of State for the appointment of a liquidator.

Duties and powers of the liquidator
He is not a trustee for the individual creditors but is the agent of the company. However he will be liable in damages to any creditor for breach of any of his statutory duties.

He must

1. assist the official receiver
2. take into his custody the property of the company
3. settle the list of contributories
4. summon meetings of creditors
5. summon a final meeting in accordance with S.146.

He may

1. bring and defend actions in the name of the company

2. carry on the business of the company so far as is necessary for the winding-up
3. pay any classes of creditors
4. compromise or make arrangements with creditors
5. he may disclaim any onerous property such as unprofitable contracts or any property which is unsaleable.

Voluntary winding up

The main attraction of voluntary winding up from the members' point of view is that there are not a great many formalities to be complied with.

A voluntary winding up may be either

1. a members' voluntary winding-up or
2. a creditors' voluntary winding-up. S.90.

Whether the winding-up is a members' or creditors' voluntary winding-up, it is initiated by the members of the company passing an appropriate resolution to that effect and not, as in the case of a compulsory winding-up, by a petition to the court.

Voluntary Winding-up Resolutions
Under section 84 of the *Insolvency Act 1986*, a company may be wound up voluntarily:

1. When the period, if any, fixed for its duration by the articles expires, or the event, if any, occurs, on the occurrence of which the articles provide that the company is to be dissolved, and the company in general meeting passes a resolution requiring the company to be wound up (in this case an *ordinary resolution* will suffice) or
2. If the company resolves by special resolution that the company be wound up voluntarily; or
3. If the company resolves by *extraordinary resolution* to the effect that it cannot by reason of its liabilities continue its business, and that it is advisable to wind up.

The reason for allowing an extraordinary, instead of a special resolution in the last case is to dispense with the requirement of twenty-one days' notice when the company is insolvent and that winding-up is urgent.

What determines the type of voluntary winding-up is whether or not a *declaration of solvency* can be made by the directors. This is a statement by the majority of them that they have inquired into the company's affairs and have formed the opinion that the company will be able to pay its debts in full together with interest within a specified period not exceeding 12 months from the commencement of the winding-up.

The declaration must be made within the five weeks immediately preceding the date of the passing of the winding-up resolution. The declaration must be filed with the registrar within fifteen days of the passing of the resolution. It must embody an up to date statement of assets and liabilities of the company.

If the declaration is made, the winding up proceeds as a member's voluntary winding up. If the declaration is made by the directors without reasonable grounds, the makers are liable to a fine or imprisonment or both. The fact that after the declaration the company's debts are not paid in full within the stipulated time raises a presumption that it was made by the directors without reasonable grounds. S.89(5).

Members' voluntary winding-up

This is entirely managed by the members and the liquidator is appointed by them. No meeting of creditors is held. Until the liquidator has been appointed the directors cannot exercise their powers without the sanction of the court; except those which relate to the disposal of perishable goods.

If the liquidator is of the opinion that the company will in fact be unable to pay its debts in full in accordance with the declaration of solvency then he must call a creditors meeting within 28 days, giving them 7 days notice by post and advertising it in the Gazette.

The liquidator must lay before the meeting a statement of the affairs of the company. The effect of holding this meeting is that the winding-up proceeds as if a declaration of solvency had not been made i.e. as a creditors' voluntary winding-up. S.96.

Creditors' voluntary winding-up

The company must call a meeting of the creditors for a date not later than 14 days after the passing of the resolution for voluntary winding up. This meeting must also be advertised in the Gazette.

The notice must name the insolvency practitioner who will act.

The business of the meeting is for the creditors:

1. to receive the directors' statement of the company's affairs together with a list of the creditors and the estimated amount of the claims; S.99
2. to appoint a liquidator. S.100
3. to appoint a liquidation committee. S.101.

The effect of a voluntary winding-up

1. As from the date of the passing of the resolution to wind-up, the company must cease to carry on business except so far as is required for beneficial winding-up.
2. No transfer of shares can be made without the sanction of the liquidator.
3. On the appointment of the liquidator the powers of the directors cease except so far as the company in general meeting, the liquidator (in a members' voluntary winding-up) or the creditors or committee of inspection (in a creditors' voluntary winding-up) may sanction their continuance. S.103.

Powers and duties of the liquidator in a voluntary winding-up

1. He can without sanction, commence or defend legal proceedings on behalf of the company.
2. He can carry on the business of the company, so far as it is beneficial for the winding-up.
3. He can exercise all the powers of a liquidator in a compulsory winding-up.
4. He may apply to the court to determine any question arising in the winding-up or to exercise any of the powers

which the court could exercise if the company were being wound up by the court.

In the case of a compulsory winding up, when the affairs of the company have been completely wound up the liquidator may give notice to the Registrar that the final meeting has been held and that the winding-up is complete. Three months after the registration of the notice the company will be automatically dissolved.

In a voluntary winding-up the three months period begins with the registration of the liquidator's final account and returns.

When a company has been dissolved the court may within 12 years make an order declaring the dissolution void.

Individual Insolvency

Voluntary arrangements

Deeds of arrangement

A debtor is sometimes able to make a private arrangement with his creditors known as a deed of arrangement (or assignment) as prescribed by the *Deeds of Arrangement Act 1914*. By such a deed a debtor assigns his property to a trustee as a repesentative of the creditors, and this deed must be distinguished from a scheme or arrangement.

A deed of an arrangement is any instrument, whether under seal or not, made for the benefit of creditors generally or made by an insolvent debtor for the benefit of three or more creditors. It may be

1. An assignment of property.
2. A deed or agreement for a composition; and in cases where the creditors obtain control over the debtor's property.
3. A letter of licence.
4. An agreement for the carrying on or winding up of the debtor's business.

A deed of arrangement will be void unless it is registered at the Department of Trade within seven days after first execution and is properly stamped. A deed for the benefit of creditors generally is also void unless assented to by a majority in number and value of the creditors before or within twenty-one days of registration, and within twenty-eight days of registration a statutory declaration must be filed confirming that the assents have been obtained. Within a further seven days the trustee under the deed must give security unless the creditors dispense with it, and in default the court may declare the deed void or appoint a new trustee.

The problem with a deed of arrangement is that it does not prevent a dissenting creditor from petitioning for a bankruptcy order. A deed of arrangement is outside the bankruptcy provisions. In addition, voluntary arrangements may be made under the *Insolvency Act 1986*.

Composition and Scheme of Arrangement
The debtor may submit a *composition* or a *scheme of arrangement* to a meeting of his creditors. The distinction between a *scheme* and *a composition* is that where a debtor makes over his assets to be administered by a trustee, that is a scheme; but a debtor keeps his assets and undertakes to pay over to the creditors a certain sum, that is a composition: *Re Griffith (1986)*. Any composition or scheme of arrangement must normally offer at least 25p in the £, and must be approved by a majority in number and three-fourths in value of the creditors. Where this is done, the composition or scheme will be considered by the court and if it provides for the payment of the preferential creditors and is one which the court considers reasonable, and calculated to benefit the general body of creditors, the court will sanction it. However, if the debtor fails to pay any instalment due under the scheme, or the scheme cannot, in consequence of legal difficulties or for any sufficient cause, proceed, or where approval of it was obtained by fraud, the scheme may be annulled and the court retains the right to adjudicate without starting bankruptcy proceedings again.

Interim Order

When an individual intends to make a proposal to his creditors on the above lines then an application may be made to the court for an "interim order". The application may be made by the debtor, or, if he is an undischarged bankrupt, by him, the trustee of his estate or the official receiver.

An "interim order" lasts for 14 days in the first instance and its effect is to stay any actions against the debtor and no bankruptcy petition may be presented against him.

An "interim order" will only be made if the court is convinced that the debtor is serious in attempting to reach agreement with his creditors. A nominee, who must be an insolvency practitioner, is appointed and the debtor must give him details of the arrangements he is trying to make.

The petition for a bankruptcy order to be made against the debtor
The petition may be filed by:

1. the debtor himself
2. the supervisor of a voluntary arrangement
3. the Official Petitioner where a criminal bankruptcy order has been made
4. more usually by a creditor who must show:
   a. that he is owed at least £750,
   b. it is a liquidated sum,
   c. it is unsecured,
   d. the debtor is unable to pay the debt.

Inability to pay his debts is proved by the creditor showing

1. that he has served a *statutory demand* on the debtor and it has been ignored for three weeks, or
2. enforcement proceedings in relation to a judgment against the debtor have not been satisfied.

The three weeks may be dispensed with and the petition may be filed earlier if it can be shown that the assets of the debt may be reduced during that petition.

After the presentation of the petition

Any disposition of property or payment of money made after petition has been presented is void if the debtor is eventually adjudged bankrupt, unless the court approves the transaction. If a person has dealings with the debtor after the presentation of the petition and before the granting of the bankruptcy order then that person may be protected if he acted in good faith for value and without notice of the presentation of the petition.

The court can stay any action, execution or legal process against the property or person of the debtor. Also the court may consider it necessary, for the protection of the debtor's estate, to appoint an interim receiver. This will usually be the Official Receiver. He will have all the powers of a receiver and manager appointed by the High Court. He will have power to sell perishable goods and any goods which are likely to diminish in value if not sold.

Bankruptcy Order

It is within the discretion of the court whether or not to make a bankruptcy order. If it does so then it will terminate any interim receivership and the debtor becomes an undischarged bankrupt and loses ownership of his assets.

The Official Receiver becomes the manager of the bankrupt's estate pending the appointment of a trustee in bankruptcy. He can sell perishable goods and goods which will diminish in value if not sold.

The bankrupt must prepare a statement of affairs within 21 days and if he refuses or neglects to do so can be punished for contempt of court.

The Official Receiver can at any time apply to the court for a public examination of the bankrupt.

The Trustee in Bankruptcy

Appointment. The trustee may be appointed by creditors, the court or the Secretary of State. Usually the creditors will appoint. They will do so when the Official Receiver, who commences to act when the bankruptcy order is made, calls a meeting to consider the appointment. The meeting must be called within 12 weeks of his taking office. If the Official Receiver decides not to call a meeting then he will become the trustee in bankruptcy.

The court may appoint as trustee the insolvency practitioner who reported on the debtor's affairs or if the bankruptcy order follows upon a scheme or composition it can appoint the supervisor of the scheme.

If the creditors fail to appoint a trustee then the Secretary of State may do so.

Functions. The trustee must collect, realise and then distribute the assets of the bankrupt. He has all the powers of a receiver appointed by the High Court. He has power to carry on the business of the bankrupt and to mortgage assets to raise money. He also has power to disclaim onerous contracts which are unprofitable and property which is unsaleable.

Control of the trustee. The trustee is subject to the general control of the court. The creditors may also appoint a committee to exercise certain function. The trustee is of course liable for misapplication of the estate, misfeasance or breach of duty and the court has full discretionary powers to order a remedy.

Assets in the bankruptcy

The bankrupt's estate "comprises all property belonging to or vested in the bankrupt at the commencement of the bankruptcy". The bankruptcy commences on the date when the bankruptcy order is made. The bankrupt's tools, books, vehicles and other items used by him in his employment and provisions necessary for the domestic needs of the bankrupt and his family are exempt.

If an income payments order is made then a proportion of the income of the bankrupt will automatically pass to the trustee as in the case of profits of the business.

The trustee succeeds to the bankrupt's property on the "commencement of the bankruptcy". Bankruptcy commences on the day of the bankruptcy order.

Any disposition of property by the bankrupt between the date of presentation of the petition and the date when the bankrupt's estate vests in the trustee in bankruptcy is void.

However persons who took property or money from the bankrupt before the date of the bankruptcy order in good faith, for value and without notice of the presentation of the petition may be allowed to keep these transfers.

Persons who took property from the bankrupt after the bankruptcy order are given no protection and will have to appeal to the court.

Family homes

The *Matrimonial Homes Act 1983* gives a right to a spouse who is not the legal owner of the matrimonial home to register a charge on the home which cannot be upset except by an order of the court. This situation is accepted by the *Insolvency Act* and application must be made to the court if it is desired to realise the bankrupt's interest in the home.

Duration of Bankruptcy

In the majority of cases bankruptcy will end automatically after 3 years have elapsed since the bankruptcy order was made. The Official Receiver can inform the court that the bankrupt has failed to comply with his obligations and the court may order that the time under the 3 year period shall stop running.

Where the bankrupt has been an undischarged bankrupt within 15 years before his current bankruptcy he will not be discharged automatically but must apply to the court for discharge after 5 years have elapsed.

Principles common to corporate and individual insolvency

1. It is a well founded principle of insolvency law that all creditors must be treated equally or pari passu.

   Exceptions to this rule are

   1. preferential creditors are paid out in preference to ordinary creditors
   2. secured creditors also get priority.

Any contractual arrangement for a creditor e.g. a bank to receive priority would be unacceptable but non-contractual rights such as a right of combination or lien will be unaffected.

British Eagle International Airlines Ltd v Compagnie Nationale Air France (1975)

2. It is important to consider the effect upon a bank account of the presentation of a petition to make an individual bankrupt or for a company to be wound up. In this connection Sections 127 and 284 are of importance.

Section 127 provides that "In a winding-up by the court any disposition of the company's property and any transfer of shares, or alteration in the status of the company's members made after the commencement of the winding-up is, unless the Court otherwise orders, void".

The effect of this section is that cheques paid out of an account in credit may have to be refunded to the liquidator and cheques paid into an overdrawn account may have to be returned to the liquidator. Also debts in an overdrawn account arising after the date of the petition would cause an increase in the debt owed to the bank which the bank could not prove.

Thus, once a winding up petition has been presented against a company the bank must stop the account. *Re Grays Inn Construction Co Ltd (1980)*.

More recent cases include *Re Tramway Building and Construction Co Ltd (1988)* and *Re Pressdee Ltd (1985)*.

In the cases of an individual insolvency *Section 284* will apply. The effect of this section is similar to that of section 127. It provides that any payment to a bank, after the presentation of the petition, shall be held by the bank for the trustee unless it can show that it acted in good faith, a transaction took place for value, and had no notice that the petition had been presented.

Once the bank becomes aware of a bankruptcy petition, it should stop the account and allow no further payments to be made from it: Sometimes it may be possible for the liquidator or trustee in bankruptcy to recover money or property transferred to third parties. This situation may arise because the bankrupt or company has been involved in a transaction at an undervalue, a fraudulent transaction or a preference. See items 3, 4 and 5.

3. Transaction at an undervalue

This will arise where the debtor has transferred property and has either received no consideration for it or the consideration was less than the market value of the property. It also arises where the debtor has entered into a transaction in consideration of marriage. Liability will arise from the fact of the transaction and the state of the debtor's mind will be irrelevant.

The period during which transactions at an undervalue may be avoided by the trustee in bankruptcy is 5 years before the presentation of the petition for a bankruptcy order.

If the trustee can "avoid" a transaction it means that the trustee can recover the property from the person who acquired it. The bankrupt must have been insolvent at the time of the transaction. Transactions within 2 years of the petition are affected irrespective of the bankrupt's insolvency. Also, if an "associate" is involved, insolvency is presumed. If any property is transferred at an undervalue during the relevant periods, it may be recovered by the trustee.

An associate includes spouses and other relatives, partners etc. The same principles apply in the case of companies and transactions at an undervalue may be avoided by the liquidator. However, where a company is concerned the basic period is 2 years and not 5 years before the relevant time and in the case of a company this is the date of the presentation of the petition (compulsory winding up) or the date of the resolution (voluntary winding up).

4. Preferences

These arise if the debtor does anything which results in the creditor being in a better position, in the event of a bankruptcy of the debtor, than he would have been in if that things had not been done. The periods during which the preference transactions must have occurred are:

1. if the transaction is not at an undervalue and is entered into with an associate of the debtor – *2 years* before the presentation of the petition. (An associate is the bankrupt's spouse or former or reputed spouse and any brother, sister, uncle, aunt, nephew or niece of them) or
2. if the person preferred is not an associate and the transaction is not at an undervalue – 6 months before the presentation of the petition.

The same periods apply in the case of a company.

For a transaction to amount to a preference there must have been the intention on the part of the debtor to improve the position of the recipient of the preference.

Also the debtor must have been insolvent at the time of the transaction. Insolvency is defined as "where the debtor was unable to pay his debts as they fell due; or where the value of the debtor's assets was less than his liabilities, including contingent and prospective liabilities."

The recipient of the preference may not always be a creditor who receives payment but may sometimes be a bank to which the debtor makes payment, not to favour the bank, but to favour the guarantor of his debt. However the bank may be protected so long as it received the benefit in good faith, for value and without notice of the relevant circumstances.

Where a bank is involved in a possible preference transaction it will be protected

1. If it received payment in good faith and for value and without notice of bankruptcy proceedings.
2. If the bank has to repay a credit received, the court may permit it to retain the security.
3. In practice a bank will include a clause in its security forms allowing it to retain the security until the danger of preference has disappeared.

Re. KM Kushler (1943)
In practice banks will usually include a clause in their security documents by which they will be allowed to keep the security until the danger of preference has disappeared.

The periods which apply are 6 months in the case of an ordinary guarantee but 24 months if the guarantee was given by a spouse, partner or company with which the customer was connected.

In the case of preferences as in undervalues the court may make an order, the effect of which will be to put the parties back to their original positions which they occupied before the transaction.

Preferences are not prohibited unless the individual is insolvent at the time of the transaction or becomes insolvent because of it.

5. **Fraudulent transactions**

Sometimes a transaction may be at an undervalue and is made with the intention of putting the assets beyond the reach of actual or potential claimants. Undervalue has the normal meaning of the word mentioned above. However a fraudulent undervalue has no restriction as to when it is made and so the periods which are relevant to an ordinary undervalue transaction do not apply to a fraudulent undervalue. *Insolvency Act 1986* Ss.423–425.

Realisation and Distribution of Assets

When it is desired to realise any security of an individual or of a company it may become necessary for a person to be appointed to deal with the business of realising the assets and distributing the proceeds amongst the debenture holders or creditors. Under the Act, there are a number of "office holders" who may act in connection with an insolvent company. These include an *administrator* appointed under an administration order, a *liquidator* whether under a compulsory or voluntary winding-up and an *administrative receiver* under a floating charge. The

Insolvency Act 1986 allows the court to order anyone who holds information or has records concerning the company to produce these to the "office holder". Clearly, this could affect the bank. Similar powers may also be obtained by the trustee in a personal bankruptcy.

Where individuals are concerned a receiver will only be appointed if it is desired to realise land. The power to appoint a receiver will arise and become exercisable in the same way as the power of sale. In practice an individual will probably only consider appointing a receiver if the land has been leased and it is considered that the proper course is to defer selling the land, and to continue to receive the rents.

Such rents collected by the receiver must be applied by him in:

1. discharge of expenses in connection with the property such as taxes and rates.
2. payment of interest on prior incumbrances.
3. payment of insurance premiums.
4. payment of repairs and his own commission.
5. payment of interest under the mortgage.
6. discharge of the principal debt.

More commonly a receiver will be appointed by a bank when it is owed money by a company or by an individual. The bank will have such power conferred in its debenture form. The receiver may realise the security whether or not a liquidation or bankruptcy has occurred.

Administrative Receiver

The receiver appointed under a floating charge is called an administrative receiver if the charge covers the whole of the company's property. He must be an insolvency practitioner.

If an application is made for the appointment by the court of an administrator under the *Insolvency Act 1986 S.9* then the court will give notice of this application to any holder of a floating charge. If the court is satisfied that an administrative receiver is in office it shall dismiss the application to appoint an administrator. If the creditor has not appointed an administrative receiver then he will have 5 days in which to do so. If he does not do so within that period the court will make an administration order.

The effect of the administration order is that the creditor may be prevented from realising his security. The creditor will not be deprived of his security rights but may only receive the proceeds when the security has been realised. Once an administrator is appointed no debenture holder can realise his security except with the court's consent. An administrator must consider the interests of the company and of the general creditors.

For this reason a creditor will in future usually take a floating charge so that it will be in a position to appoint an administrative receiver. The creditor will then be able to realise its security if he wishes.

Within 3 months of appointment the administrator must produce proposals for the creditors and if he fails to do so the administration order will lapse.

A receiver may be appointed by the creditor under the power conferred on it by the debenture form. He must be appointed in writing not necessarily under seal. The appointment takes effect when it is received by the receiver who must accept by the end of the following business day and the acceptance must be confirmed within 7 days.

After appointment the receiver must notify the company and the creditors within 28 days. The debenture holder must notify the Registrar of companies within 7 days and a note is made in the register of charges.

As stated earlier, a receiver appointed under a floating charge is an administrative receiver and is merely a receiver under a fixed charge.

A receiver is the agent of the company and so can bind the company by his transactions. However he is also personally liable on contracts he makes. He must have regard for the interests of the company and when selling the assets he must take reasonable care to get the best price available *Cuckmere Brick Co. Ltd. v Mutual Finance Ltd. (1971)*.

The powers of an administrative receiver are contained in the *Insolvency Act 1986* (Part III) and include the making of reports and the calling of creditors' meetings.

The order in which the disposition of assets is to take place follows that used by a liquidator i.e.

1. The rightful owners of the property.
2. Costs and expenses.
3. Holders of fixed charges.
4. Preferential creditors.
5. Holders of floating charges.
6. Unsecured creditors.
7. Any surplus for the members of the company.

It very often happens that soon after a receiver has been appointed a liquidator is appointed to wind up the company. When that occurs the receiver's powers cease. He ceases to be the agent of the company but he does not automatically become agent of the debenture holder.

Distribution of the Assets

To prove a debt means to claim for it in a bankruptcy or winding up proceeding. Debts which may be claimed are said to be provable and they are

1. Debts which existed before the date of the bankruptcy order/winding up order.
2. Debts for which the debtor may become liable because of an obligation incurred before the commencement of the bankruptcy/winding up.
3. The interest on a debt but that does not apply to interest payable after commencement of the bankruptcy/winding up.
4. Amounts specified in a criminal bankruptcy order.

The first three of these apply to companies and individuals alike. The last one only to individuals.

Order of application of assets in payment of debts

Once the liquidator/trustee has "collected" in all the property of the bankrupt or company he must proceed to pay those creditors who are entitled to be paid.

Secured creditors

The respective rights of secured and unsecured creditors must be maintained.

A secured creditor is one who has some mortgage, charge or lien on the debtor's property. In order that the respective rights of secured and unsecured creditors may be maintained secured creditors are allowed to rely primarily on their security for payment. In this respect they have four clear choices:

1. they may rest entirely on their security and not prove in the bankruptcy or winding up at all; or
2. they may realise their security and prove only for the deficiency; or
3. they may value it and prove for the deficiency, after deduction of the assessed value, in which case the liquidator/trustee may redeem the security at such assessed value; or
4. they may surrender the security to the liquidator/trustee and prove for the whole debt in the winding up or bankruptcy.

Once a secured creditor has exhausted his rights against his security, any balance of the debt owed to him is owed to him as an ordinary unsecured creditor.

As soon as the above considerations are disposed of, the liquidator/trustee can proceed to make actual payments to unsecured creditors in the following order.

1. Costs, charges and expenses properly incurred in the winding up/bankruptcy, including the remuneration of the liquidator/trustee.
2. Preferential debts

    a. Deductions from wages which should have been made under the PAYE scheme in the 12 months

before the relevant date or the date of the making of the winding up/bankruptcy order.
b. Value added tax payable in the 6 months before the relevant date.
c. Social security contributions for 12 months before the relevant date.
d. State and occupational pension scheme contributions which the debtor should have made.
e. Employees' arrears of wages for 4 months before the relevant date up to a maximum of £800 per employee.

   Loans made for the payment of wages would be included here, consequently a bank which lends money for this purpose would be treated as a preferential creditor.

The "relevant date" in a compulsory winding up means, when a provisional liquidator was appointed, the date of his appointment; otherwise it means the date of the winding up order. In the case of a voluntary winding up the date of the passing of the resolution for winding up. Schedule 19 *Companies Act 1985.*

3. Holders of floating charges. These rank behind the preferential creditors even though the floating charge crystallises before liquidation. This provision only applies to companies.
4. Ordinary unsecured creditors: If after payment of the preferential creditors in full, there are still funds left, the next class of creditors to be paid is the ordinary unsecured creditors. They also rank equally amongst themselves and abate *pari passu* if the company's/individual's assets are insufficient.
5. Interest on debts since the bankruptcy/winding up commenced.
6. Non-provable debts: In the unlikely event that the liquidator is able to pay all the above creditors in full, and if there are still assets available, he must then pay the debts which are normally not provable in winding up, such as unliquidated damages in tort. This is because, in

such a case, the company is solvent and by section 611, *Companies Act 1985*, all debts may be proved.
7. If after paying the above, there is still some money left, it goes to the members of the company according to their rights in a winding up. Sometimes preference shareholders take the capital in preference to ordinary shareholders.

The order of priority in the case of an individual is the same, except that "floating charges" do not apply and any assets remaining after "interest on debts" has been paid goes to pay any debts owed to the bankrupt's spouse. Finally any surplus is returned to the bankrupt.

Wages Accounts
In 2(e) above we have seen that arrears of wages rank as a preferential debt. By subrogation this privilege applies also to persons who have made advances for the purposes of paying the wages. The person who lent the money shall rank as a preferential creditor to the extent that the employee would rank as a preferential creditor i.e. £800 per employee.

A person (company, partnership or sole trader) which is borrowing from a bank for the payment of wages is often requested to open a special wages account to which all cheques for salaries and wages may be debited. It becomes essential therefore for bankers and the borrowers to know precisely what payments may be debited to the wages account with a view to obtaining preferential treatment.

It is not legally necessary to open a separate wages account to establish a preferential claim – *Re Rampgill Mill Ltd. (1967)* however the advantages of doing so are:

1. it avoids disputes as to the reason for borrowing money.
2. it avoids the operation of the "Rule in Clayton's case".

If a bank has a preferential and a non-preferential debt then any money it receives it would obviously wish to appropriate to the non-preferential debt so as to keep the preferential debt as large as possible to be proved in the winding up.

In *Re Unit 2 Windows Ltd. (1985)* the court held that the correct solution was to apply the money received proportionately between the preferential debt and the non-preferential debt.

All preferential payments rank equally among themselves and must be paid in full *in priority* to all other debts. If there are insufficient funds to pay them in full they abate proportionately.

Part 4

International

Finally in Part 4 we look at the international aspects of commercial law. In particular we must consider the effect of our membership of the European Community.

It is of the most vital importance that every businessperson should have some knowledge of European Law so that at least he/she is able to decide whether any particular business situation has a European aspect.

Chapter Twenty-One
European Community Law

After two devastating conflicts in Europe within a period of twenty years there was a general desire in 1945 for some type of organisation that might prevent any repetition of the horrors of war.

A series of Treaties was entered into with the purpose of establishing some form of co-operation between States.

In 1951 the Treaty of Paris created the European Coal and Steel Community (ECSC) which was concerned with creating a single market in coal and steel. The signatories to the Treaty were Belgium, France, Germany, Italy, Luxembourg and the Netherlands.

In 1957 a Treaty of Rome brought in to being the European Atomic Energy Community (EURATOM) and again the signatories were Belgium, France, Germany, Italy, Luxembourg and the Netherlands. However also in 1957 in Rome the European Economic Community Treaty was signed and it is this Treaty that we are concerned with when we speak of the primary source of Community Law.

Thus after 1957 there were three European Communities, the European Coal and Steel Community (ECSC), the European Atomic Energy Community (EURATOM) and the European Economic Community (EEC). Each of these communities had its own interests but obviously the EEC had wider interests than the other two. Each community had its own institutions until 1965 when the Merger Treaty was passed. From that date there was one Council, and one Commission for all three communities. Prior to 1965 only the Assembly and the Court of Justice were common to all communities.

In 1973 the United Kingdom, Denmark and Eire joined the

Community. In the United Kingdom this was achieved by Parliament passing the *European Communities Act 1972*.

In 1979 Greece joined and in 1986 Spain and Portugal followed.

The need for some type of co-operation to prevent future conflicts was expressed in the preamble to the ECSC Treaty where it was stated that it was necessary "to substitute for age old rivalries a merging of essential interests; to create, by establishing an economic community, the basis for a broader and deeper community among peoples long divided by bloody conflicts; and to lay the foundations for institutions which will give direction to a destiny hence-forward shared."

These aims eventually became wider and involved other forms of economic activity.

Single European Act
Although originally the concept was for various forms of economic co-operation, gradually these aims were widened until in 1986 the *Single European Act* was signed by the twelve participating States.

This Act added further goals e.g. of economic and monetary co-operation, health and safety of workers, research and technological development, environmental and consumer protection and co-operation in the field of foreign policy. In addition by late 1985 it had become apparent that the community's seven year timetable for abolition of barriers to movement and trade within the community was running late. There were 300 detailed decisions which the Council had agreed must be made before 1992. The reason for the delay was the requirement that every agreement in the Council of Ministers must be unanimous. Eventually therefore it was decided that the Treaty of Rome should be amended by substituting majority voting for unanimity in certain areas. The whole question of majority voting versus unanimity is a serious stumbling block to any further progress in the community because if majority voting were to be allowed then certain States would not be able to get their own way. In this connection what is known as the Luxembourg compromise was adopted and in effect this gives any Member State a right of veto if its "vital national interests" are at stake.

Court of First Instance
In addition the *Single European Act* provided for the setting up of a new court known as the Court of First Instance (CFI). The court commenced operations on September 1st 1989 and its jurisdiction is confined (a) to disputes between the Community and its servants. These are called "Staff cases". (b) cases involving EC competition law and applications for judicial review and (c) damages in respect of certain matters within the authority of the European Coal and Steel Community.

There is a right of appeal on matters of law from the Court of First Instance to the Court of Justice.

Principles on which the Community is based

Article 2 sets out the aims of the EEC as being to promote "throughout the Community a harmonious development of economic activities, a continuous and balanced expansion, an increase in stability, an accelerated raising of the standard of living and closer relations between the States belonging to it".

These aims are to be achieved by establishing "a Common Market and progressively approximating the economic development of member States".

In greater detail Article 3 enumerates the activities of the Community which will bring about not only a considerable uniformity of the economic systems of the member States, but will also establish the Community as a unit in the world market. These activities include:

a. the elimination, as between member States, of custom duties and of quantitative restrictions on the import and export of goods, and of all other measures having equivalent effect.
b. the establishment of a common tariff and of a common commercial policy towards third countries.
c. the abolition, as between member States, of obstacles to freedom of movement of persons, services and capital.

d. the adoption of common policy in the sphere of agriculture.
e. the adoption of a common policy in the sphere of transport.
f. the institution of a system ensuring that competition in the Common Market is not distorted.
g. the application of procedures by which the economic policies of member States can be co-ordinated and disequilibria in their balance of payments remedied.
h. the approximation of the laws of member States to the extent required for the proper functioning of the Common Market.
i. the creation of a European Social Fund in order to improve employment opportunities for workers and to contribute to the raising of their standard of living.
j. the establishment of a European Investment Bank to facilitate the economic expansion of the Community by opening up fresh resources.
k. the association of the overseas countries and territories in order to increase trade and to promote jointly economic and social development.

Thus it can be seen that the foundations of the economic community laid down in the Treaty include

1. Free movement of goods, which in effect transforms the Community into a customs union to be achieved through the elimination of customs duties between member States.
2. A common agricultural policy. (C.A.P.).
3. Free movement of persons, services and capital based on the right of establishment and non discrimination.
4. A common transport policy.

In addition to the objectives stated in the Treaty of Rome the Single European Act 1986 added the further goals of economic and monetary co-operation, Health and Safety of Workers, Research and Technological Development, Environmental and Consumer Protection and co-operation in the field of Foreign Policy. In order to enable the Community to carry out the activities stated in Article 3 of the Treaty of Rome Article 4 provides that certain Institutions shall be established.

The Institutions of the EEC

Every organisation is run according to rules or law. In each organisation there must be a body which proposes new laws or changes to existing law, a body to pass the laws – a legislature, a body to apply the laws and finally a body to act in the event of disputes arising.

In the United Kingdom the proposing body is the Cabinet. The body which passes laws is called Parliament consisting of the House of Commons, the House of Lords and the Queen. The body which applies the laws is the Civil Service and in the event of any dispute arising these will be resolved by the Courts of Law.

Some countries have a written constitution and in that case this written constitution is supreme and must be interpreted by the Supreme Court of the particular state.

As far as the EEC is concerned then there are similar institutions to those mentioned but their functions are not entirely identical with those stated above.

Article 4 of the Treaty provides that there shall be: an Assembly – now called the European Parliament, since the passing of the Single European Act

The Council
The Commission
The Court of Justice

Article 4 also provides for the setting up of an Economic and Social Committee and a Court of Auditors.

The Merger Treaty provides for the creation of a Committee of Permanent Representatives of the member States (COREPER).

The European Parliament

Unlike the Parliament of the United Kingdom the European

Parliament does not make laws. Its functions are advisory and supervisory.

It consists of 518 members. France, Germany, Italy and the United Kingdom have 81 representatives, Spain 60, the Netherlands 25, Belgium, Greece and Portugal 24, Denmark 16, Ireland 15 and Luxembourg 6. The Members of the European Parliament (MEP) sit not as national delegates but they divide themselves into broad party groupings irrespective of the State from which they come. Parliament is not permanently in session but meets 5 days once a month except in August. Its meetings are now held in Strasbourg. Originally they were divided between Strasbourg and Luxembourg but owing to the lack of facilities available in Luxembourg their meetings are now held in Strasbourg although the headquarters still remain in Luxembourg. As will be seen later the Commission prepares proposals for new laws but usually consults Parliament during their preparation. The Treaties also require that Parliament be consulted (along with the Economic and Social Committee) by the Council.

In its supervisory role Parliament can now call on both the Commission and the Council to account for their actions by putting questions to both Institutions and by requiring them to defend their actions before sessions of Parliament. Furthermore individual commissioners and the President of the Council of Ministers may be questioned in detail by members of Parliament. Finally, Parliament has gradually increased its powers in one area namely that of the budget. Even so its powers are not particularly significant although it does have power to accept or reject the budget as a whole.

The *Single European Act 1976* has introduced a co-operation procedure that applies to qualified majority decisions that bear on the internal market, social policy, economic and social cohesion and research. The procedure can be summarised as follows:

1. The Council, on a proposal from the Commission and after obtaining the opinion of Parliament, adopts a common position. This is then referred to Parliament

which has three months in which to endorse it (expressly or implicitly), reject it or amend it. The Commission has one month in which to decide whether or not to accept any amendments proposed by Parliament.
2. The Council then proceeds to a second reading.
3. If Parliament has rejected the Council's "common position" unanimity is required. If Parliament has proposed amendments, the Council votes by qualified majority where the Commission has endorsed them and unanimously where the Commission has been unable to do so.
4. If the Council fails to reach a decision within three months, the Commission proposal is deemed not to have been adopted.

While the Commission remains the driving force behind the drafting of legislation, this procedure gives Parliament a direct influence on decisions, even though the final word still rests with the Council.

The Council of Ministers
The Council is the Community's decision making body. The membership of the Council fluctuates according to the matters with which the Council is dealing. Thus the Council of Ministers may consist of Ministers of Agriculture, Finance, Social Affairs and so on. Where the matter under discussion is a high level policy matter then the Council may consist of Heads of State. It is then named the European Council. It received formal recognition in the Single European Act and is required to meet at least twice a year.

Article 2 of the *Single European Act* stipulates "The European Council shall bring together the Heads of State or of Government of the member States and the President of the Commission of the European Communities. They shall be assisted by the Ministers for Foreign Affairs and by a member of the Commission. The European Council shall meet at least twice a year." The most recent meeting has been that which took place in Maastricht in December 1991. The purpose of the European Council, consisting as it does of Heads of Government and the

President of France, is to give renewed political impetus to the Community. It limits itself to deciding matters of policy and is not a law making body as is the Council of Ministers.

As the Council of Ministers is not a permanent body much of the work of the Council has been taken over by the Committee of Permanent Representatives (COREPER) (Comité des Representants Permanents). COREPER is the administrative arm of the Council and is in two parts, one composed of the Permanent Representatives who are high level civil-servants with ambassador rank and the other of ambassadors to the Community. If an agreement on community policy is reached at COREPER level then it will be formally ratified by national ministers in the Council without discussion by them. Whenever possible less contentious issues are resolved at the level of COREPER and are then passed on to the Council of Ministers as an "A" point for formal agreement without discussion. The Committee of Permanent Representatives is either COREPER 1 in the case of deputies or COREPER 2 in the case of ambassadors.

The Council and the Commission must work closely together because the latter can propose but the Council must decide.

Since the Council has the power of decision then the methods of voting to be used are crucial. Article 148 of the Treaty provides that if voting is not unanimous then it may be by simple majority or by qualified majority.

Qualified majority is a system of weighted voting and each State's vote is weighted in proportion to its size and importance. Under this formula the United Kingdom, France, Italy and West Germany each have 10 votes, Spain has 8 votes, Belgium, Greece, Holland and Portugal each have 5, Denmark and Ireland have 3 and Luxembourg 2 votes. Out of a total of 76 votes, 54 are now required for a qualified majority. Thus the United Kingdom will require the support of at least 2 other States to provide the 23 votes to block any legislation it objects to.

Majority voting has been on the increase and has been given encouragement by the passing of the *Single European Act*. Decisions of major importance however are likely to continue to be taken on the basis of unanimity. Tax matters, measures relating to the free movement of persons and to the rights and interests of employed persons and measures relating to professional training and standards all now require a unanimous vote. However even though a larger number of matters can now be decided by a majority vote, the Luxembourg compromise still remains effective. This means that the "veto" will remain if "vital national interests" seem to be under attack. This is, in truth, really a commentary on the main problem facing the European Community which is to what extent each member State is willing to give up some or all of its sovereignty.

The Commission

The Commission is an unusual organisation to British eyes. It appears to be the civil service of the European Community but on the other hand has much more power than our civil service. On the other hand the Commission has no power to legislate, that remains with the Council of Ministers.

The Commission can only formulate policy in the main but can sometimes make legislation under powers delegated to it by the Council. This arises in competition matters.

In the Commission there are 17 commissioners and they act as a college. All 17 must agree upon any proposal before it can be sent to the council. The college is headed by a president and at present there are 6 vice presidents. The present President of the Commission is Jacques Delors.

Each commissioner is responsible for one or more portfolios and each of these portfolios is administered by a Directorate General at the head of which is a Director General. The Directorates General (DGs) are as follows:

DGI   External Relations
DGII Economic and Financial Affairs
DGIII Internal Market and Industrial Affairs
DGIV Competition
DGV   Employment, Industrial Relationships and Social Affairs
DGVI Agriculture

DGVII Transport
DGVIII Development
DGIX Personnel and Administration
DGX Information, Communication and Culture
DGXI Environment, Nuclear Safety and Civil Protection
DGXII Science, Research and Development Joint Research Centre
DGXIII Telecommunication, Information Industries and Innovation
DGXIV Fisheries
DGXV Financial Institutions and Company Law
DGXVI Regional Policies
DGXVII Energy
DGXVIII Credit and Investments
DGXIX Budgets
DGXX Financial Control
DGXXI Customs Union and Indirect Taxation
DGXXII Co-ordination of Structural Policies
DGXXIII Enterprises Policy, Distributive Trades, Tourism and Social Economy

President Jacques Delors has said that a commission official has six professions;

1. To innovate, as the needs of the Community change.
2. To be a law maker, preparing the legal texts needed for Community decisions.
3. To manage the growing number of Community policies.
4. To control respect for Community decisions at all levels.
5. To negotiate constantly with all the different actors in the Community process.
6. To be a diplomat in order to be successful in the five other professions.

From this it can be seen that the Commission has the responsibility of acting as the power house for the Community. It prepares action programmes in consultation with all other interested parties. Any one commissioner must of course consult with his fellow commissioners in preparing any proposals. Apart from acting as the power house of Community work, the Commission must ensure that the rules promulgated by the community are adhered to. In order to do this the Commission has powers of its own. In the case of the day to day operation of major policies such as the Common Market, the Common Agricultural Policy and the rules of Fair Trade in Competition then the Commission has a direct role and these will be considered later when we look at these particular areas of interest.

The Commission is a very important part of the Institutions of the European Community and it has three main functions:

1. To act as initiator or promoter of Community action.
2. To act as the watch dog of the Community. In this connection it has a number of investigative powers.
3. The Commission functions as the executive of the Community and once a policy decision has been taken by the Council of Ministers then the detailed implementation of that policy, which may require further legislation, will fall to the Commission.

The European Court of Justice

The Court of Justice sits in Luxembourg and its function is to ensure that in the interpretation and application of the Treaty of Rome the Law is observed. The ECJ is a permanent Institution consisting of 13 judges, 1 nominated by each member State, plus 1 additional judge. The President of the Court is elected from among their number by the judges themselves. The decisions of the Court are taken in secret by simple majority and no dissenting opinion is published.

Advocates General
In addition to the judges there are 6 Advocates General for whom there is no real equivalent in English Law. Their job is to sum up in public the case before the court and to give an expert legal opinion before the judges make their ruling.

The Advocates General have the same qualifications as the judges and they represent neither party. They act on behalf of the Law and Justice. They deliver their opinions to the Court and in the majoriy of cases the Court accepts their conclusions. The Court is not, of course, bound by their opinions and gives a "collegiate decision". If that differs from that of the Advocate General than that would be a dissenting opinion.

Thus it can be seen that the practices and procedures used in the Court of Justice are taken from Continental models. However in developing a substantive rule the Court draws on principles and traditions from all the member States.

Lord Diplock stated in *R v Henn (1981)*, "The European Court, in contrast to English Courts, applies teleological rather than historical methods to the interpretation of the Treaties and other Community legislation. It seeks to give effect to what it conceives to be the spirit rather than the letter of the Treaties; sometimes, indeed, to an English judge, it may seem to the exclusion of the letter. It views the Communities as living and expanding organisms and the interpretation of the provisions of the Treaties as changing to match their growth."

It should be noted that the European Court does not consider itself bound by precedent as is the case in the English legal system. The European Court seeks to achieve consistency in its judgments but remains free to depart from previous decisions in the light of new facts. Finally the European Court of Justice in Luxembourg should not be confused with the Court of Human Rights in Strasbourg or the International Court at the Hague. The former deals obviously with a very specific aspect of the human situation and the International Court is concerned where disputes arise between States.

The above are the main four Institutions of the European Community. In addition however there are a number of other sometimes informal groupings. The Economic and Social Consultative Assembly acts in a consultative capacity to the Community when decisions are being taken. The members of this assembly are appointed by the Council and represent a variety of different interests such as farmers, trade unionists and members of the general public. Where the Treaty requires consultation to be taken then it is an essential requirement that any matter must be referred to this Economic and Social Consultative Assembly.

The Court of Auditors was established in 1975 and the purpose of this body is to scrutinise the financial operations of the Community.

Chapter Twenty-Two

Sources and Application of Community Law

European Community Law may be found in:
1. The Constitutional Treaties e.g. the Treaty of Rome and the Single European Act.
2. Legislation – Community legislation has to be published in the Official Journal of the European Communities before it may come in to force.
3. Case Law – the judgments of the European Court of Justice are published by the court itself in European Court Reports.
4. International Treaties – all treaties entered into by the Community are published in the Official Journal.

So, laws are primarily made by the European Council of Ministers or they may be found in the decisions of the Court of Justice.

As regards the Council of Ministers Article 189 of the Treaty of Rome states "In order to carry out their task the Council and Commission shall, in accordance with the provisions of this Treaty, make Regulations, issue directives, take decisions, make recommendations or deliver opinions."

Regulations

The Treaty of Rome states "A regulation shall have general application. It shall be binding in its entirety and directly applicable in all member States." Thus a regulation does not require further implementation by a member State in order for it to take effect. It gives rise to rights and obligations for states and individuals as it stands.

Article 191 provides "Regulations shall be published in the

official journal of the Community. They shall enter into force on the date specified in them or, in the absence thereof, on the twentieth day following their publication.

Directives and decisions shall be notified to those to whom they are addressed and shall take effect upon such notification."

It may be that the direct effect of a regulation is not automatic. It could be that a provision in a regulation is conditional or not sufficiently precise or it may require further implementation before it can take full legal effect.

Directives

The Act provides (Article 189) that "A directive shall be binding, as to the result to be achieved, upon each member State to which it is addressed, but shall leave to the national authorities a choice of form and methods."

Thus a directive does not become binding on the citizen until his Government or Parliament has transformed it into national law. Thus the European product liability directive of the 25th July 1985 became immediately effective when it was published in the Official Journal. It was left to the individual member States to enact a similar piece of legislation and this occurred in the United Kingdom in the *Consumer Protection Act 1987*. A difficulty that may arise with a directive is – what is the position if a member State fails to implement a directive of the Community or does so inadequately?

The point was raised in *Grad v Finanzamt Traunstein (9/70)*. In that case the court stated that both directives and decisions are directly effective provided they are clear and precise, unconditional and leave no room for discretion in implementation.

Before a person can rely upon Community legislation it must have "direct effect". In other words it must create directly effective rights which individuals can enforce against a member State or against other individuals. Such Community rights must be enforced by the courts and override any existing or subsequent national laws to the contrary.

The test of direct effect is:-
The provision must impose on the member State:
1. A clear and precise obligation.
2. It must be unconditional i.e. not accompanied by any reservation.
3. The application of the Community rule must not be conditional on any subsequent legislation whether of the Community Institutions or of the member States; and must not lead to the latter having an effective power of discretionary judgment as to the application of the rule in question. (i.e. the provision must be "directly applicable" in the sense of not needing implementing legislation).

However a directive cannot be directly effective before the time limit for implementation has expired. In *Publico Ministero v Ratti (148/78)* the Court of Justice held that as the time limit for the implementation of one of the directives on which Mr Ratti sought to rely had not expired it was not directly effective. He could however rely on the other directive for which the implementation date had passed.

So even if a directive is strictly not "directly applicable" it is intended to apply to the member States once the implementing procedure has been followed. Directives are published and in any case states are obliged by Article 5 of the Treaty of Rome "to take all appropriate measures – to ensure fulfilment of the obligations arising out of this Treaty or resulting from action taken by the Institutions of the Community."

Vertical and Horizontal Effect
If a State has not implemented a directive why should it not be answerable to the litigant? This is known as the *vertical effect*.

On the other hand can an individual invoke against another individual a directive which has not been implemented? This is the *horizontal effect*.

In *Marshall v Southampton & South West Hampshire Area Health Authority (Teaching) (152/84)* the question of horizontal and vertical effects was discussed. In Marshall's case she was challenging the Health Authority's compulsory age of 65 for men and 60 the women as discriminatory, in breach of the equal treatment directive 76/207. The difference in age was permissible under the *Sex Discrimination Act 1975*, was it also in breach of directive 76/207? Could directive 76/207 could be relied on by Mrs Marshall?

The European Court of Justice held that the different compulsory retirement age was in breach of directive 76/207 and could be invoked against the Area Health Authority. On the other hand since a directive is binding only on each member State to which it is addressed then it follows that a directive may not of itself impose obligations on an individual and that a provision of a directive may not be relied upon as such against such a person. The court went on to say that if this distinction was arbitrary and unfair then it could easily be avoided if the member State concerned has correctly implemented the directive in national law. It does seem therefore that Marshall's case has put an end to the dispute concerning vertical and horizontal effects and has stated that a directive which has not been implemented will only have a vertical effect and cannot therefore be used by one individual against another (horizontal effect).

Problems still remained after the Marshall case in particular as to the interpretation of "public body" or "agency of the state". It would appear that where a member State has neglected to implement a directive or has inadequately done so then an individual will be unable to invoke the directive in the context of a private claim. In two cases which were decided before the Marshall case i.e. *Von Colson v Land Nordrhein-Westfalen (14/83)* and *Harz v Deutsche Tradex Gmb H (79/83)* there were claims by the litigants that they had been unfairly treated contrary to the equal treatment directive 76/207.

The Von Colson Principle
In the Von Colson case the decision of the court did not focus on the vertical or horizontal effects of the directive but turned to Article 5 of the EEC Treaty. Article 5 requires States to "take all appropriate measures" to ensure fulfilment of their Com-

munity obligations. The ECJ stated that this applied to all authorities of the member States including the courts. Thus it expected the courts to interpret national law so as to ensure that the objectives of the directive could be achieved. The result of this approach is that although Community law may not apply directly, in other words it is not directly effective – it may still be applied indirectly as domestic law by means of interpretation. This principle is known as the *Von Colson Principle*.

This principle has been discussed in the courts of the United Kingdom in a few cases. The latest view of the House of Lords is in *Litster v Forth Dry Docks Engineering Co. Ltd (1989)*. This concerned a private claim against an employer based on directive 77/187 which safeguards employee's rights in the event of a transfer of undertakings. The House of Lords in that case was prepared to interpret a domestic regulation in such a way as to comply with a directive as interpreted by the Court of Justice. It did this because the domestic regulation had been introduced for the purpose of complying with the directive. Thus the situation seems to be that where domestic legislation has been introduced for the purpose of complying with a Community directive the courts of the United Kingdom have a duty following Litster to apply the Von Colson principle and to construe domestic law so as to comply with EC Law.

Finally a limit to the Von Colson principle occurs where criminal proceedings are involved. In *Officier van Justitie v Kolpinghuis Nijmegen (80/86)* the Court of Justice stated that where an interpretation of domestic law would run counter to the legitimate expectations of individuals then the Von Colson principle will not apply.

Decisions

"A decision shall be binding in its entirety upon those to whom it is addressed" (Article 189).

Decisions are similar to regulations but may apply to member States or to individuals of these states. Like directives they are not "directly applicable", as are regulations, but they may be directly effective provided the appropriate criteria are present. This was established in *Grad v Finanzamt Traunstein (9/ 70)*. The application of a decision does not pose the same problem as a directive since a decision will be addressed to an individual addressee and not generally. The agreement by the Council of Ministers to admit Greece to a membership of the Community, for example, was a decision and not a regulation nor a directive.

Regulations, directives and decisions are the main legislative instruments used by the Community. In addition there are recommendations and opinions but these have no binding force and are ineffective in Law. However they do have a persuasive authority. It should be noted that directives and decisions shall be notified to those to whom they are addressed and shall take effect upon such notification.

Application of Community Law

As has been noted when dealing with regulations, certain laws made by the Community may become part of the national law of a member State without any further steps being taken. This situation may also occasionally apply to directives.

Some member States may automatically receive international law into their national law in which case it is said to have been "adopted". In others, such as the UK, the Member States will receive the international law by "transformation". This may be by the passing of a statute such as the *European Communities Act 1972*.

However although the Community law in these situations may be received by the courts of member States, the possibility of a conflict between the Community law and the national law may still remain. In that case which body of law will prevail?

Supremacy of EC Law

In *Van Gend en Loos (26/62)* the European Court of Justice stated uncompromisingly that where there was a conflict between Community law and domestic law then the Community law must take precedence. In that case there was a conflict between an Article of the Treaty of Rome and a Dutch Law.

In *Internationale Handelsgesellschaft mbH (11/70)* the case was concerned with a conflict between an EC Regulation and a provision of the German Constitution. The European Court of Justice stated quite definitely that Community law must take precedence over any rule of national law "of any nature whatever". Also it matters not whether the national Law preceded or was subsequent to the Community Law.

The reasoning behind the European Court's decision is that as states have freely signed the Treaty and by doing so have agreed to take all appropriate measures to comply with EEC Law (Article 5) then they must have agreed to give priority to EC Law otherwise the Community would not survive if member States were allowed to go their own individual ways.

Eventually it appears that member States have now accepted the principle of supremacy of EC Law provided they regard it as directly effective.

Conflict between EC Law and national Law
A problem may still remain for judges in the member States where there is a conflict between a national rule and the European rule – must the judge wait for the national law to be repealed or legally annulled before he can give precedence to the EC Law?

This problem came before the European Court in *Simmenthal SpA v Commission (92/78)*. In that case the European court of Justice stated that the national judges must shut their eyes to the domestic law and they need not, indeed must not, wait for the law to be changed.

The reaction of the member States to this very forthright statement of position by the Court of Justice was initially a little diffident.

As far as the United Kingdom is concerned it is the *European Communities Act 1972* which determines its position with regard to Community Law. Section 2(1) of that Act provides that EC law shall be directly applicable in the United Kingdom – "All such rights, powers, liabilities, obligations and restrictions from time to time created or arising by or under the Treaties, and all such remedies and procedures from time to time provided for, by or under the Treaties, as in accordance with the Treaties are without further enactment to be given legal effect or used in the United Kingdom, shall be recognised and available in law, and be enforced, allowed and followed accordingly; and the expression 'enforceable Community right' and similar expressions shall be read as referring to one to which this subsection applies."

Section 2(2) in addition provides power to the United Kingdom legislature for Community law to be implemented by means of secondary legislation. This power is subject to Schedule 2 which lists areas where the United Kingdom legislature cannot adopt the Community Law. These areas are taxation, the introduction of retrospective measures or the creation of new criminal offences.

As always Lord Denning M R made his comments on Community Law and in *HP Bulmer Ltd. v Bollinger S.A. (1974)*. He stated "The Treaty is like an incoming tide. It flows into the estuaries and up the rivers. It cannot be held back." However in *Felixstowe Dock & Railway Company v British Transport Docks Board (1976)* Lord Denning stated "It seems to me that once the bill is passed by Parliament and becomes a statute, that will dispose of all this discussion about the Treaty. These courts will then have to abide by the statute without regard to the Treaty at all".

Gradually the dispute has seemed to resolve itself between (1) those judges who accept the European view as expressed in *Macarthys Ltd v Smith (1979)* and are prepared to give priority to European Law and (2) those judges, amongst whom was Lord Denning, who prefer the "rule of construction" approach. This means that they are prepared to interpret any United Kingdom act of Parliament in a generous way provided that Parliament has made it clear that it intends to comply with Community Law.

In *Litster v Forth Dry Docks Ltd (1989)* the House of Lords interpreted United Kingdom regulations in such a way as to comply with an EC directive. In that case it was suggested that where the United Kingdom had introduced regulations specifically in order to implement an EC directive then the courts of this country must interpret the national Law so as to comply with the directive.

Thus in the United Kingdom there still seems to be some divergence of opinion amongst the judges as to the supremacy of EC Law. It is probably true to say that in the case of an EC regulation which is directly applicable then that will be acceptable. However in the case of a directive which may not be directly applicable then the EC rule may only be adopted provided the United Kingdom legislation can be interpreted in such a way as to comply with the EC directive. Whether or not this can be done will depend on whether the court considers that Parliament did have the intention to comply with the Community Law.

The courts of Italy, France, Germany and Belgium have had similar difficulties in deciding whether or not to accept the supremacy of EC Law. However it can be said that in general all the courts of the member States seem to be reaching the position where they will agree to the supremacy of EC Law even though they may insist that political and judicial control must still remain with the member State.

In 1991 the European Commission claimed that the United Kingdom Government had failed to ensure that the environment would remain unaffected, contrary to an EC directive, in connection with major building projects such as the Channel tunnel. Commenting on this Britain's judge in the European Court of Justice said that if the European Commission took the government to court over major building projects, including the Channel tunnel high speed rail link, EC law would prevail.

Sir Gorden Slynn, before his move to become a law lord, said: "If the commission makes a directive then we (the European Court) would be bound to say that the commission rule overrides any decision by the UK government, assuming that the rule was valid.

"It is as plain as a pikestaff," Sir Gordon said in Brussels. "You can't say, 'No surrender of sovereignty'. It has gone, in a limited way. Pooling of sovereignty is a better expression."

The government will have two months in which to respond to the commission's complaints that its laws are in breach of the EC directive on environmental assessment. Under a procedure contained in article 169 of the Treaty of Rome, if the commission is not satisfied with the government's explanation, then it will take the matter to the European Court of Justice and seek a ruling. This could take up to two years because of the backlog at the court.

There is no right of appeal against a ruling by the European Court. Although the court has no sanctions to ensure compliance, the government is morally obliged to comply with its treaty obligations.

In the meantime, the commission may seek an injunction from the court, a suspensory order, to freeze the projects until the matter comes to a full hearing. Obtaining such an injunction could take six months.

Chapter Twenty-Three

The European Rules Relating to Competition

It is a fundamental principle of the common market that competition is not distorted (Article 3).

The Treaty seeks to establish a system of sound competition based on three sets of rules:

1. Rules applying to undertakings.
2. Rules against dumping.
3. Rules governing State aids.

Rules Applying to Undertakings

Articles 85 and 86 are concerned with the main rules relating to undertakings in general. Article 90 is concerned in particular with public undertakings.

An undertaking is not defined in the Treaty of Rome but is accepted as being any person or organisation that carries on some economic or commercial activity. It includes limited companies, partnerships, sole traders, individuals, state corporations and trade associations. It may also include Sovereign States and local authorities carrying out commercial activities.

In a recent case, decided on June 10th 1991, in the Queens Bench division it was held "Regulatory bodies performing the function of a public authority with the power to levy charges are not thereby a commercial organisation and not therefore subject to the provisions against anti-competitive practices of Article 86 of the EEC Treaty" – *Irish Aerospace (Belgium) NV v European Organisation for the Safety of Air Navigation.*

Thus it is necessary to ensure that each party to an agreement comes within the definition of an "undertaking".

Not only that but the agreement in question must have some actual or potential effect on inter-State trade. It does not follow that merely because an agreement is made between two UK companies that in fact such an agreement would escape the EC competition rules. For example an agreement could be made between two companies in this country and one term of the agreement might be that the activities of one of the parties could be restricted and so inter-State trade might be affected.

The competition rules of the EC are basically contained in Articles 85 and 86. Article 85 prohibits anti-competitive agreements and Article 86 prohibits abuses of a dominant position.

Article 85

This Article relates to anti-competitive behaviour by two or more undertakings or decisions by their associations that it prohibits agreements or other practices which distort competition and which are liable to affect trade between member States.

Article 85

1. The following shall be prohibited as incompatible with the common market: all agreements between undertakings, decisions by associations of undertakings and concerted practices which may affect trade between member States and which have as their object or effect the prevention, restriction or distortion of competition within the common market, and in particular those which:

a. directly or indirectly fix purchase or selling prices or any other trading conditions;
b. limit or control production, markets, technical development, or investment;
c. share markets or sources of supply;
d. apply dissimilar conditions to equivalent transactions with other trading parties, thereby placing them at a competitive disadvantage;

e. make the conclusion of contracts subject to acceptance by the other parties of supplementary obligations which, by their nature or according to commercial usage, have no connection with the subject of such contracts.

2. Any agreements or decisions prohibited pursuant to this Article shall be automatically void.

3. The provisions of paragraph 1 may, however, be declared inapplicable in the case of:
- any agreement or category of agreements between undertakings;
- any decision or category of decisions by associations of undertakings;
- any concerted practice or category of concerted practices;

which contributes to improving the production or distribution of goods or to promoting technical or economic progress while allowing consumers a fair share of the resulting benefit, and which does not:

a. impose on the undertakings concerned restrictions which are not indispensable to the attainment of these objectives;
b. afford such undertakings the possibility of eliminating competition in respect of a substantial part of the products in question.

Thus it can be seen that the following activities will be prohibited by Article 85 –

a. Price fixing either directly or indirectly. This includes an agreement whereby an undertaking will restrict itself as to the trading conditions applied in business dealings such as on what basis discounts are granted, credit terms etc.
b. Market or production sharing. Arrangements as to control production itself such as limitations imposed by quotas as well as long term plans regarding production will normally not be allowed.
c. Agreements to discriminate. This may arise where A and B agree to apply more advantageous conditions to buyer C than to buyer D.

The European Rules Relating to Competition

d. Collective boycotts. This would arise where there is an agreement between undertakings with the objective of forcing a potential competitor out of the market or preventing market entry by others.
e. Tie-ins. These are agreements which impose tie-in arrangements which oblige a buyer of one product or service also to buy another product or service. Such agreements are not allowed.

The above agreements are known as horizontal agreements. These are agreements between competitors or potential competitors. They should be contrasted with vertical agreements which are agreements between undertakings in different stages of the process through which a product or service passes from the manufacturer to the final consumer.

Further horizontal agreements which may pose problems are:

1. Joint purchasing agreements between competitors and even between non-competing firms which may lead to a restriction on competition.
2. Joint selling agreements which limit the freedom of the parties to fix their selling prices.
3. Sales promotion e.g. trade fairs, joint advertising and the use of a common quality control label.
4. Exchange of information through a central agency on quantities, prices, discounts and other terms of business.
5. Trade associations or market for closure. Usually undertakings may validly pursue common interests by creating a trade association. But problems may arise if the activities of the trade association tend to deprive members of their freedom to determine their own business policies.
6. Non-competition clauses in connection with the sale of an undertaking.

All these situations are not invalid automatically but they may in fact violate Article 85.

The other type of agreement is called a vertical agreement. These agreements are concerned with the distribution of the product of an undertaking unlike a horizontal agreement which is concerned with arrangements by competitors restricting their independent business behaviour.

Whether or not a vertical agreement concerned with distribution will contravene Article 85 will depend on the extent in which the parties i.e. the supplier and his distributor agree to restrict their commercial freedom. A simple distribution agreement where neither the supplier nor the distributor is bound by any restrictive obligations will not fall within Article 85. However an exclusive distribution agreement by which the supplier agrees to supply only one distributor in a determined territory may be affected by Article 85. Such an exclusive distribution agreement may be beneficial by contributing to market unification. For this reason an exclusive distribution agreement may be given a block exemption. Provided certain specific provisions are complied with. These are:

1. The agreement must involve two parties only.
2. The products must be supplied for resale.
3. The sales area must be either a defined part of the common market or the entire territory of the common market.
4. The only permitted restriction on the supplier is the obligation not to sell to other re-sellers in the sales area allocated to the exclusive distributor.
5. The supplier may not be required to guarantee absolute territorial protection for the distributor.
6. The supplier may agree not to make direct sales himself to customers within the distributor's territory.
7. The distributor may agree to purchase all his requirements from the supplier.
8. The agreement must not involve competing manufacturers since this could lead to horizontal market sharing.
9. There must be no effort by the parties to create absolute territorial protection for the distributor.

Any agreement which satisfies these conditions will be automatically exempted and the parties do not need to notify the agreement to the Commission.

In the same way there may be an exclusive purchasing agreement. This is an agreement by which a re-seller is obliged to buy his supplies exclusively from a stated manufacturer or other supplier without being allotted an exclusive sales territory.

An exclusive purchase obligation is permitted as part of an exclusive distribution agreement. Otherwise it is only allowed within the terms of the exclusive purchase block exemption. The maximum duration of the exclusive purchasing obligation must be limited to five years (renewable) and the range of products covered by the obligation must be limited to products which either by their nature or by commercial usage are connected to each other.

There are special provisions in the new group exemptions for exclusive purchasing agreements relating to beer (and other drinks) and petrol.

Selective Distribution Agreements

Certain manufacturers may want their products to be sold only by approved dealers. This is true in the case of technically sophisticated products such as electronic equipment, watches or automobiles. This gives the manufacturer control of the way in which their product is sold. However it is also a way of maintaining retail prices and of isolating dealers from competition. It is therefore regarded with suspicion by the Commission and the only block exemption for selective distribution is for motor vehicle distribution.

Outside the motor vehicle sector, manufacturers or importers wishing to sell through dealer networks must either ensure that the agreements fall outside Article 85 or they must seek an individual exemption.

Agreements will only fall outside Article 85 if:

1. The products concerned require specialist retailers i.e. they are technically complex.
2. The dealers are selected on the basis of their ability to do the job or the suitability of their premises, but nothing else.

3. There are no anti-competitive clauses in the dealer agreements which might influence retail prices or restrict classes of customers or ban exports.

Franchising

A franchising agreement enables the franchisor to establish a uniform distribution network without the need for major investment. It will also allow an independent trader to set up an outlet more rapidly and with a greater chance of success than if he had to do so without the experience and assistance of the franchisor.

In 1988 the Commission enacted a Block Exemption Regulation in the field of franchising agreements. The Commission treats franchise networks differently from selective distribution networks.

Industrial Property

Industrial property rights include patents, copyrights, trademarks, performing rights, registered designs and models. These rights can be obtained and used by members of each member State according to the national laws of each State. The owner of an industrial property right has a legal monopoly in his protected product process or name because he can prevent others from infringing his rights. Furthermore he has the sole right to permit others to do what otherwise would be an infringement. Thus the owner of an industrial property right has the opportunity to restrict competition and divide up the common market and place restrictions on licensees. However European Community competition law recognises and respects the existence of monopolies created by industrial property rights. However although the mere existence of an industrial property right cannot infringe Articles 85 or 86. An improper or abusive exercise of these rights can. In *Consten SA and Grundig v EC Commission* the German firm Grundig entered into an agreement with Consten a French firm whereby Consten became the sole representative of Grundig for France, and

Corsica. Consten undertook to buy Grundig products, carry out publicity, and set up repair workshops and also undertook not to sell similar products or to compete with Grundig. On the other hand Grundig undertook to retail sale rights and not to deliver either directly or indirectly to other persons within the area covered by the agreement. Furthermore Grundig authorised Consten to use the name and emblem of Grundig as registered in Germany and Consten registered in France, in its own name, the trademark of Grundig GINT. In April 1961 Consten found that another Company, UNEF was buying Grundig products from German traders and reselling these in France at more favourable prices than those charged by Consten. So Consten brought actions against UNEF for unfair competition and for infringement of the GINT trademark. Eventually the matter came before the Court of Justice which considered the affect of the arrangement of inter-State trade notwithstanding the fact that the volume of trade between the States had been increased. The court decided that the agreement was capable of endangering freedom of trade between member States which could harm the attainment of the object of a single market between States.

Patent Licensing

Patent licensing agreements may present problems in view of the territorial restriction they impose which may result in the isolation of national markets. They also confer on the licensee an exclusive right to manufacture and/or sell the products covered by the patent.

However patent licensing confers a number of benefits. The agreements allow firms to obtain access to newly developed technologies and they also encourage the innovative activities of smaller firms which lack the financial resources to exploit their inventions themselves throughout the whole community.

In recognition of the beneficial effects the Commission has adopted a group exemption in the area of patent licensing which is characterised by three main principles:

1. It recognises a need for certain degree of protection for the holder of the patent (licensor) and his licensees.
2. It aims to assure effective competition and subject to certain limitations, a freedom of intra-community trade for the patented products.
3. It provides security for the parties to the contract.

In patent licenses the following are prohibited:

1. The charging of royalties or the imposing of restrictions after the patent has expired
2. An obligation on the licensee to assign to the patentee any rights in improvement in the patented product or process.
3. No challenge clauses which mean that the licensee is not allowed to challenge the validity of the patents.
4. Non-compete clauses which means that the licensee is not allowed to manufacture or sell competing products.
5. Charging royalties on the manufacture of non-patented products.

Know-how Licensing

Know-how licensing agreements are also covered by a block exemption dated November 30th 1988. A know-how agreement is not actually an industrial property right but it is sometimes treated in a similar manner. The duration of clauses granting the licensee exclusive rights and restricting exports in a know-how licence is limited to ten years (five years for bans on passive exports).

In copyright and trademark licences the same principles apply. "Know-how", for this purpose, is defined as "a body of technical information that is secret, substantial, and identified in any appropriate form".

Activities Outside the Scope of Article 85(1)

Notification – Negative clearance
If the parties to an agreement consider that it may violate Article 85 and want to be informed on this particular point they

may apply to the Commission for a decision. This procedure is known as "notification". One type of notification is known as "an application for negative clearance". This means that the parties want the Commission to confirm that their agreement falls outside Article 85(1) altogether. Another type of notification is called "a notification for exemption". In this case the parties may consider that their agreement falls within Article 85(3) but are now asking the Commission for an exemption. If of course an agreement falls under one of the group exemptions then notification is necessary.

The procedure for notification requires that it must be made in writing or an official form A/B issued by the Commission. The applicants must give detailed information on the form relating to the parties to the agreement, the essential features and aims of the agreement. The form together with a copy of the agreement must be sent to the Commission.

The procedure for granting a formal exemption or negative clearance is an expensive one and sometimes the parties may decide that a less expensive method will be acceptable. In this case the Commission will be asked to issue a formal or an informal "comfort letter". Such a document falls short of a formal exemption but for practical purposes serves the same purpose and is much quicker to obtain. If the Commission issues a formal "comfort letter" it will first publish brief details of the agreement in the official journal and invite comments from third parties. It will subsequently publish details in its annual report on competition policy. If it issues an informal "comfort letter" it will merely agree to close its file and take no action.

The De Minimis Rule (agreements of minor importance)
Small or medium sized firms should be aware that many of the agreements they conclude will not be considered as violating the competition rules because the economic effect involved is not significant enough. This can be measured by market share and turn over.

As a guide-line the Commission has stated that normally agreements will not be caught by Article 85(1) if two conditions are met:

1. Market share – the goods or services which are the subject of the agreement and other goods or services of the participating undertakings, considered by consumers to be similar by reason of their characteristics, price or use, must not represent more than 5% of the total market in the area of the Community where the agreement has effect.
2. Turn-over – the aggregate turn-over of the participating undertakings must not exceed ECU 200 million.

Relations between Undertakings to which the Competition Rules do not apply

Commercial Agents

The Commission has stated in 1962 that a contract with a commercial agent transacting business on behalf of a principal does not fall under Article 85(1). The agent must not assume financial risks as part of his duties e.g. buying and selling goods, providing marketing support or providing an after-sales service. Also he must not act for more than one principal.

Parent Companies/Subsidiaries

Article 85(1) can only apply where the competition which exists between undertakings is capable of being restricted. Agreements between a parent company and its subsidiaries or between subsidiaries themselves – in other words undertakings forming one economic unit – will not be caught by Article 85(1) where the subsidiary does not have any real freedom to determine its course of action on the market and the agreement relates merely to the allocation of tasks within the concern.

Activities which by their nature are not anti-competitive

The Commission has stated that certain forms of co-operation between undertakings and certain types of subcontracting agreements do not conflict with the competition rules. The size of the undertakings involved is generally not relevant in this context.

Co-operation Agreements
The Commission has indicated that the following 18 types of agreement are considered not to restrict competition where their object is one of the following forms of co-operation:

- a. an exchange of opinion or experience.
- b. joint comparative studies of enterprise or industries.
- c. joint preparation of statistics and calculation models.
- d. joint market research.
- e. co-operation in accounting matters
- f. joint provision of credit guarantees.
- g. joint debt collecting association.
- h. joint business or tax consultant agencies.
- i. joint implementation of research and development contracts.
- j. joint implementation of research and development projects.
- k. joint placing research and development contracts.
- l. sharing out of research and development projects among participating enterprises.
- m. joint use of production, storage and transport equipment.
- n. joint execution of orders (but only when the participants do not compete with each other as regards the work to be done).
- o. joint selling arrangements by non-competing firms.
- p. joint after-sales and repairs services when the participants are non-competing firms, or even if they are competitors, when these services are provided by an undertaking independent of them.
- q. joint advertising (but no restriction is allowed on the participants also to advertise independently).
- r. joint quality marks (but only where the label is available to all competitors on the same conditions).

Sub-contracting
A sub-contracting agreement is a form of work distribution

whereby one firm – the sub-contractor – supplies goods, work or services for another firm – the contractor – in accordance with the latter's specifications. This distinguishes it from an ordinary sale of goods or supply of services.

Exemptions – Article 85(3)

As has been stated the general rule is that restrictive practices which affect inter-State trade are not allowed and undertakings engaged in such activities will be ordered to stop doing so as well as running the risk of incurring a fine. However there is an important exception to this rule. The prohibition of Article 85 can be declared inapplicable by the Commission (not by the national courts) if the harmful effects of a restrictive agreement or practice are sufficiently counter-balanced by a number of beneficial elements.

The following are four conditions which must be met before an exemption can be granted by the Commission –

1. The agreement must contribute to an improvement in production or distribution or economic progress.
2. A fair share of the resulting benefits must be allowed to consumers in the form of lower prices or an improvement in the quality of the goods or services.
3. Only restrictions of competition which are indispensible in order to achieve the beneficial results will be allowed.
4. Competition in respect of a substantial part of the goods or services in question must not be eliminated.

If the above four requirements are met then an exemption may be granted either on an individual basis or by way of a group/block exemption. For the Commission to grant an exemption in an individual case the parties must first have notified their agreement to the Commission as mentioned earlier.

Agreements need not be notified but will nevertheless benefit from an exemption if they fulfil the requirements contained in the so-called group exemption regulations which exist with respect to certain categories of agreements. At present, block exemptions are in force with respect to the following types of agreements:

1. Specialisation agreements.
2. Exclusive distribution agreements.
3. Exclusive purchasing agreements.
4. Patent licensing agreements.
5. Research and development agreements.
6. Distribution agreements in the automobile sector.
7. Franchising agreements.
8. Know-how licensing agreements.

Consequences – Article 85(2)
If an agreement falls within the prohibition of Article 85(1) the following consequences apply:

a. It is null and void from the outset. An agreement can be declared void and thus unenforceable by a national court, if the parties are involved in a law suit about the agreement. The Commission can also order parties to put an end to such a prohibited agreement.
b. The Commission has the power to order the parties to terminate the illegal conduct and it may impose fines of up to ECU 1 million, or a larger sum up to 10% of the annual turn-over of the undertakings concerned. Fines are paid to the Commission, not to any parties injured by the anti-competitive behaviour. The latter, however, may seek damages in the national courts.

Article 86 – Abuse of a dominant position

Whilst Article 85 prohibits certain arrangements which may affect inter-State trade and are likely to distort free competition within the Community, Article 86 prohibits abuse of a "dominant position" which has a similar effect.

Article 85 will involve more than one party where as Article 86 may be infringed unilaterally by one party itself.

Article 86 provides – any abuse by one or more undertakings of a dominant position within the common market or in a substantial part of it shall be prohibited as incompatible with the common market in so far as it may affect trade between member States.

Such abuse may, in particular, consist in:

a. Directly or indirectly imposing unfair purchase or selling prices or other unfair trading conditions;
b. Limiting production, markets or technical development to the prejudice of consumers
c. Applying dissimilar conditions to equivalent transactions with other trading parties, thereby placing them at a competitive disadvantage
d. Making the conclusion of contracts subject to acceptance by the other parties of supplementary obligations which, by their nature or according to commercial usage, have no connection with the subject of such contracts.

The elements necessary for Article 86 to apply are:

a. The undertaking must be in a dominant position. Although market share is the major element in assessing dominance (as a rule a share below 40% precludes a finding that the undertaking is dominant) it is by no means the only factor. An undertaking can be deemed to be dominant if, because of various factors, such as ready access to raw materials or capital, it has the power to act independently without having seriously to take into account its competitors, purchasers, or suppliers.
b. The dominant position must be in the common market or a substantial part of it.
c. There must be an abuse of the dominant position in the sense that advantage is taken of the dominant position which causes injury to third parties. Examples of abusive conduct are:

1. Charging unfair purchase or selling prices.
2. Discriminatory prices, e.g. charging customer A more than customer B for exactly the same transaction, thereby placing customer A at a competitive disadvantage.
3. Refusal to sell to a customer without valid, objective reasons.
4. Attempts to hold on to customers for example by granting fidelity rebates.

5. Acquisitions of competing undertakings, thereby affecting the competitive structure within the common market.

It will be seen that Article 86 will usually apply to the major market leaders or to State or privatised monopolies. It would not normally be a problem for small or medium sized businesses. However it can apply to smaller businesses which produce very specialised products or services for which there can be no substitute, especially if protected by patents, designs or copyright.

It is more likely that it will be small businesses who will find themselves the victims of breaches of Article 86 and these may consist of refusals to supply or discriminatory treatment.

If it is found that an infringement has occurred then the Commission may be notified of this or may become aware of such an infringement in any other way. In that case the Commission must give the parties concerned notice of its objections to their behaviour in the form of a written communication known as "the statement of objections". The parties concerned may examine the Commission's documents supporting their allegation and they must prepare their response. They must also respond in writing to the Commission's objections.

After the written response has been filed then the parties can also request an opportunity to argue their case orally. This oral hearing is organised by the Directorate General for Competition and is conducted by the "Hearing Officer" of that department. Following the oral hearing the Commission must consult the advisory committee on restrictive practices and dominant positions and after these procedural steps have been taken the Commission can come to a final decision.

If the Commission decides that an infringement does in fact exist then it will order the undertakings involved to put an end to it forthwith. This order is known as a "cease and desist" order. If the parties have already terminated the infringement then the decision may simply consist of a declaration that the behaviour in question did in fact constitute an infringement.

The Commission also has power to impose fines of up to ECU 1 million or 10% of the world annual turn-over of the undertaking concerned in the previous business year whichever of the two is greater. Such a fine may be imposed where it is found that an undertaking has infringed Articles 85(1) or 86 intentionally or through negligence.

If it is found that owing to the complexity of any case it may take the Commission a substantial period of time to reach a final decision then it is possible for the Commission to take immediate action in the form of so-called "interim measures" to stop the objectionable behaviour.

Many cases that can come before the Commission are concluded by way of an informal settlement. This will occur where the undertaking concerned voluntarily eliminates any objectionable practices. In the case of an informal settlement this would take place by way of "administrative letters" in which the Commission informs the party that there is no reason to take any action under the competition rules and that the relevant file will therefore be closed. These letters do not have the legal binding effect of decisions but may be useful as guidance.

Control over the Commission by the European Court of Justice

The E.C.J. has the following powers of review over decisions taken by the Commission:

1. The court has the power to confirm, reduce, cancel or increase fines and penalty payments imposed by Commission decisions.
2. All formal decisions by the Commission – negative clearances, decisions granting or refusing exemption, orders to terminate infringement, decisions requesting information, orders to submit to an investigation and provisional decisions relating to the immunity from fines – can be reviewed and, if necessary, annulled or varied by the court.

In addition appeals can be brought before the court where the Commission has failed to act for example, failure to examine a formal complaint that has been submitted to it or to inform the complainant of its reasons for not purusing the matter after preliminary examination.

State Aids

In this connection Articles 92 and 93 of the Treaty of Rome set out the control that may be exercised by the Commission.

Article 92
This Article provides that as a general rule all government aid to business is forbidden. "Save as otherwise provided in this Treaty, any aid granted by a member State or through State resources in any form whatsoever which distorts or threatens to distort competition by favouring certain undertakings or the production of certain goods shall, in so far as it affects trade between member States, be incompatible with the common market."

Aid in this connection covers not only government grants, cheap loans and interest subsidies but also tax concessions, public guarantees of corporate borrowing from banks or the capital market, provision of goods and services on preferential terms and in some circumstances, the acquisition of public share holdings in public businesses.

However the Article goes on to provide that certain types of aid are compatible with the Common Market namely aid having a social character which is granted to individual consumers or aid to make good damage caused by natural disasters. The following categories of aid may be considered compatible with the common market.

1. Aid to promote the economic development of areas where the standard of living is abnormally low or where there is serious under-employment
2. To promote the execution of an important project of common European interest or to remedy a serious disturbance in the economy of a member State
3. Aid to facilitate the development of certain economic activities or of certain economic areas, where such aid does not adversely affect trading conditions to an extent contrary to the common interest.

4. Such other categories of aid as may be specified by a decision of the Council acting by a qualified majority or a proposal from the Commission.

Article 93
Under this Article member States are required to notify the Commission in advance, of any plans to introduce new aid schemes or to alter existing ones. The member State may not implement the aid scheme until the Commission has taken a final decision. The Commission has two months in which to state its position on a notified scheme. If the Commission does not think it will be able to authorise the scheme then a special procedure is followed by which the Commission must give the member State a certain period, usually one month, in which to defend its scheme against objections raised by the Commission. At the end of the procedure, the Commission takes a final decision in which it takes into account the arguments of the member State concerned and the reactions of the other member States and interested parties who have been notified of the scheme in the Official Journal of the European Communities.

The Commission then reaches a decision and if the member State disagrees with this it has two months in which to demand a judicial review by the European Court of Justice.

Dumping

Dumping has no place in the internal market, governed, as it is, by the free movement of goods.

However anti-dumping rules exist to protect the EC from having its trade affected by goods being dumped in the EC by third countries.

Dumping occurs when the export price of the goods is less than the normal value of a like product.

If a member State considers that dumping is taking place, it may complain to the Commission which will hold and investigation. It may then impose an anti-dumping duty.

Chapter Twenty-Four

The Foundations of the European Community

The four freedoms that form the foundations of the European Community are:

Free movement of goods.
Free movement of persons.
Freedom of establishment and provision of services.
Free movement of capital.

Public purchasing also accounts for 15% of the Community's gross domestic product.

The Common Agricultural Policy and the Common Transport Policy are very specialised areas and are not dealt with here.

Free Movement of Goods

The idea of a Common Market was the underlying philosophy of the American constitution of 1787. It implies a geographical area in which, unhampered by restrictions, the market forces of supply and demand are brought face to face. This means in practical terms, the elimination of economic frontiers between the member States of the Community and the creation of a customs union in which the market will operate on the basis of free movement of goods, persons, services and capital.

However the mere removal of customs barriers and obstacles to the inter-play of supply and demand would be insufficient to create a single economic area. Economic policies themselves must be harmonised.

The abolition alone of customs duties and similar charges will not be sufficient to guarantee the free movement of goods within the common market. Therefore other protectionist practices which hinder the free flow of goods from one State to another must also be abolished.

Quantitative Restrictions
Article 30 prohibits quantitative restrictions on imports.
Articles 31–33 provide for the gradual abolition of import restrictions during the transitional period.
Article 34 prohibits quantitative restrictions on exports.

Quantitative restrictions have been interpreted as any measures amounting to total or partial restraint on imports, exports or goods in transit.

The above Articles 30–34 are addressed to member States and in addition they are binding upon community institutions and individuals. However community institutions may depart from these provisions where they are authorised to do so.

Article 36 provides "the provisions of Articles 30–34 shall not preclude prohibitions or restrictions on imports, exports or goods in transit justified on grounds of public morality, public policy or public security; the protection of health and life of humans, animals or plants; the protection of national treasures possessing artistic, historic or archaeological value; or the protection of industrial and commercial property. Such prohibitions or restrictions shall not, however, constitute a means of arbitrary discrimination or disguised restriction on trade between member States".

Article 36 has been restrictively interpreted by the European Court of Justice. The court has held that the purpose of Article 36 is not to reserve certain matters to the exclusive jurisdiction of the member States.

In an important case known as *Cassis de Dijon (1979)* the European court has made it clear that:

1. Only requirements strictly necessary for such protection can be justified.
2. There should be a mutual recognition of other States' safety standards.

This judgment has been used as the basis for the commission's "new approach" to harmonisation directives in the

Single Market campaign. In other words the commission does not expect that the relevant laws of the member States should be harmonised to a single European standard (except in certain areas like telecommunications). But, instead, a mutual recognition of national standards should be ensured by providing that standards meet the essential protection laid down in the directives. This approach has been applied in relation to services, capital, workers' qualifications and rights of establishment e.g. for banks.

Apart from departing from Articles 30 and 34, as provided in Article 36, derogation is also permitted in the interests of national security and in regard to measures to meet short term economic difficulties, balance of payment difficulties and measures to meet deflections of trade which might obstruct the application of community commercial policy or economic difficulties in any member State resulting from the implementation of commercial policy.

Article 37 is complimentary to Articles 30 and 34 and this requires a member State "to adjust any State monopolies of a commercial character so as to ensure that when the transitional period has ended no discrimination regarding the conditions under which goods are procured and marketed exists between nationals of member States". Article 37 is not intended to abolish monopolies but to ensure that they do not operate in a discriminatory manner thus obstructing the free movement of goods and distorting competition within the community.

Equivalent measures
In addition to quantitative restrictions on imports and exports there are also other measures which have an equivalent effect. In *Procureur du Roi v Dassonville (1974)* the European Court of Justice held that "all trading rules enacted by member States which are capable of hindering, directly or indirectly, actually or potentially, intracommunity trade are to be considered as measures having an effect equivalent to quantitative restrictions".

Measures which have been prohibited include:

1. Import and export licences and similar requirements, even where they are purely a formality.
2. Customs formalities.
3. "Buy national" campaigns even where they are non binding – *Commission v Ireland (1982)*.
4. Excessive road worthiness tests on vehicles imported from other member States – *Schloh v Auto Contrôle Technique Sprl 50/84*.

The Rule of Reason and Proportionality
In the *Cassis de Dijon* case also known as *Rewe – Zentral A G v Bundesmonopolverwaltung für Branntwein (1979)*, the above two principles were stated. This case was concerned with a German law which required certain alcoholic drinks to have a minimum alcohol level. This had the effect of excluding cassis from the German market. The ECJ held in this case that if a member State takes measures to prevent unfair practices in regard to the import of products, then such restrictions are subject to the condition that they should not act as a hindrance to trade between member States and should be available to all community nationals.

The Rule of Reason is qualified by the statement that such measures must not constitute an arbitrary discrimination or a disguised restriction on trade between member States. The Rule of Reason has been upheld on the grounds that it;

a. Maintains fair competition.
b. Permits fiscal supervision.
c. It protects consumers.
d. It protects the environment and biological resources and promotes community wide cultural interests.

The other principle is the proportionality test and this has been described as meaning that the measures taken to prevent unfair practices in regard to the import of goods must be no more than is necessary to achieve the desired objective. The measures must be proportionate to the end to be achieved and so barriers to trade will only be permitted to go as far as is necessary for the achievement for the reasonable purpose for which they were introduced. Thus, in the *Cassis de Dijon* case the ECJ held that the German laws on alcoholic content went beyond what was required for consumer protection.

Free Movement of Persons

The Treaty makes a distinction between

a. wage earners (workers) – anyone who pursues an activity as an employed person and,
b. non-wage earners i.e. professional people, tradesmen etc. These persons include not only human persons but companies.

Free Movement of Workers

Article 48 provides for freedom of movement for workers within the community, and for the abolition of any discrimination based on nationality as regards employment, remuneration and other conditions of work. Freedom of movement of workers may be interfered with by:

1. Imposing restrictions on the ground of nationality.
2. Treating family and dependents less favourably than the nationals of the host state.
3. Depriving the worker of social security rights.

All these impediments have been discarded by community law and the provisions of the Treaty in regard to these are directly enforceable in the courts of the member States.

The latest cases on these points are *Cowan v Le Trésor Public (186/87)*. In this case the court gave judgment in 1989 and found against the member State, France, because Cowan had been refused compensation for assault because the victim, Cowan, was not domiciled in France.

Delbar v Caisse d'allocations familiales (114/88). In this case also decided in 1989 it was decided that family allowances should be payable even when the dependants do not live in the same member State.

Thus, it is the intention of the European Community to allow nationals of member States to enter another member State in order to accept an offer of employment and to look for employment provided that they can produce a passport or identity card. Member States are obliged to issue entry documents and to allow the worker to leave his home country. All these rights apply to EC nationals, the spouse and descendants who are under the age of 21 or who are dependants. The nationality of a member of the family is irrelevant provided that the worker is an EC national and he has exercised his right to move to a different member State.

The Treaty in Article 48(3) does permit member States to limit the free movement of workers on "grounds of public policy, public security or public health". For these reasons member States may refuse entry into or residence within their territory or expel workers who are nationals of another member State. Furthermore the principle of non-discrimination on the ground of nationality does not apply to employment in the public service.

Freedom of Movement of Non-wage Earners

This topic may be considered under the headings of "Right of Establishment" and "Services".

Right of Establishment

This includes the right to take up and pursue activities as self-employed persons and to take up and manage undertakings, agencies, branches or subsidiaries "under the conditions laid down for its own nationals by the law of the country where such establishment is effected." (Article 52(2))

The difference between freedom of establishment and freedom of services is that the former implies the setting up in the host State of a base from which services or other activities are provided inside that State. Services on the other hand are normally provided directly from the home country and might require only occasional, or temporary entry into the other member State.

In regard to both these freedoms the principle of non-discrimination applies as it does in the case of freedom of movement of wage-earners.

Again, the principle of non-discrimination does not apply to activities which are connected, even occasionally, in the member State with the exercise of official authority.

Freedom to Provide Services

Article 52 of the Treaty provides that the freedom to provide services concerns, in particular, activities of an industrial or commercial character and activities of craftsmen and the professions. Again the principle of non-discrimination on the basis of nationality will apply. However a member State may impose specific requirements upon a person providing services because of the particular nature of the service to be provided. It may be that there are some professional rules which are for the general good; or particular rules relating to the organisation, qualification, professional ethics, supervision and liability which are binding upon a person providing that kind of service.

To facilitate the exercise of the freedom to provide services and also freedom of establishment there are provisions for the mutual recognition of diplomas, certificates and other qualifications.

Finally an exception to the freedom to provide services is the same as those provided for the freedom of establishment i.e. activities which are connected, even occasionally, with the exercise of official authority and limitations resulting from provisions laid down by law, regulation or administrative action providing special treatment for foreign nationals on grounds of public policy, public security or public health. (Article 56).

Movement of Capital

Articles 67–73 of the Treaty provide that restrictions on the movement of capital belonging to persons resident in member States and any discrimination based on the nationality or place of residence of the parties or on the place where such capital is invested shall be progressively abolished. This elimination is, however, only required "to the extent necessary to ensure the proper functioning of the common market".

It has of course been established that persons must be allowed to finance their needs in the exercise of one of the freedoms already mentioned such as freedom to work in a different member State and to set up a new home.

Again Article 106 provides for the free movement of payments. This means that member States must authorise payments from a debtor in one member State to a creditor residing in another member State, but only in so far as they are connected with the free movement of goods, services and capital.

If the free movement of payments were interfered with then the other freedoms could not be used because the financial results of their application could not then be brought back to the member State of the person involved.

Public Purchasing in the European Community

Selling to public purchasers in the European Community makes up about 15% of the European Community's gross domestic product. National Governments have traditionally favoured domestic suppliers of goods and services and this of course is not compatible with the principle of a Single European Market.

Public purchasing has been agreed by the European community heads of Government to be one of the top five single market priorities. Some changes have already occurred and others have been agreed or are under discussion. Eventually public purchasing rules will cover the following areas:

1. Supplies – the supply of goods to central, regional and local government and similar bodies.
2. Works – building and civil engineering projects for central, regional and local government and similar bodies.

3. Utilities (formerly known as excluded sectors) – the provision of supplies and works to public and private purchasers in the energy, water, transport and telecommunications sectors. This directive was adopted in 1990 and will be brought into force in most member States by 1 January 1993.
4. Services – the supply of certain services to entities covered by the Supplies and Works' directives. A proposed directive was published in 1990. A separate directive will be made for entities covered by the Utilities directive.
5. Remedies – the effective enforcement of the public purchasing directives. A directive applying to the Supplies and Works directive was brought into force at the end of 1991.

Common Elements

Some of the most common features of the public purchasing rules are as follows:

Contract award procedures
The existing directives set out three ways in which contracts can be awarded. These are:

a. *Open procedures*
   In this case all interested suppliers may submit tenders.
b. *Restricted procedures*
   Only suppliers invited by the purchaser may submit tenders.
c. *Negotiated procedures*
   In this case direct discussions between the purchaser and one or more suppliers of the purchaser's choice take place, to negotiate terms.
d. In addition to the above there are also *design contests*. In this case the authority is provided with a plan or design and a jury selects on the basis of competition. This particular procedure usually applies to contracts in architecture, engineering, town planning or data processing.

Public Service Concession

In this case an authority transfers the performance of a public service to another body in return for the right to seek payment for the service. This arrangement excludes broadcasting services.

Qualification and Contract Award Criteria
Suppliers tendering or wishing to be invited to participate may need to meet conditions laid down by the purchaser. These conditions may include the need to provide evidence of their economic, financial or technical standing.

Purchasers are allowed to apply one of two criteria in deciding which bid to accept. The criteria are:

1. Price alone
2. A combination of factors which persuade the purchaser that a tender is the most economically advantageous of those received. Factors involved in this second criterion might include price, quality and delivery. Purchasers must say in advance which factors they intend to apply and they must then assess bids on the basis they have described.

Standards
Rules on the use of standards are important to the achievement of a more open public purchasing régime. Standards and technical specifications must not be used as barriers to trade. In order to promote a proper non-discriminatory use of standards there must be reference to national standards. In the absence of relevant European standards, the directives set out the following hierarchy of standards which may be used by purchasers:

1. National standards implementing international standards
2. Any other national standards
3. Any other standards.

The Supplies Directive – *Directive 77/62 amended by 80/767 and 88/295*
The Supplies directive covers the purchase, lease and

hire of goods by central government, local and regional authorities and similar bodies such as health authorities and police forces. Contracts exceeding the following thresholds are covered:

1. 200,000 ECU (£140,000 approx) for regional and local government
2. 130,000 ECU (£91,000 approx) for central government.

Contract award procedures
Purchasers may use open or restricted procedures or negotiated procedures when no tenders are received under an open or restricted procedure; or goods are for research and development purposes only; or goods may only be supplied by a particular supplier for technical or artistic reasons; or extreme urgency resulting from some unforeseeable event.

Purchasers are required to publish an indicative notice of their procurement plans by product area, where purchases above the thresholds in each area concerned are likely to exceed 750,000 ECU (£525,000 approx) per year in total. A contract notice advertising individual contracts must be published before the selection of applicants can begin or tenders be received.

When open procedures are used there must be at least 52 days between the despatch of a contract notice and the deadline for the submission of tenders.

In restricted and negotiated procedures at least 37 days must elapse between the despatch of a notice and the deadline for receipt of requests to participate. In restricted procedures at least 40 days must be allowed between the date of despatch of a written invitation to tender and the dead-line for the receipt of bids. The time limit may be reduced to 15 days and 10 days respectively in cases of urgency.

Works Directive – *Directive 71/305 amended by 89/440*
The directive applies to contracts involving construction or civil engineering works for central government, local and regional authorities and similar bodies such as health

authorities and police forces. Contracts exceeding a threshold of 5,000,000 ECU (£3.5 million approx) are covered.

If a work is divided into several lots, each the subject of a separate contract, the overall value must be used determining whether the threshold is exceeded. Lots worth less than 1 million ECU (£662,000) may be excluded provided they do not exceed 20% of the overall value.

Contract award procedures
Purchasers may use open or restricted procedures. Negotiated procedures with a call for competition may only be used when:

1. tenders under open or restricted procedure are irregular or unacceptable.
2. works are carried out purely for R & D purposes
3. in exceptional cases, the nature of the work does not permit prior overall pricing.

Negotiated procedures without a call for competition may only be used when:

1. no suitable tenders are received.
2. only one contractor may carry out the work for technical or artistic reasons.
3. extreme urgency resulting from an unforeseen event.
4. additional works cannot be separated from a main contract.
5. under certain specified circumstances works repeat a previous contract.

Purchasers are required to publish

a. indicative notices, which give the essential characteristics of works contracts which they intend to award, whose estimated value exceeds the threshold and
b. contract notices for individual works above the threshold except in certain circumstances under the negotiated procedure.

When a contract has been awarded the purchaser must

publish a contract award notice. He must also tell unsuccessful applicants, if asked, why they were rejected.

Time limits

When open procedures are used, at least 52 days must be allowed between the date of despatch of a contract notice and the deadline for submission of tenders, unless an indicative notice has been published, in which case the limit is 36 days.

In restricted and negotiated procedures at least 37 days must be allowed between the despatch of a notice and the deadline for receipt of requests to participate. In restricted procedures, the period between the date of despatch of a written invitation and the deadline for the receipt of tenders must be at least 40 days or 26 days if an indicative notice has been published.

Utilities – Directive 90/531

This covers the four sectors which are specifically excluded from the provisions of the Supplies and Works directives. These are energy, water, transport and telecommunications. Public authorities in the telecommunications sector are covered by the Works directive.

The rules cover public contracting entities in the four sectors. Private sector bodies will be covered if they possess special or exclusive rights granted by the competent authority of a member State and if they;

1. provide or operate a network producing or distributing drinking water, electricity, gas or heat, or
2. exploit a geographical area to explore for or extract oil, gas, coal or solid fuel, or
3. provide terminal facilities to carriers by air, sea or inland waterways, or
4. operate public transport services by rail, tram, trolley or bus, or
5. provide or operate one or more public telecommunication services.

Contracts worth more than 600,000 ECU (£420,000 approx) in the telecommunications sector and 400,000 ECU (£280,000 approx) for supplies, or 5 million ECU (£3.5 million approx) for works will be covered.

Contracts Award Procedures
All three types of award procedure will be available namely, open, restricted and negotiated.

Purchasers will need to publish regularly a "periodic indicative notice" (PIN) setting out details of their planned purchases of supplies and works over the following 12 months. The information provided will need to cover contracts exceeding the relevant supplies threshold where the value of such contracts in total exceeds 750,000 ECU (£550,000 approx) in a particular product area. Similar notices will have to be published covering the essential characteristics of works contracts worth more than 5 million ECU (£3.5 million approx). Unless tenderers are selected from a qualified list or all candidates responding to a PIN are given a chance to confirm their interest, purchasers will have to publish a contract notice. In all cases, they will have to produce a contract award notice from which some details will be published.

As regards the minimum time limits, there should be at least 52 days between the dispatch of a notice and the deadline for the receipt of tenders under open procedures (36 days if advance notice is given). Under restricted or negotiated procedures there should be at least 35 days and in any case not less than 15 or 22 days (depending on publication times) between the date of dispatch of a tender notice and the deadline for the receipt of requests to participate. The time for receipt of tenders will be a matter for agreement between purchasers and potential tenderers but in the absence of agreement, the relevant period will need to be at least 21 days and in any case not less than 10 days between the date of an invitation to tender and the dead-line for the receipt of tenders, except in the case of extreme urgency.

Contract Award Criteria
A successful tender will need to be either the cheapest of those on offer or the "most economically advantageous". However,

purchasers will be allowed to reject a tender for a supplies contract where less than 50% of the value of the products in the tender is of EC origin, even if it is the cheapest or the "most economically advantageous" bid. In addition, tenders where 50% or more of the value of the products is of EC origin, will have to be preferred if they are equivalent to tenders where less than 50% of the value of the products concerned is of EC origin. The directive defines "equivalent" as being up to 3% more expensive.

To summarise then, there are in existence directives on:-
Supplies 77/62
Works 71/305
Utilities 90/531
A *remedies directive* in relation to the Supplies and Works directives 89/665

Proposed legislation will comprise:-

A *remedies directive for Supply* and Works contracts in the excluded sectors.

A *directive on public Service* contracts in the previously excluded sectors of transport, energy water and telecommunications.

A *public Services directive* which was submitted in 1990 and sets out Community procedures for procurement of services by entities covered by the Supplies and Works directives. The proposed directive (now amended) splits services into priority and residual services.

Priority services are likely to be:

Maintenance and repair services. Land transport and courier services. Air transport of passengers and trade. Land and air transport of mail except by rail

Telecommunications, certain financial services, computer and related services, research and development services, accounting, auditing and book-keeping services, market research and public opinion polling, management consultancy and related services, architectural services, engineering, urban planning and landscape services, related consultancy services, technical testing and analysis.

Advertising services, cleaning of buildings and property management, publishing and printing on a fee or contract basis, and sewage and refuse disposal, sanitation and similar services.

Residual services would be hotel and restaurant, rail transport, water transport, supporting and auxiliary transport; some financial, legal, personnel, investigation and security; educational and vocational education; health and social; recreational, cultural and sporting and services not covered by categories one and three.

Services to be excluded would include real estate transactions; the provision of services "in house"; services related to particular professions and some arbitration and conciliation services.

Contracts covered by special procurement rules e.g. international agreements will be exempt.

Procedures are specified by the proposed directive for the award of public service contracts and they may be open, restricted, negotiated or design contests. One further type of permitted procedure is the award of public service concessions whereby an authority transfers the performance of a public service to another body, in return for the right to seek payment for the service.

Award of Contracts
Member States may either make awards on the basis of the lowest price only or on the most advantageous tender when criteria of quality, technical assistance, delivery date, period of completion are taken into account.

Remedies Directives

There is a remedies directive 89/665/EEC which is intended to ensure that the public purchasing rules laid down in the Supplies and Works directives may be properly enforced at national level. The directive provides that the Commission can bring member States to the European Court of Justice if it is not satisfied that the rules are being implemented. It can ask that interim measures such as the suspension of a contract award be granted.

It is recognised that it is more effective if member States have power to enforce the public purchasing rules. Thus the directive requires that there should be a national system set up to ensure that decisions by contracting authorities can be rapidly reviewed. The body responsible for reviewing decisions will have power to take interim measures to correct any infringements. The Commission will also be able to ask a member State for an explanation of what appears to be "a clear and manifest infringement" of the community rules. The member State will be required to respond to the Commission within 21 days, either confirming the correction of the infringement or stating that the contract award procedure has been suspended.

There is another remedies directive proposed which is designed to ensure compliance with community rules contained in the Utilities directive. Its purpose is to provide remedies at the national level for suppliers harmed, or at risk of harm, from breaches of the rules in the water, energy, transport and telecommunications sectors.

It follows to a large extent the remedies available under the directive for compliance with the Supplies and Works directives.

Member States must establish national systems to review decisions taken by contracting entities. The review body may take interim measures to suspend contract award procedures and to set aside procurement decisions or to order a payment if a breach of the rules in not corrected or avoided.

Damages may be awarded and decisions by a non-judicial review body will be subject to judicial review.

The Commission may ask the member State for an explanation for what it considers to be a "clear and manifest infringement". If this has not been corrected then a reasoned submission of why it has not been corrected should be provided within 30 days.

Member States may set up attestation (audit) systems, under which contracting entities can have their purchasing practices accredited by an independent attestor.

A supplier who considers that he has been harmed by an infringement may make a request to the Commission for conciliation as an alternative to judicial review proceedings.

Chapter Twenty-five
Conflict of Laws

This subject is sometimes called Private International Law. It has been defined by one writer on the subject as "that part of law which comes into play when the issue before the court affects some fact, event or transaction that is so closely connected with the foreign system of law as to necessitate recourse to that system."

Each State in the world has its own system of law which is used in connection with that State and to decide disputes that arise within that State. Within a country there may be more than one State. This arises of course in the United States of America but also arises in the United Kingdom where Scottish law is different from the law used in England and Wales.

Conflict of laws or Private International Law must be distinguished from Public International Law. This is a set of rules which determines the relations between countries in the world. Thus there can be international agreement between one country and another and Public International Law includes the laws relating to armed conflict, to salvage of ships and international air travel.

Also Private International Law must not be confused with European Community law. In that case the intention is to make the European Community a single State eventually. It will then have its own system of law which will apply to each of the member States. At present this political fusion has not occurred but nevertheless where there are transactions between the member States then European community law may apply and in some cases will be superimposed upon the national law of the member States. The body of rules known as Conflict of Laws will be used to determine any dispute which may arise in a number of situations. It can arise where property has been purchased which is situated abroad. It may arise where a couple have been married in a foreign country. It can arise where there is a question of legitimacy or adoption or very frequently where there is a negotiable instrument. From a commercial law point of view the most obvious example would be where there is a contract with a foreign element. This could arise where A is an Englishman who is visiting France and enters into a contract with B who is a German. The purpose of the contract is to perform some service in Spain. It will be apparent that a number of systems of law may be called upon to solve any dispute that may arise.

If a dispute does arise and the matter is brought before an English court then this court must first of all decide whether it has jurisdiction to hear the case in the first place. If it does so decide that it has jurisdiction then it must secondly decide which system of law must be applied in resolving the dispute.

It should be noted that as a rule any person can sue and be sued before an English court. The main exceptions are if the defendant has diplomatic immunity and secondly if the plaintiff is an alien enemy. In all other cases then the action may be heard by an English court but whether or not it is so heard will of course depend upon the circumstances. It may be that the parties when entering into the contract agree at that time that in the event of any dispute arising it should be resolved by reference to an English court of law.

In deciding whether or not to bring an action before an English court then the obvious consideration must be that in the event of the plaintiff succeeding in his action will he be able to enforce any judgment? Thus if the defendant is domiciled abroad then it may be impossible, or at least very difficult, for a successful plaintiff to proceed against any assets of the defendant in the foreign country. Of course if the defendant is a company in this country with large assets then the problem will have disappeared.

If the problem is then brought before a court of this country then it must decide whether or not it has jurisdiction to hear the case. If the court does decide that it has jurisdiction then it must then consider what system of law is to be applied to the problem.

This process is known as classification. This means that the English judge, because of course this is a matter for English law, makes his own analysis of the question before him and then assigns it to a particular legal category. The legal categories may be wider than the categories of the internal law of the State. Nevertheless in practice the classification process will place the problem into:

1. Law of property divided into the Law of Immovables and the Law of Movables.
2. Family law i.e. relationship between husband and wife, Marriage and Divorce.
3. Legitimacy, Legitimation and Adoption.
4. Torts.
5. Contracts.

Lex Causae
Having classified the problem into one of the particular categories then the court must decide which particular body of law to apply to the problem in order to resolve it. The law to be applied to the case is known as the lex causae. This means the law applicable to the case. If the lex causae is a foreign system of law then this law must be proved before an English court in the same way as any other evidence. The evidence as to what is the foreign law must be brought into court by an expert witness. This does not mean that the witness must be a lawyer but he must have practical experience. In one case a Roman Catholic Bishop was allowed to testify as to the matrimonial law of Rome. A secretary to the Persian Embassy was allowed to depose to the law of Persia and the evidence of a London bank director with experience of banking in South America was preferred to that of a young man who had been at the Chilean bar for a number of years when the problem concerned the meaning of a bill of exchange given in Chile.

Contracts
As far as commercial law is concerned, of course contract is its basis and we must now consider the actions of the courts of this country where there is a contract with a foreign element.

Where a contract is concerned then there may be a dispute between the parties in regard to any of the essentials of the contract. Capacity is one of the essentials leading to the formation of the contract. This includes offer and acceptance, consideration and intention to create legal relations. Other aspects are the essential validity of the agreement and such matters as mistake, the effect of mistake, misrepresentation, duress and illegality. Finally there is the interpretation and effect of the contract and the manner of performance as well as the methods of discharge. In all these cases a dispute may arise between the parties and the question that remains, if there is a foreign element, will be which body of law must be used in order to solve the particular dispute.

The Proper Law of the Contract

In English law where there is a contract with a foreign element then it is the proper law which is used in order to solve any dispute.

Dicey's view is that "the term proper law of contract means the law or laws by which the parties intended, or may fairly be presumed to have intended, the contract to be governed". This is known as the subjective view and the emphasis of course is placed upon the intention of the parties.

The other view is the objective view which Lord Denning favoured. He stated that "the proper law of the contract depends not so much on the place where it is made, nor even on the intention of the parties or on the places where it is to be performed but on the place with which it has the most substantial connection" – *Boissevain v Weil (1949)*.

It should always be remembered of course that the parties, when they enter into their agreement, may state the body of law which they wish to make use of in the event of any dispute arising. Again Lord Denning said "It is clear that if there is an express clause in a contract providing what the proper law is to be, that is conclusive in the absence of some public policy to the contrary." – *Tzortzis v Monark Line A/B (1968)*.

In cases where the parties have not themselves stated which

body of law is to be used in the event of a dispute then a case called *The Assunzione (1954)* provides a good example of how the courts determined which is the proper law of a contract. In that case there was a charter party entered into between the plaintiffs who were French and the owners of the ship, the Assunzione, who were Italian. The ship was to carry grain from Dunkirk to an Italian port and the question was whether French or Italian law governed the situation. Neither party contended that English law applied although the case was heard before the courts of this country. There were points of contact with French law namely:

a. the charter party was headed Paris 7th October 1949 and was therefore concluded in France.
b. the charter party itself was written in English but was followed by a supplement written in French.
c. the bills of lading were written in French and in the French standard form.
d. the charterers were French brokers and were acting on behalf of the French government.

On the other hand there were the following points of contact with Italian law:

a. the ship flew the Italian flag and was owned by two Italian brothers carrying on business at Genoa and Naples.
b. Italy was the place of performance in the sense that delivery was due at Venice.
c. freight and demurrage were payable at Naples in Italian currency.
d. the bills of lading had been indorsed with the consignees in Italy.

Thus it appeared that both the French and Italian elements of the contract were in equipoise. There was obviously no outstanding fact which was decisively significant and so the question was what would a reasonable man decide; should the contract be regarded as Italian or French? Eventually the Court of Appeal decided that the contract must be decided according to Italian law. The Court of Appeal did make the point that the crucial factors were that the charterers had to pay freight and demurrage at Naples in Italian currency.

Since these cases, the matter of the proper law of the contract has been considered by the European Community and in 1990, in Rome, a Convention was made which had the aim of providing a uniform method for deciding the law governing international contracts. The Convention is world-wide in effect and applies to all international contracts.

The law contained in the Convention has been ratified by the United Kingdom Parliament and now appears in the form of a statute named *Contracts (Applicable Law) Act 1990*

Section 2 of the Act provides that the Rome Convention signed by the United Kingdom on 7 December 1981, shall have the force of law in the United Kingdom. This Convention provides uniform rules which apply where there is a conflict of laws in relation to contractual obligations. It is world-wide in effect and applies to all international contracts which come within the scope of the Convention and which come before the United Kingdom courts.

The Act came into force on 1 April 1991.

The Rome Convention

Article 3 provides that the parties are free to choose any law whatever to be applied to their contract. An exception is where all the other elements relevant to the situation are concerned with one country only then the rules of that country, called "mandatory rules", shall be applied.

Article 4 provides that in the event of the parties not choosing a particular law to govern the contract then the contracts shall be governed by the law of the country with which it is mostly connected. The Convention would appear to be complying with the rules used in English law to decide which is the proper law of the contract. In English law, before the Convention, the court determined all the elements of the contract and decided which body of law should govern it and made use of no presumptions. However in the Convention, Article 4(2) provides "in the absence of choice by the parties then the law governing the contract shall be the law of the country where the party who is to effect the performance of the contract shall have his residence or, in the case of a company, its central administration."

In the case of a contract of sale the question is where does the characteristic performance of the contract take place? It has been held that in a contract of sale the characteristic performance of the contract takes place in the country where the seller has his residence. The law governing other types of contracts will of course be determined in other ways. In the case of an individual employment contract, then the law governing that contract will be the law of the country in which the employee habitually carries out his work in performing the contract or, if the employee does not habitually carry out his work in any one country, then it will be governed by the law of the country in which the place of business through which he was engaged is situated.

The validity of a contract shall be determined by satisfying the formal requirements of the law which governs it according to the Convention or of the law of any one of the countries.

When the applicable law has been determined then this will govern such matters as

a. interpretation.
b. performance.
c. the consequences of breach including the assessment of damages.
d. the ways of extinguishing obligations and limitation of actions.
e. the consequences of nullity of a contract.

All these matters therefore are to be determined by the applicable law. Article 10(2) does provide that in relation to the manner of performance then regard shall be had to the law of the country in which performance takes place.

From the above it is apparent that determining the applicable law of the contract may sometimes be quite a difficult task so to avoid any difficulties it is obvious that the parties to any contract which has a foreign element in it should at the outset determine and agree which body of law shall govern that contract in the event of a dispute.

International Sale of Goods
In international trading it is customary to incorporate special trade terms in the contract. These terms sometimes differ between countries and so the International Chamber of Commerce has published a set of INCOTERMS so as to prevent any misunderstanding.

These terms will apply to all contracts of international sale of goods if the parties have incorporated them into their contract.

The terms are changed from time to time to take into account different methods of payment, transport and documentation. A new term is DDU (Delivery duty unpaid). This has been introduced to apply to exports within the EC when duties between member States have been abolished. In this case the seller must deliver the goods to a named place in the country to which they are being exported. The seller must bear the costs of transport but not duties, taxes or import charges. The alternative term is DDP which is the same as DDU except that the seller must bear the payment of duties, taxes and import charges.

The latest version of the INCOTERMS is identical in both English and French.

These terms state the duties and responsibilities of the seller of the goods. Some other examples are :–
FCA – Free carrier. Here the seller is not liable once he has handed the goods to a carrier at a named place.
FAS – Free alongside ship and FOB – Free on board have obvious meanings.
CFR – cost and freight. The buyer assumes risk of damage or loss when the goods have passed the ship's rail.
CIF – Cost, insurance and freight. Is similar to CFR but the exporter must pay for the insurance.
CPT – Carriage paid to a named place and CIP – Carriage and Insurance are similar and are used when the goods are being carried in containers.
DAF – Delivered at frontier, DES – delivered ex ship and DEQ – delivered ex quay a named port of destination have obvious meanings.

These are some of the latest examples of INCOTERMS and may be incorporated in a contract by the parties to it.

Uniform Laws on international sale of goods contracts.
When Parties in different States enter into a contract it will sometimes result in difficulties because of the varation in the rules applying in each of the States. In order to achieve some sort of uniformity in the laws which in different States apply to contracts for the international sale of goods some Conventions were entered into at the Hague. The first as the Uniform Law on the International Sale of Goods. The second was the Uniform Law on the formation of Contracts for the International Sale of Goods. These are contained in schedules 1 and 2 of *The Uniform Laws on International Sales Act 1967*. However on April 11th, 1980, the UN convention on contracts for the international sale of goods was signed in Vienna. This convention was based on the two Hague conventions and supersedes them.

This convention has now been brought into operation. It applies to business (non-consumer) sales between parties who have places of business in different States provided the States concerned have accepted the Vienna Convention and the proper law of the contract is that of the acceding State. The Vienna Convention becomes part of the law of the State but it does not apply to issues of liability for death or personal injury caused by the goods supplied and the parties to the contract may exclude or vary any of its provisions by express agreement or by usage.

The Vienna Convention has incorporated a number of concepts which are strange to English lawyers such as the avoidance of a contract in part, the buyer's right to demand specific performance, repair or replacement of defective goods and the seller's right to remedy his deficiency.

Whether or not business men will incorporate the terms of the Convention into their contracts will remain to be seen.

General Index

Agency 3
  – creation of Agency 7
  – duties of agent 10, 11
  – duties of principal 13
  – liability of Agent 4
  – liability of Principal 7
  – Power of attorney 8
  – ratification 7
  – rights of agent 13
  – rights of principal 13
  – signatures of Agent 5, 6
  – termination of Agency 13
Arbitration 62
  – ADR (Alternative Disputes Resolution) 69
  – Arbitration agreement 66, 67

Bills of Exchange 230
  – acceptance 232
  – definition 231
  – dishonour 235
  – holder in due course 238
  – noting and protesting 236
  – payment 234
  – transfer 237

Cheques 240
  – bearer cheques 246
  – crossings 242
  – order cheques 248
  – protection of collecting banker 255
  – protection of paying banker 250
Companies 25
  – articles of association 31
  – borrowing by 45
  – capital 39
    – ordinary shares 40
    – preferences shares 39
    – redeemable preferences 40
  – debentures 47, 48, 49, 56
  – directors 32
  – disqualification of 36
  – fixed and floating charges 47, 53
  – formation of 26
  – meetings 37
  – memorandum of association 27
  – name of 30
  – objects, alteration of 29
  – personal liability of 35, 36

- rule of Turquard's case 34
- shadow directors 44
- ulton? vira reform 28
Conflict of laws 358
- proper law of the contract 361
Consumer credit 193
- cancellation 204
- exempt agreements 195
- fixed-sum credit 196
- hire agreement 199
- regulated agreements 202
- running-account credit 197
Consumer protection 161
- defences 165
- who is liable 163
- who may sue 162
Contract 73
- acceptance 80
- notification of 80
- postal 81
- agreement 76
- Battle of forms 108
- consideration 82
- rules of 84
- discharge 115
- by agreement 117
- by breach 120
- by frustration 118
- by performance 115
- duress 100
- essentials of 74
- exemption clauses 109
- formation of contract 86
- illegality 101
- intentions 74
- invalidating/vitiating factors 87
- as to identity of party 90
- as to type of contract signed 92
- mistake as to subject matter 88
- misrepresentation 93
- definition 94
- form? 95
- innocent 95
- remedies 122
- damages 122
- injunction 127
- rescission 127
- restraint of trade 102
- offer 76
- counter offer 80
- death of offerer or offeree 79
- lapse 79
- rejection 80
- resolution 78
- terms of contract 105
- undue influence 100
- unfair contract terms 111
- utmost good faith/ utmost disclosure 97
- rescission 98
Copyright 179

Data protection 222
- principles of 224
- register 223, 226

– rights of an individual 225

Electronic transfer of funds 264
European Community Law 299
– article 85 323
– article 86 335
– Commission 307
– conflict between EC and national
law 318
– competition rules 322
– Council of Ministers 304
– Court of Justice 309
– decisions 316
– directives 313
– European Parliament 303
– free movement of capital 347
– of goods 341
– of persons 345
– institutions 303
– public purchasing 348
– remedies directives 356
– supplies directives 350
– utilities 353
– works directives 351
– regulations 312
– Single European Act 300
– Sources and application of 312

Financial Services Act 1986 209

– Investments – definition 210
– Rules for conduct of business 218
– SLB 212
– SRO 212

INCOTERMS 365
Insolvency 269
– administrator receiver 289
– bankruptcy order 282
– corporate 268
– individual 279
– order of distribution 292
– preferences 286
– realisation and distribution of assets 288
– transaction of an underdue? 286
– winding up 270
 – by court 271
 – voluntarily 276
Insurance 168
– insurable interest 169
Intellectual Property 173
– copyright 179
– passing off 183
– patents 173
– trade marks 183
– unregistered design right 182
Investments
– regulation of 209
– rules for the conduct of business 218

– securities and Investments Board 212
– types of 210

Partnership 15
– bankruptcy of 23, 24
– definition of 15, 16
– dissolution of 21, 22
– firm name 17
– liability of partners
  – joint and personal 19, 20
  – of retiring partner 20
– property of 22
– relationship of partners interse? 19
– relationship with third parties 18
Patents 173
Power of attorney 9
– enduring powers of attorney 9, 10
Product liability 161

Sale of Goods 129
– conditions 134
– delivery 149
  – by instalments 150
– implied conditions 135
  – by sample 139
  – correspond to description 136
  – fitness for purpose 138
  – merchantable quality 137
  – of title 145
  – right to sell 135
  – Romalpa clause 144
  – specific goods 141
  – transfer of property 140
  – unascertained goods 142
– ownership and possession 130
– property 131
  – transfer of 140
  – protection of purchaser 132
  – against the goods 157
– remedies of buyer 153
  – of seller 155
– warrantes 134

Vitiating factors in contract 88